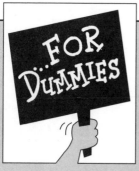
™

References for the Rest of Us

D1072952

COMPUTER BOOK SERIES FROM IDG

Are you intimidated and confused by computers? Do you find that traditional manuals are overloaded with technical details you'll never use? Do your friends and family always call you to fix simple problems on their PCs? Then the *. . . For Dummies*™ computer book series from IDG is for you.

. . . For Dummies books are written for those frustrated computer users who know they aren't really dumb but find that PC hardware, software, and indeed the unique vocabulary of computing make them feel helpless. *. . . For Dummies* books use a lighthearted approach, a down-to-earth style, and even cartoons and humorous icons to diffuse computer novices' fears and build their confidence. Lighthearted but not lightweight, these books are a perfect survival guide to anyone forced to use a computer.

> *"I like my copy so much I told friends; now they bought copies."*
>
> **Irene C., Orwell, Ohio**

> *"Quick, concise, nontechnical, and humorous."*
>
> **Jay A., Elburn, IL**

> *"Thanks, I needed this book. Now I can sleep at night."*
>
> **Robin F., British Columbia, Canada**

Already, hundreds of thousands of satisfied readers agree. They have made *. . . For Dummies* books the #1 introductory level computer book series and have written asking for more. So if you're looking for the most fun and easy way to learn about computers, look to *. . . For Dummies* books to give you a helping hand.

IDG BOOKS

THE INTERNET
FOR MACS
FOR
DUMMIES™

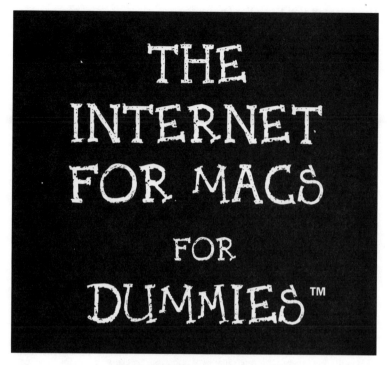

THE INTERNET FOR MACS FOR DUMMIES™

by Charles Seiter

Foreword by David Pogue
Macworld Contributing Editor, and author of *Macs For Dummies*

IDG BOOKS

IDG Books Worldwide, Inc.
An International Data Group Company

Foster City, CA ♦ Chicago, IL ♦ Indianapolis, IN ♦ Braintree, MA ♦ Dallas, TX

The Internet For Macs For Dummies

Published by
IDG Books Worldwide, Inc.
An International Data Group Company
919 E. Hillsdale Blvd.
Suite 400
Foster City, CA 94404

Library of Congress Catalog Card No.: 94-77623

ISBN: 1-56884-184-1

Printed in the United States of America

10 9 8 7 6 5 4 3

1B/SQ/RS/ZU

Distributed in the United States by IDG Books Worldwide, Inc.

Distributed by Macmillan Canada for Canada; by Computer and Technical Books for the Caribbean Basin; by Contemporanea de Ediciones for Venezuela; by Distribuidora Cuspide for Argentina; by CITEC for Brazil; by Ediciones ZETA S.C.R. Ltda. for Peru; by Editorial Limusa SA for Mexico; by Transworld Publishers Limited in the United Kingdom and Europe; by Al-Maiman Publishers & Distributors for Saudi Arabia; by Simron Pty. Ltd. for South Africa; by IDG Communications (HK) Ltd. for Hong Kong; by Toppan Company Ltd. for Japan; by Addison Wesley Publishing Company for Korea; by Longman Singapore Publishers Ltd. for Singapore, Malaysia, Thailand and Indonesia; by Unalis Corporation for Taiwan; by WS Computer Publishing Company, Inc. for the Philippines; by WoodsLane Pty. Ltd. for Australia; by WoodsLane Enterprises Ltd. for New Zealand.

For general information on IDG Books in the U.S., including information on discounts and premiums, contact IDG Books at 800-434-3422 or 415-655-3000.

For information on where to purchase IDG Books outside the U.S., contact IDG Books International at 415-655-3021 or fax 415-655-3295.

For information on translations, contact Marc Jeffrey Mikulich, Director, Foreign & Subsidiary Rights, at IDG Books Worldwide, 415-655-3018 or fax 415-655-3295.

For sales inquiries and special prices for bulk quantities, write to the address above or call IDG Books Worldwide at 415-655-3000.

For information on using IDG Books in the classroom, or ordering examination copies, contact Jim Kelly at 800-434-2086.

is a registered trademark of
IDG Books Worldwide, Inc.

About the Author

Charles Seiter wrote his first computer programs on ancient IBM iron in the 1960s and, at one point, had a college summer job writing FORTRAN code for Atlas missile guidance simulation. That's right, he *is* a rocket scientist.

Well, not really. He got a Ph.D. in chemistry from Caltech and then worked as a chemistry professor for years. His academic career was derailed by winning a pile of money on a television game show, at which point he freed himself from the job of flunking a certain percentage of premed students in freshman chemistry every year and moved away to a redwood forest in northern California.

He began consulting on the design of DNA sequencing equipment and other biochemistry hardware for firms in the Bay Area and, by chance, just happened to be hanging around when Macworld was founded. Over the course of ten years, he has probably reviewed more Mac technical software than anyone in history. *The Internet For Macs For Dummies* is his tenth computer book and his first in the . . . *For Dummies* series.

Welcome to the world of IDG Books Worldwide.

IDG Books Worldwide, Inc. is a subsidiary of International Data Group, the world's largest publisher of computer-related information and the leading global provider of information services on information technology. IDG was founded more than 25 years ago and now employs more than 7,000 people worldwide. IDG publishes more than 220 computer publications in 65 countries (see listing below). More than fifty million people read one or more IDG publications each month.

Launched in 1990, IDG Books Worldwide is today the #1 publisher of best-selling computer books in the United States. We are proud to have received 3 awards from the Computer Press Association in recognition of editorial excellence, and our best-selling ...For Dummies™ series has more than 12 million copies in print with translations in 25 languages. IDG Books, through a recent joint venture with IDG's Hi-Tech Beijing, became the first U.S. publisher to publish a computer book in the People's Republic of China. In record time, IDG Books has become the first choice for millions of readers around the world who want to learn how to better manage their businesses.

Our mission is simple: Every IDG book is designed to bring extra value and skill-building instructions to the reader. Our books are written by experts who understand and care about our readers. The knowledge base of our editorial staff comes from years of experience in publishing, education, and journalism — experience which we use to produce books for the '90s. In short, we care about books, so we attract the best people. We devote special attention to details such as audience, interior design, use of icons, and illustrations. And because we use an efficient process of authoring, editing, and desktop publishing our books electronically, we can spend more time ensuring superior content and spend less time on the technicalities of making books.

You can count on our commitment to deliver high-quality books at competitive prices on topics consumers want to read about. At IDG, we value quality, and we have been delivering quality for more than 25 years. You'll find no better book on a subject than an IDG book.

John J. Kilcullen
President and CEO
IDG Books Worldwide, Inc.

Acknowledgments

The author would like to thank Janna Custer at IDG Books for approaching me about this project, and Jim Heid and Maryellen Kelly for talking me into it. Thanks also to Nancy Dunn for getting me into this racket in the first place. The staff at Macworld, particularly Carol Person and Galen Gruman, have shown great forbearance about my frequent and unseemly disappearances into cyberspace.

I would like to thank Laurie Smith, my project editor at IDG's Indianapolis office, for floating some deadlines so that we could include late-breaking develop-ments. She worked straight through Memorial Day weekend in *Indianapolis*. That's dedication. I would also like to thank those members of the editorial and production staff who gave of their time and talents to make this book a success: Shawn MacLaren, Pam Mourouzis, Barbara Potter, Valery Bourke, Chris Collins, Tricia Reynolds, and Angela Hunckler.

Thanks also to Suzanne Stefanac for tech editing and for last-minute help with the project; to K. Calderwood for discussions on TCP/IP, gateways, and other matters; and to David Pogue for the hilarious Foreword.

Loretta Toth, rather than seeing an acknowledgment about my wife "putting up with long hours blah, blah, blah," realized at once that she should just do her own book project at the same time. Brilliant! I hope this sparks a domestic-tranquillity revolution in publishing, in which contracts are issued in pairs.

Finally, I would like to thank the pioneers of the Internet, some famous and some unsung, who put together this remarkable system. Bit by bit they made an entity with its own living intelligence and its own strange dreams.

The publisher would like to give special thanks to Patrick J. McGovern, without whom this book would not have been possible.

Credits

**Executive Vice President,
Strategic Product Planning
and Research**
David Solomon

Editorial Director
Diane Graves Steele

Acquisitions Editor
Megg Bonar

Editorial Managers
Tracy L. Barr
Sandra Blackthorn

Editorial Assistant
Tamara S. Castleman
Stacey Holden Prince
Kevin Spencer

Acquisitions Assistant
Suki Gear

Production Director
Beth Jenkins

**Associate Project
Coordinator**
Valery Bourke

Production Pre-Press
Tony Augsburger
Steve Peake

Project Editor
Laurie Ann Smith

Editors
Shawn MacLaren
Pam Mourouzis
Barbara Potter
Andy Cummings

Technical Reviewer
Suzanne Stefanac

Production Staff
Chris Collins
Angela F. Hunckler
Dwight Ramsey
Gina Scott
Patricia R. Reynolds

Proofreader
Henry Lazarek

Indexer
David Heiret

Book Design
University Graphics

Cover Design
Kavish + Kavish

Contents at a Glance

Cartoons at a Glance

By Rich Tennant

page 7

page 30

page 69

page 68

page 142

page 157

page 132

page 191

page 215

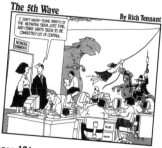

page 184

Table of Contents

· ·

Foreword

• •

by David Pogue
Macworld **Contributing Editor, and author of** *Macs For Dummies*

Some topics don't make good *Dummies* books. I doubt the phrase "flying off the bookstore shelves" would ever apply to *Escalators For Dummies, Flossing For Dummies,* or, for that matter, *Neurosurgery For Dummies.*

The Internet, however, begs — pleads — *screams* to be a *Dummies* book.

You must understand that the Internet is our solar system's largest information network, accessible only by computer modem. It's a tangled, seething mass of cobbled-together wiring and computers, designed by a bunch of tangled, seething scientists and government bureaucrats 30 years ago. When I *picture* the Internet, I usually envision something like a set design out of *Alien* or *Brazil.* Abandon hope, ye who enter.

Those Internet designers had in mind a secret network, a huge underground maze of circuitry, so cruelly cryptic that invading Russians would throw up their hands and march right back to their submarines in disgust. The Internet requires its own silly language, in which things like

```
sumex-aim.ncsa.uiuc.edu@ftp(*)
```

means "Yo." The Internet was designed to run on huge humming mainframe computers that dwarfed Manhattan warehouses and had 4K of memory. The Internet is so complex that even complete reclusive computer nerds with few social opportunities had to write utilities like SLIP and WAIS and WWW to manage the Internet's utilities.

And during every step of the tangled, seething construction of the Internet, there's one thing nobody ever stopped to consider.

You.

Nobody intended for the typical, well-meaning American of above-average intelligence and a decent education to be able to make any sense of the Internet. Until *Time* and *Newsweek* and *The New York Times* began hailing the Internet as the biggest news story since Baby Jessica, it was the sole domain of scientists and hackers (the Internet, not the baby).

You haven't a prayer for making your way through the snarled, tangled techno-mass of the Internet without Charles Seiter. He was born with some kind of double-recessive gene, a freak rarity, that lets him make technical topics as accessible as the fridge. Good grief, sometimes I even catch myself reading his *Macworld* articles on things like statistical analysis and quantum physics, just because they're funny and interesting.

In this book, Charles offers two ways for you to get onto the Internet without losing unduly large hair tufts. First — the Great *Internet For Macs For Dummies* Dirty Little Secret — you can avoid the crumbling, archaic dirt roads of the military/university computers entirely. Instead, you can drive on the new, smoothly paved freeways provided by friendly services like America Online.

Second — if clicking a few colorful icons is too sissified for you — Charles also shows you how to get onto the Internet the *regular* way (huge humming main-frames, and so on). And he tells you what few silly Internet-language codes you really need to negotiate the hostile electronic waters — but friendly fellow cybernauts — of the Internet.

Either way, you're likely to be blown away and probably consumed for hours a day by the awesomeness and depth of the information and people you'll find there. Billions of Mac programs. Trillions of facts. 100 messages a day about *Seinfeld*.

And 30 million people.

Correction: 30 million and one.

Welcome to the Internet.

David Pogue

New York City

Introduction

 ·

*W*elcome to *The Internet For Macs For Dummies*! When I started taking my Macintosh onto the Internet, I found that there was a lot to learn, mainly because the Internet was not built with the Mac in mind. But I'm going to save you plenty of Internet time and trouble because

   ✔ I've already chewed my way through all the hassles.

   ✔ You were kind enough to buy this book.

The Internet is a gold mine of information, but most of the programs you can use to access Internet services were based on early-1980s state-of-the-art programming — in other words, stuff people admired before the Macintosh was invented. The Internet is a large part of what experts call the information superhighway; I must say, however, that the paving is chock full o' potholes.

I assume that because you're a Mac user, you don't want to learn a bunch of mysterious three-letter commands from a different computer operating system just to send an e-mail letter to someone. In the Mac world, of course, things are supposed to be easier. Every chance I get, I'm going to show you ways to work around the complicated old style of Internet access.

Lately, there's been some good news for us Mac users. Most Internet services providers have been improving their Macintosh interfaces during the last year. Thank goodness. In January 1994, you still had to learn bits of the notoriously complex UNIX operating system to get anything like real Internet access. Now you don't.

This book is full of cutting-edge material. In fact, it may be the first non-obsolete Internet book for the Macintosh because it was written *after* the interface revolution.

About This Book

I wrote this book to get you onto the Internet and point out its many interesting features. All the material here has been tested on ordinary users. By *users,* I don't mean the people who hang around at users' groups comparing shareware; I mean people who call me with questions about using the spell checker in MacWrite.

This book will be easier to follow than, say, a *Macworld* article. But be sure to skim most of this book before picking a way to sign on the Internet: I compare the costs and benefits of many different approaches.

Here are some key points explained in this book:

- ✔ What the Internet is (and isn't)
- ✔ How you get connected
- ✔ What you'll find
- ✔ How to get free software
- ✔ How to make friends on the Net
- ✔ How to access a whole universe of computers

Using This Book

If you just want to get on and get out there, this is the right book for you. This is a reference book, but that doesn't mean that it's a computer-systems manual. It's a guide to launch you onto the Net, and it's a map to help you navigate the system after you're out there.

I prefer real Macintosh, point-and-click software. Nonetheless, some of the services described here still have a plain old text interface. When you have to type something (such as file name, directory name, Internet address, or newsgroup), I'll indicate it in a monospaced font like so:

```
upload goodies.txt
```

In general, it makes a difference whether you type a command in lowercase or in capital letters, so do it exactly as shown.

Not Just a Job, It's an Adventure

Learning about the Internet is not just another computer chore, such as learning Aldus PageMaker shortcuts. When you sign on to the Internet, you are participating in one of the most exciting intellectual adventures in history. Out there on the Net is a big chunk of all the information accumulated by the human race since the dawn of time, from satellite photos to Shakespeare. Many of the coolest people on the planet are out there, too.

Nobody knows where all the Internet is headed, how big it's going to get, or how it will evolve next. All I know is that tens of millions of intelligent people will be able to communicate all over the planet (or *off* the planet, according to some Internet UFO discussion groups). Because you're reading this book, you're going to be able to help determine the future.

Being a Newbie

Newbie is a term for Internet newcomers. Presumably, that means you.

Sometimes it's a term used in a neutral context, as in "Newbies are asked to review the FAQ (*f*requently *a*sked *q*uestions) file after joining the conference." (Translation: Before you ask on-line a question that has been asked and answered a hundred times already, the old-timers want you to check out a file written for beginners.)

At other times, *newbie* is an insulting term. It's not rare to find a Net old-timer *flaming* a newbie — that is, answering an innocent question with a string of nasty remarks. To tell the truth, back when the Internet was a sort of exclusive club, people were a bit more patient with beginners. Of course, when you have 30 million people communicating with each other, the law of averages predicts that some will be classic grouches.

In this book, I offer tips for

✔ Being an impeccably-mannered newbie

✔ Dodging flames

✔ Finding a style of your own

What's in This Book

This book is divided into five parts; each has a different function.

Part 1: Mac Internet Basics

In this part, I explain the world of the Internet — what's in it, how it came to be, and who's there. You can read this part to learn some Internet background so that you can impress your friends and associates, or you can use the new knowledge to plan real adventures.

Part II: National On-Line Services

The easiest Internet access is through the big on-line services. Not only do these people want your business, they are furiously upgrading their Internet capabilities on a monthly basis, just to make you feel welcome.

Part III: Do-It-Yourself

If you want to play in the big leagues, I tell you what you need in this part. Sometimes it makes sense to be your own Internet site and sometimes it doesn't, so I cover the options.

Part IV: The Part of Tens

Some of these top-ten lists are serious, and some are just for fun.

Part V: Appendixes

In the appendixes, I reveal some extra hints and tips. I also offer you some useful lists that are too long to put in the middle of the book.

Icons Used in This Book

Hey, look here, everyone: Pictures in a computer book.

Technical Stuff

Believe me, the Internet has plenty of technical aspects. You can skip these sections if you like, but read them if you're curious.

Tip

A Tip is a recommended way to accomplish an Internet task with your Mac. Often, a Tip is a shortcut.

Remember

This icon flags background information that you should keep in mind. "Eat your dinner first and then eat the salad" would be a Remember for traveling in Italy.

Warning

Drive on the left would be a Warning for traveling in Britain.

Navigate

This icon alerts you that I'm going to tell you how to get to some cool places on the Internet. Hey, on the highway, do it my way.

Mac Psychology

Every time I can turn the Internet into a Mac-friendly environment, I signal so with this icon. Here you'll find some of the distinctively Mac stuff in the book.

What's Next?

It's time to take the plunge.

But first, I'd like to offer a few words of encouragement: Some parts of the Internet world are fairly confusing. If you find them confusing, it's not just you. Some aspects are hard — the way English-language spelling is hard — because the Internet evolved through a series of historic accidents.

I've been the editor in charge of stuff-that's-too-hard-for-English-majors at Macworld for nine years. And I've found some aspects of Internet use to be as hard as, say, advanced topics in Microsoft Excel. So if you are puzzled by the Internet from time to time, remember that it's not your fault.

IDG is paying me to make this easy for you. I think that this addition to the good ole . . . *For Dummies* series will make Internet access almost as easy as word processing — and considerably more fun.

Tell Us What You Think

Please send me your comments; you can reach me at

IDG Books Worldwide
7260 Shadeland Station
Suite 100
Indianapolis, IN 46256

I'd give you my Internet e-mail address, but it's already so jammed with stuff that I'm more likely to find your comments on paper!

Part I
Mac Internet Basics

The 5th Wave   By Rich Tennant

"EXCUSE ME- IS ANYONE HERE <u>NOT</u> TALKING ABOUT THE INTERNET?"

In this part...

The Internet is the wild and woolly frontier of electronic communication. A huge part of all the information ever accumulated is out there somewhere on the Internet. It's just a matter of finding a way to navigate this digital ocean with your Macintosh.

That's why I'm here. This is the first second-generation Internet book. It assumes that you want to use the Internet the same way you use a Macintosh, with icons, menus, and lots of the little details smoothed over.

In this part, you'll travel the Internet, seeing what it has to offer and how you get it for yourself. I hope you enjoy the journey!

Chapter 1

Welcome to the Net — Internet Basics

• •

• •

What Is the Internet?

At one time, people thought that the Internet was the natural habitat of rocket scientists. But lately, every newsmagazine in America has told us that the Internet is The Next Big Thing. Newspapers talk about *netsurfing*, a peculiar sport played by people who rarely get wet. And commercials about the so-called information superhighway promise that you'll soon have data coming out of your ears and that a portable fax machine strapped to your wrist will be proper fashion for a beach vacation.

Whew.

Well, when you get into the Internet, you'll find out two things:

✔ It really is pretty amazing.

✔ You don't have to be a rocket scientist anymore to use it. And it won't follow you on vacation, unless you insist.

Caught in the Net

Most computers in offices or universities can talk to each other over *networks*, or sets of wiring and software that let computers communicate with each other.

The Internet is a way for these computer networks to connect to other computer networks. In fact, you can contact people all over the world from your computer through the Internet.

You see, the Internet lets you send files from one computer to another over a big, high-speed system of computer network connections, which the U.S. government paid for and installed. Because all these computers all over the planet can transfer files anywhere, anyone (even you) can access any information that someone wants to place in the *public domain*, meaning that it's available to everyone with no restrictions.

That's right, people develop programs and other valuable stuff and give them away. And a lot of the programs are really good! The next time someone cuts you off in traffic, tell yourself it's probably someone hurrying home to post a free file.

Combining all this information with *electronic mail* (or e-mail) means the following:

- ✔ You can send messages to anyone across the Internet, and they get the messages in a few minutes, usually.
- ✔ You can find thousands of useful files and free (!) programs.
- ✔ You can *chat* on-line with people anywhere (computer chatting is like talking via CB radio).
- ✔ You can get all sorts of instant, up-to-date news.

Macintosh, the easy network machine

Even if you're just sitting at your own Mac and aren't wired to anyone else, you have network capability anyway. The Mac's survival originally hinged on its success in the graphics/printing market, so Apple had to provide a way for several Macs to hook up to one (expensive) laser printer. (Three Macs and a printer is your basic example of a small network.) AppleTalk, a piece of software that lets Macs talk to each other and to a printer, became an essential part of the Macintosh system.

AppleTalk is too slow for larger networks, so vendors produced Mac-compatible hardware for Ethernet, a much faster networking connection. Fortunately, Ethernet is simple enough that lazy Mac users like you and I can use it without daily access to a network guru.

If you're having trouble visualizing the Internet as a network of networks, check out the schematic known as Figure 1-1. Still confused? Read on. (Sure, sure: I know that a picture is worth a thousand words. But, hey, give me a break: I get paid to write, not draw.)

That's you, at your own Macintosh, in the lower left of Figure 1-1. Using a modem, you dial into a computer *bulletin board*, or a central computer that many users can connect to. The bulletin board computer has a direct connection to the Internet, so it can dial up a computer at a university across the country. And that computer can look for files, at your request, on the big, federal computer located just outside Washington, D.C. To summarize: After you make an Internet connection, you can reach tons of files on any Internet computer. This process isn't *hacking*, or gaining illegal access to files; it's legitimately accessing files that people on other networks *want* you to see.

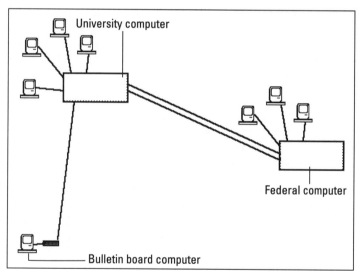

University computer

Federal computer

Figure 1-1:
The Internet is a network of networks.

Bulletin board computer

Mail: Snail versus electronic

Snail mail is computerese for letters delivered by the U.S. Post Office. *E-mail* is computer messages (which can now include sound and pictures) that get sent over a network. When you send a piece of e-mail, it gets there almost immediately. (The only catch is that the person receiving the mail has to connect to the network to receive it.) As a result, the Internet is evolving into an international instant Post Office because it can pick up e-mail on one network and deliver it to another.

Internet Archaeology

How did all this Internet stuff happen? In the 1970s, the Defense Department decided that research efforts would speed up if investigators with funding from the Advanced Research Projects Agency (ARPA) could communicate from one network to another. Usually, these networks were at big national labs like Los Alamos or universities like MIT.

ARPANET, as the new networking setup was called, originally linked about 30 sites, most of which used computers that are now ancient (Burroughs, Honeywell, ancient DEC hardware). Some of the first ARPANET designers were hired for another project that would let ARPANET connect to radio- and satellite-based computer communications. This effort defined the communications hardware and software that make an Internet connection.

In the 1980s, the old ARPA sites converted to the new Internet connections. Then the National Science Foundation (NSF) put together a high-speed network for Internet sites. Companies selling gateway hardware and software (a *gateway* is the actual connection from one network to another) for connecting to the NSFNET began to appear. Commercial Internet service networks were born.

Letting all existing networks connect to the single big Internet produced the well-documented explosion of Internet connections; now every techno-hipster business card has an @ address. At the heart of the system is the nationwide, high-speed NSFNET, which has been funded for the next five years as a sort of government experiment in communications infrastructure.

The number of people connected to the Internet has simply exploded in the last three years (see Figure 1-2). Some authorities are guessing that the system can handle 100 million users without too much trouble. After that, the Internet may need to handle e-mail addresses differently — just as phone companies have had to adjust over the years to the increase in telephone use.

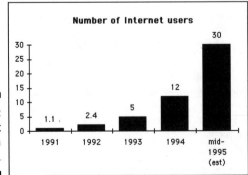

Figure 1-2: Internet users (in millions).

This amazing growth is one of the reasons that Internet access is still "under construction," at least in terms of a decent interface for Mac users. In January 1993, the typical Internet user had a research job and was used to dealing with a clunky interface (for example, see the archaic Internet commands listed in Figure 1-3). Very few people involved in designing the Internet foresaw that you and I would be pounding on the gate(way)s by 1994, demanding a user-friendly Mac interface to Internet services.

```
& help
cd [directory]          chdir to directory or home if none given
d [message list]        delete messages
e [message list]        edit messages
f [message list]        show from lines of messages
h                       print out active message headers
m [user list]           mail to specific users
n                       goto and type next message
p [message list]        print messages
pre [message list]      make messages go back to system
mailbox
q                       quit, saving unresolved messages in mbox
r [message list]        reply to sender (only) of messages
s [message list] file   append messages to file
t [message list]        type messages (same as print)
top [message list]      show top lines of messages
u [message list]        undelete messages
v [message list]        edit messages with display editor
x                       quit, do not change system mailbox
z [-]                   display next [previous] page of headers
!                       shell escape
```

Figure 1-3: Internet commands circa 1992.

E-Mail, the Internet, and @

If you glance at a business card for someone who works in a high-tech business or large company, it's likely that a line on the card will list an e-mail address (look for the @). (And to think, six years ago most cards didn't even list a fax number.) For example, an Apple employee named Kermit T. Frog could have the following e-mail address:

```
kermitf@apple.com
```

The @ is the tip-off that this code is actually an Internet-valid e-mail address; the notation .com (the Internet *zone designation*) means that the address is a business. When you read this address, you say "kermit-eff at apple dot com" (the @ is pronounced "at" and the . [period] is pronounced "dot").

Here's why addresses are important: If you have an @ address, you can communicate with anyone else on the planet with an @ address — that includes everyone who's anyone in the computer business and many of the powerful people at most organizations. To be taken seriously as a computer user or businessperson in the next few years, you're going to need your own @ address.

For example, today you can send a message to

vicepresident@whitehouse.gov

and help educate Al Gore on environmental issues ("Sir, I'd like to volunteer several distant states as nuclear waste dumps.").

By the way, the zone designation .gov means that the e-mail address is at a government site. Professors at universities usually have addresses that end in .edu (for education). Sometimes, an address will be a location instead of a job category. For example, I have an address at well.sf.ca.us, which means that you can reach me at a bulletin board site called the WELL near San Francisco, California, in the good old United States. See Table 1-1 and/or Appendix A for more examples.

When you get your own @ address, I promise that you'll feel very official. I know I did.

Table 1-1	Ten Internet Address Types
Address	*Interpretation*
@post.queensu.ca	Queen's University in Canada (.ca by itself means Canada, whereas .ca.us means California)
@coombs.anu.edu.au	Australian National University
@netcom.com	A commercial Internet service provider
@aol.com	America Online, another commercial Internet service provider
@nic.ddn.mil	A military site
@whales.org	A (mythical) nonprofit organization
@nsf.net	The National Science Foundation network
@unicef.int	An international organization
@informatik.uni-hamburg.de	A computer science department in Germany (.de means Deutschland)
@leprechaun.ie	A fantastic address in Ireland

Electronic Libraries on the Net

To recap: As an Internet user, you can exchange messages with other Internet users, from Brazil to Baltimore. By itself, that capability makes the Internet extremely useful. But, wonder of wonders, you also can use the Internet to access incredible files of information stored all over the world.

The Library of Congress, for example, contains copies of all the books (and nearly all the magazines and newspapers) published in the United States. (Of course, only 20,000 or so of the most useful books have been prepared for you to access through the Internet, but several library groups are working to get the whole collection ready for the Internet.) The U.S. Patent Office has files on all the patents it has ever issued. And university libraries across the country (Harvard, Yale, and Illinois are the largest) house all sorts of foreign research material not found in the Library of Congress. Heck, you can find comic books and campaign fliers and recipes and jokes and back issues of *TV Guide* on the Internet.

All this stuff is being merrily scanned into a text-file format that your Macintosh can read. All you must do is retrieve the file from the Internet.

Now, on-screen reading isn't great for novels — try scrolling through an 800-page paperback at the beach. It's ideal, though, if you're looking for specific pieces of information because you can search the files for key words.

Looking for books?

Here's an example: The library in the small town where I live recently got its own Internet connection. (Your library will get a connection soon because Internet access is *the* hot topic at librarians' meetings in the '90s. Come to think of it, it's about time the poor old librarians had a hot topic.) Last week, from my house, I checked the local university library for holdings on a particular topic. I didn't find what I wanted, so I clicked into libraries at the University of California at Berkeley and at the University of Illinois, Champaign-Urbana. I could have tapped into libraries at Oxford, for that matter. Finally, I came back to my own library and made an interlibrary loan request for a book at Berkeley. Not bad for ten minutes work at my own Mac!

In other words, even if you're sitting in front of your Macintosh, you can browse the stacks of most of the world's libraries. Although you may not always be able to get individual books transferred to a library near you, the information in these books is, as I write, steadily being converted to on-line files that you can download.

A connected world

The Internet isn't all serious. Sure, it has resources on programming languages and mathematical physics. But the Internet also is the planet's chief pipeline to news and plain, old, silly gossip.

For example, I regularly check comments made by fans of the strange TV program "Mystery Science Theater 3000." This program has thousands of avid fans who chatter away on-line every day in a huge open bulletin board, called a *newsgroup*. Because "MST 3K" specializes in obscure, funny references, any given line from the show is capable of generating an endless stream of linked messages from fans, explaining various perspectives on the wisecrack.

Inevitably, the Internet reflects what's on people's minds: Just as Egyptians filled their tombs with pornographic graffiti, and just as the first artsy pictures of naked ladies appeared within a year of the invention of photography, many private computer bulletin boards specialize in adult material. And many of those boards are connected to the Net. In fact, it's a matter of record that two of the newsgroups most frequently accessed are `alt.sex` and `rec.arts.erotica`.

Actually, if you want on-line access to dating service communications, bulletin boards are hotter than the Internet.

Looking for love?

The Internet has a service called Internet Relay Chat (IRC), a sort of global conference call. But the chat lines on bulletin boards and big on-line services, such as GEnie, are actually better for this stuff than the Internet. There's no point clogging up the poor old Net if you can have more fun anyway with a specialized connection.

Who Needs the Internet?

Well, the Internet is not just for universities anymore. Millions of people — cyberpunks, grandmothers, business people — have a legitimate need for Internet access. And plenty of Internet users advocate the idea that nearly everyone should be connected.

On a drizzly, spring morning in San Francisco, I decided to find out what sorts of people were willing to take a beginning Internet class. The class was organized by the WELL (415-332-4335), a San Francisco-area computer bulletin board that's probably the finest service of its kind in the country — the East Coast equivalent is ECHO (212-255-3839). The crowd, amazingly enough, consisted of equal parts of

✔ Generation X-ers, complete with the occasional nose ring and I'm-an-artist-don't-bother-me-OK? fashion

✔ Retired high-school teachers

This pattern has held through several rounds of classes (by the way, you can add entrepreneurs to the mix — to them, the Internet represents a new business opportunity). Of course, I don't quite know what this means. Lately, I've been asked to give Internet talks to every community group north of the Golden Gate Bridge, so my guess is that the sociological profile of Internet users is probably going to look just like the general population within a year or so.

Greek to me

Just about everything ever written in Latin or ancient Greek is available on-line as part of a huge project involving Classics departments all over the world. It's nice when you can read *finished* documents — I don't think that these authors will be writing new editions any time soon.

Your Mac Experience

Mac users buy a Mac for straightforward point-and-click access to serious computer power. Naturally, you and I both want Internet access that uses a traditional Mac interface. If you have free Internet access (for example, you're a university student or your employer has given you an account), you should check out the special considerations in Chapters 14 and 15. The aim of most of this book, however, is to explain Internet access to people who don't have large organizations with systems administrators supporting them.

There is no way, just now, to get full Internet access easily in a single software or service package, so I'm going to recommend an ease-into-it approach. I think that you start with partial access and graduate to full access later. In other words, go ahead and goof off for a few months and let teams of drones do all the grunt labor for you!

There are two reasons for this phased-in, lazy approach:

✔ **The Internet is big.** You can probably get comfortable with Internet e-mail in just a few days, but the amount of other material available is so vast that you can spend weeks just surveying the so-called cyberspace landscape. If you start with an easy-to-use but limited service, you can later step up to full Internet access when you have a better estimate of what you need.

✔ **The Internet is changing.** For example, the folks at the National Center for Supercomputing Applications (NCSA) who wrote Mosaic (a very nice Macintosh front-end to the Internet) as a free program have moved to California to produce a commercial version. Either they will sell an easy-to-use version of their own product, or parts of Mosaic will be incorporated into the interface for national on-line services.

One way or another, full Internet access for Macs will happen in the course of the next year. So learning that

```
!sx -a myfile.txt
```

is the command for downloading a file in some systems is a ghastly waste of time.

Using the Internet shouldn't be any harder than using, say, FileMaker Pro — this isn't true right now, but it will be soon. So I say, get on the Net immediately and don't bother with Internet tricks that will be obsolete by Christmas.

The available Internet services are wildly different. Delphi has real Internet, but it uses a text-based menu for navigation. America Online (AOL) has a real Mac interface, but some parts of real Internet are still missing. All other services provide either worse interfaces than AOL or fewer features than Delphi, but they offer some other features as a compromise.

Besides direct Internet access, I'm going to discuss the pros and cons of Internet access with

✔ America Online

✔ CompuServe

✔ Prodigy

✔ Delphi

✔ GEnie

✔ eWorld

In Part II, I detail these services so that you can see what you'll get before you pay to join. I promise, I'm going to make this Internet stuff easy. Hey, and *they* are going to make it cheap: you can find some free-trial coupons from many Internet services at the very end of the book.

Think about it. If there's a research topic that you've always wanted to pursue, you can command the resources of most of the world's universities with your fingers. If you're an Australian frustrated by America's utter lack of interest in cricket, you can get yesterday's scores by making a local call. If you just want to find a large group of people who share your obsessions, you no longer have to leave your home.

And, in most cases, as long as you observe a few basic rules of decorum, you'll find that you are welcomed into these new electronic communities. It's not just the future — it's already happened!

Check these topics

To motivate you, to give you some idea of what's out there, I list here some of the kinds of information on the Internet. You also can take it for granted that there are gigabytes of hard-core techie stuff, too.

✔ **Urban legends:** Folklorist Jan Harold Brunvand, author of *The Choking Doberman* and *The Mexican Pet,* maintains files on urban myths in a newsgroup called `alt.folklore.urban`. You can check here to convince yourself that all known poodle-in-a-microwave stories are fiction.

✔ **QuarkXPress at Indiana University:** Authors of books on Quark have downloaded files to this huge archive of tips and information on using QuarkXPress. Now you can look at this week's tips instead of last year's.

✔ **GUTNBERG:** Project Gutenberg is the name of an initiative to put almost everything important that was ever printed into on-line form. Time for a bigger hard drive, huh?

✔ **Hong Kong Polytechnic:** The address `@library.hpk.hk` takes you into the library of this college in Hong Kong (the country code is `hk`, naturally). I mention this address because most of the other places on the planet that have computers are as connected as the United States. The curious exception is Japan; the Japanese government telecommunications office hasn't quite decided what to make of all this Internet stuff.

✔ **Internet Business Journal:** This on-line journal, which exists electronically only, discusses business opportunities on theInternet. (If you send a note to `441495@acadvml.uottawa.ca`, the editor will cheerfully sign you up for a paid subscription.) Advertising businesses is a very controversial topic, and it will be interesting to see how some kinds of business revenues are brought in to support services.

✔ **Is funny, nyet?** There's an Internet service that reports jokes from the former Soviet Union. These days they can use all the humor they can get.

✔ **Agriculture:** On a huge range of university-maintained databases, every bit of agricultural research ever assembled is indexed and available. If you're a farmer, there's no need any more to wait for the agent from the ag school to get around to your county.

Chapter 2
Many, Many Nets

The Internet Is a Collection of Nets

At the same time that the Defense Department began sponsoring a communications protocol for connecting research networks, computer use by ordinary people exploded. In the early 1980s, as the old ARPA system gave way to the Internet, Apple II sales soared into the millions and the IBM PC essentially became a new industry. Meanwhile, cheap, fast modems appeared, making computer bulletin boards and assorted on-line services practical for the first time.

Who Are All These Networks Anyway?

When you start exploring the Internet, you'll find all sorts of information, opinion, and outright bafflement. Not only are there nearly 30 million Internet users, but there are comparable numbers of people connected to other nets that pass information to the Internet. Some of these other nets are just tiny private bulletin boards that service five people a day. Some of them are government networks that span the whole globe and connect thousands of solid citizens in white shirts and ties.

Although thousands of nets can exchange messages and data with the Internet, only a few are really important. Four big sources (Usenet, BITNET, university special-interest groups, and government labs and organizations) contribute most of the stuff that you find on the Net, so in this chapter I'm going to give you a quick rundown on them.

The cloudy crystal ball

When you read predictions about where the Internet is going, think about the following:

• How Steve Wozniak started Apple because he couldn't convince his bosses at Hewlett-Packard that a market for small computers existed.

• How Steve Jobs managed to "borrow" much of the Mac interface from Xerox because Xerox thought of work from its Palo Alto Research Center (PARC) as a research lab curiosity.

If you keep old computer magazines for more than a few years, you can laugh yourself silly reading the pundits' columns. Hey, in the early 1950s, Univac figured that the United States could absorb *12 computers* over the years. Wanna bet that the experts are all smarter now?

So by the time you read three chapters of this book, you can consider yourself an Internet guru qualified to make predictions.

If That's the Internet, What's This Usenet Business?

When people think of the Internet, they often think of cool characters swapping sophisticated messages on every topic under the sun. Actually, most of that action takes place on another network, called Usenet. But plenty of Internet sites also are Usenet sites, so the information tends to slosh across the two systems. On the Internet, you can talk to Usenet people, and they can talk to you.

Usenet newsgroups are the source of the most entertaining material accessible on the Internet. For example, the newsgroup `rec.humor.funny` is the most-accessed topic on the Internet; `rec.humor.funny` includes jokes selected diligently from the material found in the larger selection `rec.humor`. That's right, someone screens out the unfunny jokes for you! Is this a great service or what?

Short-sited?

After you make an Internet connection, through an on-line service or bulletin board, you can ask the system operator to add your name to the subscription lists for different newsgroups.

If your connections site does not carry a particular newsgroup, ask your system operators to add it; they almost always are willing to do so.

Usenet also is the source of serious stuff. If you want to study mathematical chaos, for example, you can join a newsgroup called `sci.non-linear`.

Getting network news

More than two million users participate in a scheme referred to collectively as network news; Usenet is the set of newsgroups at the core of the collection. Essentially it's just a set of conferences (organized discussion groups) that allow network discussions of different topics, together with an organized system for passing the discussions along to different nets.

An amazing amount of Usenet material is contributed by graduate students from various distinguished institutions of higher learning. (Considering the many afternoons I whiled away at dear old Caltech playing billiards when I should have been taking magnetic resonance spectra, I find that I envy today's students, whose every wisecrack is recorded for posterity. Now get back to work, folks.) At least they make for lively reading.

Conference calls

Table 2-1 lists a tiny sample of the conferences on Usenet that you can join from an Internet site. In the chapters where I tell you how to sign on, I tell you how to get a current list — many changes occur every few months.

Usenet sites, as a rule, use the operating system UNIX. One of my goals in writing this book is to insulate you from UNIX; I don't want you to have to learn a lot of UNIX commands just to get Internet access.

The reason UNIX appears all over the Internet is that UNIX is a real industrial-strength, bulletproof network operating system. It's also very efficient with computer resources, and both computer memory and computer time used to be more expensive. It's nerd heaven, too. If you feel the urge to learn more, just check out IDG's *UNIX For Dummies* or the UNIX command sections in *The Internet For Dummies*.

Table 2-1 Welcome, Stranger!

Newsgroup	Topic
comp.ai	Artificial intelligence
soc.culture.thai	The latest from Bangkok and elsewhere
sci.med.aids	Current AIDS information
alt.hotrod	Souped-up vehicles, natch
alt.rush-limbaugh	Please note the hyphen
alt.sports.baseball.chicago-cubs	Seminar on congenital optimism
talk.abortion	Abortion controversies of all kinds
rec.arts.poems	Write a poem, put it here
misc.answers	About Usenet itself
comp.sys.mac.wanted	Macs for sale

Drinking from a fire hose

The relatively specialized newsgroup for magnetic resonance lists about a hundred messages a day. But face it, even though magnetic resonance has elbowed its way into hospitals, it remains a pretty obscure subject. My point: Newsgroups for popular topics (in other words, where practically anyone may have an opinion) really run some high volume. Figure it out: If magnetic resonance is worth a hundred postings on a good day, how much traffic do you think shows up in alt.fan.howard-stern?

If you join lots of newsgroups indiscriminately, I promise that you won't be able to find the time to read most of the stuff.

So That's Usenet, Now What's BITNET?

BITNET, another system of computer conferences on a big assortment of topics, is a network of nearly 4,000 large computer systems. BITNET, which grew from a single funky operation in North Carolina in the early 1980s, got its name from an old IBM ad that featured the line "Because It's Time." (It's kind of an ironic slogan: at the time, IBM missed every boat leaving the harbor.)

What you have here is your basic collection of IBM mainframe computers with a special program that forwards discussions from one computer to the next on the network. It's as simple as that.

And because many of these BITNET sites are also Internet sites, there's no reason you can't join BITNET discussions from your Internet service. I give you the gory details when you need them. (FYI: The exact mechanism is the LISTSERV mailing list manager; LISTSERV (and another program called MAILSERV) puts you on a computer mailing list, just as you can be on a mailing list of community volunteers.) For now, check Table 2-2 to see some of the topics. Generally, there are more computer-oriented and serious topics on BIT than Use.

Table 2-2	Bits of BIT
Newsgroup	*Content*
`bit.listserv.frac-a`	Cool stuff about fractals
`bit.listserv.lstsrv-l`	Uncool stuff about LISTSERV mechanics
`bit.mailserv.word-mac`	Mac word processors
`bit.listserv.games-l`	Computer games
`bit.listserv.gaynet`	Gay discussion groups
`bit.listserv.catholic`	Catholic topics

Too Cool for School?

Plenty of independent commercial on-line systems offer many of the services that people expect from the Internet. You can find all sorts of shareware to download, for example. You can find special-interest groups with an unlimited (and, I dare say, unhealthy) interest in the details of old Partridge Family shows. You can track the entire universe of day-to-day data (stock quotes, sports scores, weather). The really unique feature of the Internet, aside from its unmatchable vast connectivity, is the contribution made by university networks: If you want to look up biographical details on Marilyn Monroe, you can do so in a library. If you want to keep up with developments in molecular biology, you need the Internet. Internet access means access to most of the important areas of modern scholarship.

In fact, special initiatives now exist on the Internet for a sort of virtual reality international conference for biologists, in which scientists compare data and analysis on-line — including journal figures and photos. In a more pedestrian Internet mode, Internet files are increasingly the standard repository for fast-moving information.

The Internet someday may help level the research-competitive playing fields between richer and poorer institutions. Already, Internet access has enabled people in some fields, most notably mathematics, to enjoy a level of contact that's a vast improvement on the traditional once-a-year-let's-all-meet-in-D.C. style of interaction.

Classes at Electronic U

Universities are using the Internet not just to exchange research results but to offer courses. Think for a moment about the quality of student/teacher interaction in a freshman physics course: it's not uncommon at large universities to stuff 400 students in a lecture hall (and those sitting at the back have to watch the lecture on TV monitors). Doesn't a private on-line tutor sound more desirable? The window in Figure 2-1 is an example of an early version of Internet courseware.

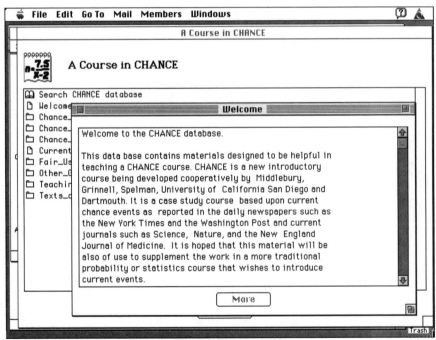

Figure 2-1: Take a chance on this Internet course.

One big argument in favor of on-line courses is the appallingly short shelf life of course material. For example, there's not much you could have learned in a digital-design course in electrical engineering ten years ago that would look very compelling in your personnel file today. In most engineering professions, it's taken for granted that the whole stock of information needs to be overhauled every five years. The need for fluid information flow keeps many schools interested in on-line education despite the hassles involved in designing a new instructional format.

If it's hot, it's here

Lots of the academic journals on the shelves of a university library now have a *one-year* lead time. That time lapse may be OK for medieval historians — the last time I looked, Charlemagne was still dead — but it's not fast enough for biotechnology or AIDS research or dozens of other hot topics. On the Internet, you can encounter not just newsgroups discussing current research but also databases that are updated almost daily by diligent university types.

Caution: People at work

Right now, there is open access to huge areas on university-maintained networks that maintain Internet connections. Stanford University and the University of Minnesota, just to name two, do heroic public interest work. Stanford, in particular, has enough Macintosh stuff to keep you happy for years.

Of course, if millions of people start logging onto these university networks in the middle of the day, users will complain. And when it becomes clear that the university network is jammed with users downloading Snoopy screen-savers, the powers that be are going to change the open-access rules.

Your Tax Dollars at Work

Universities around the world contribute a great deal to the information base of the Internet, but the U.S. government pays lots of the bills. Come to think of it, that means *you* pay a lot of the bills. Umm . . . hey, thanks!

It's pretty clear that almost no one in the government had any idea (what else is new?) what was being created when the funding for the high-speed NSFNET and another net called NASA Science Internet was approved. Actually, I'm talking about a trivial amount of money by Defense Department standards — remember, we live in a world where new fighter-plane designs cost tens of billions of dollars. It would have taken Nostradamus to realize that the world could be stood on its ear by a few hundred million doled out over a few decades to scientists.

Good guys and bad guys?

Although many Internet old-timers are convinced that the U.S. government in total is too dumb to impose any sort of regulation on the Net, lots of advanced thinkers working for the government have become quite agitated about the prospect of a high-speed, nearly anonymous, nonwiretappable international communications network.

As a result, topics of net access and security are controversial. Most traditional Internet people favor unrestricted use, and a minority favor some way of guaranteeing law-enforcement access to suspicious activities. It's probably naive to disregard the possibility that some Internet users will find a way to use the Net to foster criminal activities (send opinions to psuarez@medellin.cartel.com?), but it's also naive to suppose that there's an unobtrusive way to check a significant fraction of messages. Expect plenty of debate in these areas in the years to come.

Dear Congressman (from a concerned citizen who can afford a computer)

You can find lots of old-time government data on the Internet (I tell you where in the access chapters). Some of it is the kind of info the government's printing office still ships from Boulder, Colorado, with a hundred fun recipes for powdered milk, or pamphlets on *The Soybean, Our Versatile Friend*, or travel tips on avoiding exotic diseases.

Another way to use the Internet is to make yourself heard in the corridors of power. Because newspapers have many staffers in the forefront of the on-line revolution, you're likely to find Internet e-mail addresses for everyone with the slightest pretensions to authority, including state legislators, congressional representatives, governors, senators, and cabinet members. Usually these @ addresses are listed on the editorial page of the paper (sometimes printed as a shameless way to fill space).

The handful of people I know who have worked this contact channel (some old hands at PeaceNet and EcoNet, for example, pioneering public-interest network groups) claim to have obtained better results electronically than with traditional paper and pen.

Despite the millions of Net residents now on-line, the whole scheme is probably new enough to politicians that an Internet message still has a certain mystique. And if you send an Internet message to a politician, you're more likely to be taken seriously. The U.S. Senate, by the way, now has an anonymous FTP site with files of current Senate information. (Curiously, Teddy Kennedy was essentially the senator who sponsored this initiative. *I* was surprised, but I'm a Democrat and so thought that old Ted's mind was on other things.)

How Did All This Stuff Get Here?

Before most day-to-day Mac users heard of the Internet, people were pumping out information and discussions from Usenet, BITNET, university special-interest groups, and government labs and organizations. They were doing it in the United States, and they were doing it everywhere else, too.

Finland, for example, jumped on the Internet early. Finland is snowed-in five months of the year (they're the world champs at icebreaker-ship technology), so on-line communication makes plenty of sense compared to frozen snail mail. A big Internet presence keeps Finnish researchers in contact with the rest of the planet.

As you head out into cyberspace, I have good news and bad news. The bad news: The landscape is even more crowded. You're visiting a 30-million-user Internet, not a 2-million-user Internet. The good news: The landscape is more crowded and therefore richer.

To get your hardware set up to cruise this strange new world, turn to the next chapter.

The 5th Wave

Larry's newsgroup friends pay an in-person visit.

Understanding What a Modem Does

Despite all these hardware considerations, a modem's job is really fairly simple: it takes output from your files or your keyboard and converts the pattern of zeroes and ones into an equivalent pattern of tones. The telephone line can handle the tones reliably, so the message gets sent.

The other common communications accessory is the fax machine, so these days modem makers tend to build fax capability into the modem. A fax/modem's job isn't much harder — it converts the document into a set of lines containing dark bits and white spaces (blocks of zeroes and ones) and performs the same tone conversion on this data.

The circuit boards inside these products reflect this simplicity. They usually contain just a few chips (and there are only a few popular chip vendors for data communications circuits) and other components. In portable modems, the holder for the nine-volt battery is often the biggest physical component. Because there's really not much in them, prices for modems fall steadily every year as the chips get cheaper. Yesterday's $600 modem is today's $99 bargain, and yesterday's mainstream modem is sitting on a closet shelf.

Is old stuff good enough?

Millions of 1200-bps (bits per second) modems are floating around, and if you plan to contact an on-line service only occasionally, you can get along with one of them. Frankly, you shouldn't *buy* one — try to cajole someone into giving you one instead. The typical Mac users group includes dozens of people who have upgraded their communications and may be willing to donate their old ones to you. You won't be happy downloading Internet files at 1200 bps.

Is not-quite-old stuff good enough?

You can still buy a 2400-bps modem without a fax as a basic communications system. Sometimes you find them bundled with introductory offers for national on-line services. As the following sidebar explains, they sometimes come bundled with your Mac.

Honest, they gave me this thing!

Apple sold at least a million Performa models with built-in modems and communications software. The catch in this arrangement is that the modems are 2400-bps units, for which Apple paid about $20. The built-in modem is fine for getting oriented to Internet services, but once you start doing anything serious, it's going to be out with the old and in with the new, modem-wise.

Although 2400 bps is a bit old-fashioned in terms of current chip technology, as of 1994, most bulletin boards and network connections have more local toll-free numbers for 2400 bps than for 9600 bps. Some commercial services also tack on a surcharge for 9600-bps connection. Major vendors such as Supra and Hayes sell 2400-bps modems for street prices of $60 to $100.

What should I buy?

To be happy with a modem connecting to the Internet, you should plan on buying a 9600-bps modem — or faster if you can afford it. The reason is simple. Once you get used to file transfers at 9600, using 2400 feels like you're wading though bean dip.

With a built-in fax, 9600 bps should cost a bit more than $100 in the next year. Modems that send data at 14,400 bps and also have 14,400-bps fax send/receive capability will replace their 9600 cousins over the next couple of years. They cost about $250 today, but that price will drop pretty quickly.

If you are the kind of person who wants a $3,000 trail bike and who bought a Power Mac the first day they appeared, you should know that 19,200-bps and 28,000-bps modems are also available (see Table 3-1). These modems work with special data-compression coding schemes that speed things up further by a factor of four. It's not clear which set of high-speed tricks will become universally accepted, so consider a modem faster than 14,400 bps as a sort of experimental investment.

Table 3-1	Modem Standards
The Standard	*What It Means*
V.22*bis*	2400 bps
V.32	9600 bps
V.32*bis*	14,400 bps
V.32terbo	19,200 bps
V.Fast	28,000 bps

CompuServe, for example, is installing 14,400-bps local numbers in large cities, but few on-line services are set up yet for this speed. In many areas, the phone service needs to be improved to allow fast modems to do their thing. So telephone systems themselves are being upgraded to carry more data — at 28,000 bps, the noise in ordinary voice lines becomes a big problem. Although lots of private bulletin boards with Internet connection have 14,000-bps lines, it's going to take a while for the big services to install the appropriate hardware.

Without Me You're Nothing: The Software Connection

The modem, of course, does nothing but sit there until a piece of software tells it what to do. (Also, make sure that it's turned on — believe it or not, I've been called out on consulting calls where pressing the On button was the issue.)

Three kinds of software are important for your Internet journey. First is the software provided directly by on-line services. If you're going to connect to Prodigy for Internet service, Prodigy sends you its own software disks. The second kind of software is represented by the special communications programs you have to use with direct Internet connection (I tell you about these programs in the next two chapters). Finally, basic communications software lets you connect to bulletin boards and on-line services that have a plain, vanilla, no-icon, text-style interface.

ZTerm, the last word

David Alverson wrote a terminal program called ZTerm that shows up (in earlier versions) on bulletin boards and in the software libraries of on-line services. If you have a PowerBook with an internal modem, the vendor probably gave you ZTerm (see Figure 3-1) as part of the package. In the *Macworld* August 1994 issue, the editors picked ZTerm as the best communications software. Computers, you see, are still a funny kind of business. One good programmer — for example Mr. Alverson, working by himself in Mason, Ohio — can do better work than a whole three-story building full of mediocrities on the West Coast.

Figure 3-1:
ZTerm is fast, clean, efficient, and usually free.

Microphone LT (for lovable terminalware)

A majority of new Mac modems ship with Microphone LT from Software Ventures Corporation (510-644-3232). It lacks the automation features and some of the high-end capabilities built into the full-scale version of Microphone, but it's certainly good enough for using your Mac as a text-based terminal. For signing onto a free Internet connection at a library or for any other dial-up Internet service that works on text command, it has everything you need.

If you know your modem's speed (see Figure 3-2) and the phone number for your connection, you can pretty much leave Microphone LT's default settings in place. Microphone LT also lets you specify VT-102 as the terminal type in a simple terminal settings window (see Figure 3-3). Lots of people on the Internet still use real hardware VT-102 terminals, so you're in good company.

One of this program's great virtues is that it keeps a record of your on-line session, and it's just about impossible to lose this record by accident. Instead of downloading files, often it's more convenient to read them on-screen and then later open the Microphone LT record of the session by using your favorite word processor. (See the coupon at the end of this book.)

Figure 3-2: Microphone LT asks you to make only one or two setup decisions.

Figure 3-3:
The terminal
type you
want is
VT102. Insist
on it by
name.

ClarisWorks — I've seen better, I've seen worse

ClarisWorks, which is bundled with an amazing number of Macs sold through consumer channels, includes a communications module. It's neither as capable as Microphone nor as easy to use (see the dialog box in Figure 3-4); however, if you already own it, you can learn to live with it. It doesn't have as many friendly, built-in reminders as the best communications software and was clearly something of an afterthought to Claris, but if you use ClarisWorks all the time, it gets information into the other modules (word processing and data-base) conveniently.

Microsoft Works: Data communications for the Flintstones

You're a back-to-basics sort, right? No frills? Chip your own stone tools on weekends? Microsoft Works has a communications module just for you.

Somewhere far to the west, a brooding Bill Gates lies in bed and stares up at a vaulted ceiling in his giant mansion. What's keeping him up nights? The nagging thought that somehow, somewhere, someone got something for free from Microsoft. The word processor in Works is designed, for example, to force you to buy Microsoft Word from sheer frustration someday. Microsoft acquired the communications module from a third party in a no-cash-exchanged transaction essentially as a marketing consideration.

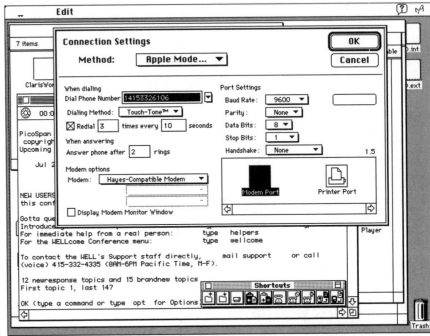

Figure 3-4:
ClarisWorks'
communi-
cations
module is a
bit fussier
than
Microphone's.

If you have Works, one of the first things you should do on the Internet is use it to download a better terminal program by using the screen shown in Figure 3-5. I tell you how in Chapter 5.

Figure 3-5:
This screen
isn't much
fun, but you
can use it to
download
ZTerm.

Fancy stuff

Figure 3-6, the sign-on screen from America Online, shows you what Mac communication software is supposed to look like. I don't show you the configuration and settings screens because usually you need to enter only modem speed and phone number, which often have been preset.

If, Against All Odds, You Find Modems Fascinating

In this book, I only want to tell you enough modem stuff so that you don't buy something that's disastrously wrong. As you can see, the Internet itself is a big enough subject to occupy your attentions. The definitive work on modems is Tina Rathbone's *Modems For Dummies,* another fine IDG product. With these preliminaries out of the way, I show you how to communicate with everyone on earth in the following chapters.

Figure 3-6:
This AOL
screen is a
vast
improvement
on terminal-
style
interfaces.

Chapter 4
E-Mail — Wired to the World

• •

In This Chapter

▶ E-mail for beginners

▶ Putting e-mail to work

▶ Understanding how the other systems do it

▶ Doing it the Macintosh way

• •

What's the Story on E-Mail?

You can send e-mail to any one of the Internet's 30 million users if

   ✔ You own a Macintosh and a modem.

   ✔ Your Mac is on a network, and the network has a modem.

   ✔ Your Mac is directly connected to a network that is an Internet *host* — a computer system with its own Internet numerical address. You don't even need a modem.

The first e-mail services open to the public (businesses have had in-house e-mail since the 1960s) were national organizations like MCI Mail and CompuServe. In the beginning, if you had an MCI account, you could send mail to anyone else with an MCI account, but you couldn't send mail out of the system. Actually, you could have had an MCI message delivered on paper to a regular street address for a discouragingly high fee.

By the early 1990s, however, everyone involved in the e-mail business had figured out that universal connection was the future of e-mail. If CompuServe, MCI Mail, and Prodigy became Internet hosts, then users could easily send messages from one service to another. It was obviously a good idea. Surprisingly, they actually followed through. Every commercial service that can afford to advertise in a magazine is now connected to the Internet.

Hosts, mailboxes, and you

Suppose that you sign up with a major Internet service provider, such as Netcom (408-554-8649). Netcom gives you a local dial-up phone number. You pick the name "Joe Cool," and you choose "joec" as your Net name. Your Internet address, then, is joec@netcom.com. Netcom is the *host*, meaning a computer system with its own Internet numerical address. You, in turn, are a user attached to that host, but you are not a host yourself.

As a service for outgoing e-mail, Netcom becomes the equivalent of the corner mailbox. You send a message to your pal Michael Nifty,

miken@world.com. Netcom routes the message to the receiving Internet host, world.com. The receiving host acts like one of those big office mailbox systems with hundreds of pigeonholes. It finds miken, stores the message, and notifies your pal that he has new mail. Usually, he sees this notice the next time he logs into the world.com system.

Oh, there really is a world.com, provided by The World. It's another big-time commercial Internet service (based in Boston, it was one of the first), and you can reach it at 617-739-0202.

These connections work, in part, because the messages are primitive. The e-mail messages I'm talking about are plain text; these messages can be created on any type of computer and read on any other. And because they're just text, they're compact — a one-page color picture file is 500 times bigger than a file containing a page of text. That makes a difference when you use a relatively slow phone line (2400 bps) for Internet connection. Someday, you may be able to send systemwide sound-plus-picture messages across the Internet. Even now, it's possible to send sound and picture *files* with a few tricks (more on this subject later), but sounds and graphics are not generally available in Internet e-mail yet.

Dear Mr. President

Using only the simplest version of a mailing system, I'm going to give a little e-mail tour now. The way I show you is not the best way to do e-mail, but this simple way is common. Some national on-line services have convenient and intuitive mail systems, and you can use a Mac-specific mail program called Eudora if you are a host (or have a direct link to a host). But the typical Internet setup uses a plain, vanilla, UNIX mail program like the one in this chapter.

First step

You get an account and log into your system. All you need is your name, your password, and a phone number. Most likely, you'll use one of the communications programs described in Chapter 3 (most chapters in this book explain the details of signing on one way or another, so for now just come along for the ride). After you log in, you get a prompt (no menus here, folks); a common prompt is the %. That's right, the computer sends you this symbol — % — to assist you in figuring what to do next. Thanks for all the help.

If you read the manual, you know that at the prompt you can type

```
mail president@whitehouse.gov
```

to start the mail program. By the way, if you find yourself stuck using this kind of interface, at the % prompt you can also type

```
man
```

and the main system (the host system — it's the host, you're the user) fills your screen with pieces of the operating system's manual.

A piece of your mind

After you type **mail** and an address at the prompt, you're rewarded with something a bit more informative. Now you see

```
mail president@whitehouse.gov
Subject:
```

You may as well compose a good general-purpose Internet presidential letter — one with a long shelf life. After you give a subject name and press Return, type this message:

```
mail president@whitehouse.gov
Subject: Such a Deal
The deficit in the Federal Budget is running nearly a billion
dollars a day. I have developed a spreadsheet in ClarisWorks
that can reschedule interest payments on the national debt by
half-day increments to save $10 billion a year, and I only
want payments of $1 million a day (it's a licensing arrange-
ment) for it. Look at it this way: I may even be right, and
$1 million a day is well within the range of accounting error
in your system. As far as you can tell, it wouldn't cost you
anything even if I were wrong!
Yours sincerely,
Joseph M. Cool
```

Now what? Well, if you read the manual, you know to press Ctrl-D (hold down Ctrl and D at the same time). The system sends you

```
EOT
```

for end of transmission.

Out into the Net

That's the end for you, but the computer system has just started working. It attaches an ID to your message and finds a path through the Internet to the target computer — in this case, a computer at the White House.

Sometimes this process is very straightforward, but the message path may go through a whole set of computers with their own weird Internet addresses.

At the receiving end, the president sees your message with a header that contains all sorts of system information. Actually, I'm just kidding about the president — it's a lead-pipe cinch that he won't see anything you send personally. But the header is there (see Figure 4-1).

Figure 4-1:
A typical
Internet
e-mail
message,
preceded by
a header
with more
than you
want to see.

```
Path:search01.news.aol.com!newstf01.cr1.aol.com!uunet!MathWorks.Com!europa.eng.gt
efsd.com!library.ucla.edu!csulb.edu!csus.edu!netcom.com!zzz
From: zzz@netcom.com (Louis Zzizz)
Subject: Re: Mac Ftp Mirrors
Message-ID: <zzzCqFHpC.AoC@netcom.com>
References: <2s1fq9$f8c@news.CCIT.Arizona.EDU> <fujii-260594031300@ts7-
38.upenn.edu>
Date: Sun, 29 May 1994 21:15:11 GMT

Subject: Re: Mac Ftp Mirrors
From: zzz@netcom.com (Louis Zzizz)
Date: Sun, 29 May 1994 21:15:11 GMT
Message-ID: <zzzCqFHpC.AoC@netcom.com>

>> Where else can I ftp to get the Umich and/or Info-Mac files?

Here are two sites that are updated every day:

ftp.univie.ac.at      131.130.1.4     mac/info-mac           1/1
ftp.ucs.ubc.ca        137.82.27.62    pub/mac/info-mac       1/1

Louis Zziz         zzz@netcom.com       San Jose, CA
```

If you make a mistake in the address, the message won't get through. Some systems tell you after a brief delay that the address isn't working. Typically, however, the message goes out on the Internet and gets bounced back to you much later — you'll find it returned the next time you connect to your host system. In other words, it's critical to get Internet addresses exactly right. Unlike the Post Office, the Internet has no way to work around your typos.

Ten Internet e-mail tips

1. The best way to find someone's address is simply to ask for it over the phone. Sometimes you can even state your message. Ain't technology neat?

2. If tip 1 fails, try looking up the address in *The Internet White Pages.*

3. Make your Internet name recognizable instead of using `squiggy@netcom.com` or something like that.

4. DON'T USE CAPITALS. THEY MAKE IT SEEM LIKE YOU'RE SHOUTING.

5. Remember the Golden Rule, because everyone else can do unto you automatically. Over and over. Over and over. Over and over.

6. E-mail jokes don't always work. In plain text, it's harder to tell when you're kidding, you lamentable buffoon (just kidding).

7. Try to keep it short. U dnt hv 2 wrt lk ths, but *Moby Dick* doesn't fit down a wire.

8. Make sure that the person receiving the message can tell who you are (put name and phone number in the text of the message).

9. Unsolicited messages should put a **?** first in the subject line, as in **?are you the joanm who went to high school in greenwood, wi.**

10. Pay attention to discussion of electronic security in newspapers. Watch Big Brother instead of letting him watch you.

Sorry about the UNIX Stuff

The Internet For Dummies includes a description of a somewhat-improved UNIX-based mailing system called elm. This program has a nice repertoire of commands and a full-screen editor. By UNIX standards, it's a big improvement. There are half a dozen other mailing programs, too.

But the fact is, they're all absolutely pitiful even compared to a simple Macintosh shareware mailing program. Nonetheless, only shareware programs are available for many kinds of basic Internet connections.

Here's why: Back when the Mac could run only MacPaint and MacWrite, UNIX was a highly evolved, nearly uncrashable operating system that could handle big networks. The best way to make a low-cost, multiuser system in the mid-1980s was to get a single, powerful UNIX computer and a bunch of cheap terminals that offered only character-oriented display. Hundreds of universities, government organizations, and businesses — the same ones that make up a big part of the Internet today — set up UNIX systems.

In the mid-1990s, therefore, Internet services often want you to take your lovely, graphics-oriented Macintosh, capable of QuickTime movies and stereo sound, and operate it as a character-oriented terminal. The machine at the other end of the wire thinks that you actually have a character-oriented terminal. Actually, I wish that some wise guy would write a program that mimics a terminal with a black screen and green dot-matrix characters to remind me of the time I spent as a child at a real VT-100 terminal.

BBS Are Bttr

Check out the mail system in Figure 4-2. It's a text-based but menu-driven system — you don't necessarily have to memorize the commands or keep a cheat sheet in your lap while you're typing because help is available at all times.

```
            COMMAND OPTIONS FOR USING EMAIL

mail userid  ...Send email to another WELL user. You will be prompted for
             a "Subject". Type a short subject header and hit Return.
             Then, enter the text of your message, hitting Return at
             the end of each line (about 70 chars wide).  To abandon
             the message without sending it, hit control-c twice.

             To send the letter, go to a new line, type a dot (.),
             and hit Return.

mail         ...Read your mail. You will see a list of your mail items
             and a prompt which looks like this: &   ...To read each
             consecutive mail item, hit Return at this "&" prompt.

             Type: r    ...to respond to the current message.

             Type: dt   ...to delete the current message.

             Type: q    ...to quit email.
```

Figure 4-2: This mail system isn't Mac software yet, but it makes a few concessions to the user.

The difference between this mail system and classic UNIX mailing systems, like so many things, has to do with money. In the stock UNIX situation, you had access to a computer system by using UNIX, and you took what you got. Don't like the mailing system? Then write people notes in purple crayon on paper towels.

A typical bulletin board system (BBS) or conferencing system wants you to sign up, wants you to be happy, and wants to charge you a fee. If the mailing system is intolerable, two problems arise: You don't want to write messages, so you won't stay connected (and the service usually charges an hourly fee). And eventually you quit, an even worse situation. Even if the BBS is free, the BBS operator pays for the software, so any way you slice it, there's more incentive to offer a decent mailing system.

Mac Access

Two years ago, I would have felt compelled to offer a few pages full of UNIX mailing commands. Now, I propose to duck the whole, ugly mess. Even UNIX hotshots themselves are converting their systems wholesale to an interface called X Windows, which looks for all the world like a small-print version of a Macintosh screen.

You can get Internet e-mail access in lots of ways. You can use the plain, guess-your-next-command style that's standard with UNIX, or you can get a really friendly mail interface from America Online. Ironically, Internet e-mail access probably costs between $10 and $20 a month, whichever type of access you pick. Allow me to underline this distinction by presenting two mail-access screens (see Figures 4-3 and 4-4) back-to-back. Look, you had enough sense to pick a Mac in the first place — make your own decision.

```
Sun Mar 13 23:50:20 PST 1994
crl1% mail
Mail version SMI 4.0 Fri Jul  2 11:55:02 PDT 1993  Type ? for help.
"/usr/spool/mail/chseiter": 1 message 1 new
>N  1 wilson        Sat Mar 12 26 05:59   36/1103  Macworld note

& mail chseiter@aol.com
Subject: comm1
Hi. If you can read this, you're not having fun.

.
EOT

New mail has arrived.
crl2% mail
Mail version SMI 4.0 Fri Jul  2 11:55:02 PDT 1993  Type ? for help.
"/usr/spool/mail/chseiter": 1 message 1 new
>N  1 MAILER-DAEMON    Sun Mar 13 23:53   24/719
Returned mail: User unknown
& d 1
& quit
|
```

Figure 4-3: The traditional Internet mail interface.

Figure 4-4:
Internet mail
meets the
Macintosh.

Names and Numbers

Once you're on the Internet and people know that you're a master of e-mail, you may find yourself called on to chitchat about esoteric topics. That is, I propose to get you up and running with minimal fuss, but if I don't fill you in on a few gory details, you won't be able to impress your friends. Already, Net old-timers are complaining that *anyone* can get on the Internet. In one plaintive newsgroup message I read recently, a hard-core Nethead complains that he just received a message from his grandmother!

A class system

Internet hosts have machine addresses composed of four numbers separated by dots. Thus the WELL in San Francisco is called

```
well.sf.ca.us
```

but other Internet machines know it as

```
198.93.4.10
```

The numbers between the dots range from 1 to 254. In other words, there are 254 x 254 x 254 x 254 possible addresses — about 4 billion.

A, B, and C

Because there are different ways to do the network address assignment, the people who assigned them made up three classes: A, B, and C. Class A networks can support about 16 million hosts (that's a big network!); class C networks can handle 254 hosts. Because a host computer on a network can handle several incoming lines, there's a lot of room out there.

Inside a big network, a method called *subnetting* simplifies addressing from one network to the next, and another method called *supernetting* lets organizations effectively address several smaller networks as though they were one big network. I wouldn't bother you with a word of this, except that it will come back to haunt you when I tell you how to make your Mac a host. Figure 4-5, for example, shows the setup screen from MacTCP. You have to know how to fill in the blanks, or you can't get connected.

Figure 4-5:
Class B?
Subnet
mask? It's
all part of
the Internet
fun.

Chapter 5
Beyond E-Mail — The InfoSphere

Piles o' Files

Here's one way to look at the Internet situation: E-mail contains everything that someone thought up yesterday and wanted to communicate. The rest of the Internet is everything that someone *ever* thought up and wanted to communicate.

Current estimates suggest that the Internet has something like 100 gigabytes of text files that ordinary users can access with no special security clearance. This book has about half a megabyte of text, so I'm talking about the rough equivalent of 200,000 average books. Besides the text files, there are programs and pictures. And, in addition to the stuff that, strictly speaking, resides on Internet hosts, gigabytes of information slosh back and forth between BITNET and Usenet sites and thousands of bulletin boards, as well.

Finding What You Want

The first problem you face is finding what you want. Thousands of big computers are on the Internet — so where's the good stuff? The next problem is hauling what you want back to your computer. You actually have to transfer a file to your own hard drive to use it. Both of these problems have a standard Internet solution and a Macintosh solution.

The most common Internet tools for finding files are the programs Archie, Gopher, and WAIS (*wide area internet search*). In this chapter, I run some basic exercises in these programs, more to demonstrate what a search is like than to give you a step-by-step demo. A program called FTP (for *file transfer protocol*) is the standard tool for retrieving files.

The Macintosh equivalents, as you may expect, are even better than the originals. The file-finding programs TurboGopher, Anarchie, and Mosaic (a program for hypertext searches of Internet databases; see Figure 5-1) are fantastic. And Fetch is a file-retrieval program that makes users of other computers drool with envy. The catch, and it's not a small one, is that you have to have a direct Internet connection to use these programs. That means that 1) you're a Mac user on a network host, 2) you pay for an expensive full-time direct connection, or 3) you bought a SLIP account (see the following sidebar).

Figure 5-1:
Mosaic, a
hypertext
gateway to
the Internet,
is as cool as
it gets.

Key to the Highway

At first, the assortment of Internet navigation tools can be somewhat bewildering. How, for example, are you supposed to figure out when to use which tool?

It's all very simple. It came to me in a blinding flash, after this book was 95 percent finished. I looked back over several chapters and realized that in 12 different sections I talk about the same thing. Here it is:

There is only *one* trick on the Internet. That trick is the capability to jump from one computer to the next. Everything else is just a file-management utility.

SLIP slidin' away

SLIP (*Serial Line Interface Protocol*), as implemented in the programs MacSLIP and InterSLIP, lets you connect directly to the Internet over an ordinary phone line. With a fast modem (at least 9600 bps) and a SLIP account from an Internet service provider, you can have your own Internet address number. You're a host!

SLIP service by phone involves a few minor difficulties. It's great for transferring files, but mail to your new address only works when you're on-line. If you hang up, the rest of the Internet thinks that you're a "Host not responding" site. That's why most SLIP account users have another way to get mail 24 hours a day, through a national on-line service like CompuServe or through a *shell* account (standard bulletin-board style dial-up access) at the SLIP provider.

Another minor difficulty is that getting SLIP up and running can be frustrating (more on this topic in Chapter 13). It's also likely that the service provider's customer support people aren't Mac authorities. And sometimes these guys are a bit strange, anyway. Here's an authentic hot-off-the-Internet joke:

Q: How do you tell an extroverted network engineer?

A: He stares at *your* shoes when he talks to you.

Two steps out

Here's the scenario: You get an Internet account and a password. Then you sign onto your host. There you are on your host computer, which probably has all sorts of interesting files itself. But face it: You want more. You want *power*. So you type the command

```
telnet fedix.fie.com
```

At this command, your own host computer calls up a big computer network that serves as another Internet host (see the sidebar "Remote possibilities"). This host is full of government databases. You see the dazzling display of character-based graphics in Figure 5-2.

You are asked to log in; fortunately, this particular system tells you how:

```
Enter your FEDIX/MOLIS USERID, or NEW if you are a new user,
  or PRIOR if you have forgotten your USERID > new
Logged in as new
```

After this point, just follow the menus. There's a ton of material there — just look at the menus in Figure 5-3. You keep answering questions, and the system keeps giving you choices.

```
Hello, Welcome to FEDIX on fedix...


Last login: Mon Jun  6 18:53:20 from uclink2.Berkeley
Up - Sat May 28 12:08:04 EDT 1994
SunOS Release 4.1.2 (FEDIX2) #1: Tue May 25 11:51:11 EDT 1993
        FFFFFFFFF EEEEEEEEE DDDDDDDD  IIIII XXX   XXX
        FFF       EEE       DDD  DDDD  III   XXX XXX
        FFF       EEE       DDD   DDD  III    XXXXX
        FFFFFF    EEEEEEEE  DDD   DDD  III     XXX
        FFF       EEE       DDD   DDD  III    XXXXX
        FFF       EEE       DDD  DDDD  III   XXX XXX
        FFF       EEEEEEEEE DDDDDDDD  IIIII XXX   XXX


*****************************************************************************
*****************************************************************************

logged in on - /dev/ttyp5
Internet
```

Figure 5-2:
Yikes! It's
the Feds
(sort of).
But they're
smiling!

```
      FEDERAL  INFORMATION  EXCHANGE
**********************************************************

   Item  Description
   ----  --------------------------------------------
    1    Federal Opportunities (FEDIX)
    2    Minority College & University Capability Information (MOLIS)
    3    Higher Education Opportunities for Minorities & Women (HERO)
    8    New System Interface (Lynx http://web.fie.com/) *** PLEASE USE ***
         (From Mosaic, Cello or Lynx; URL=http://web.fie.com/)
    9    Download FEDIX/MOLIS Files
    0    Exit

What is your choice  - > 9
          Currently files are available from:

      FEDIX System
    1 -- Air Force Office of Scientific Research (AFOSR)
    2 -- Department of Energy (DOE)
    3 -- Department of Agriculture (USDA)
    4 -- Federal Aviation Administration (FAA)
    5 -- Federal Minority Opportunities
    6 -- National Aeronautics and Space Administration (NASA)
    7 -- Office of Naval Research (ONR)
    8  MOLIS System

Which agency do you want a file from?
```

Figure 5-3:
The Feds
answer
your every
question.

One step back

You, astute reader (hey, I figure that you're all astute because you had enough
sense to get this book), may raise some questions at this point. How did I know
where to telnet? Actually, I got the information from a list provided by my own
Internet host as I experimented. Unless you picked the worst service provider
on earth, customer support at your service can send you a list of telnet sites to
try (send an e-mail message to customer support).

Remote possibilities

Telnet is a standard UNIX command that connects you to another computer network (you're on one now; it connects you to another one). The command *rlogin,* for remote login, is similar. When you type **!man telnet**, most systems give you a manual about telnet to read (the exclamation point is pronounced "bang" in UNIX).

If you don't have advance information, you usually won't know what to do at the login prompt. If you have to guess, use "guest" or "public" as your name and your Internet address as a password. A better approach is to get the information from your own host. Usually, when you read about an interesting telnet site in a magazine or newspaper, the login information is provided.

Some networks you reach with telnet have prepared a lovely menu system to help you navigate. Some haven't. If you get into a network that gives you only a % prompt, try typing **ls** or **dir**. You should get a directory of files. If the directory doesn't make sense to you, type **bye** or **quit** and read the rest of this chapter like a good Net citizen.

A Macintosh HyperCard stack called HytelNet has a big directory of resources you can search off-line. You can also try sites from Table 5-1, my list of Ten Telnet Treasures.

Table 5-1	Ten Telnet Treasures	
Telnet to	*Login As*	*It Holds*
fdabbs.fda.gov	bbs	The latest FDA warnings
michel.ai.mit.edu	guest	A strange virtual reality world
sparc-1.law.columbia.edu	lawnet	Legal databases
coast.ucsd.edu	gopher	Everything about the oceans
nisc.jvnc.net	nicol	Directory of Internet resources
bbs.oit.unc.edu	bbs	General-purpose Internet facilities
hnsource.cc.ukans.edu	history	The login says it all
mb.com	mb	A shopping service
fedworld.doc.gov	bbs	Piles of government documents
nebbs.nersc.gov	new	K-12 education

As you may expect, there is an organized way to find stuff other than logging into one computer after another in search of gems. That's why I dedicate the rest of this chapter to searching.

Another "astute" question: How do I get those files from the big computer over there to my little Macintosh over here? That's the function of FTP (*file transfer protocol*), which is a sort of telnet-with-download-built-in that's the standard file transporter for networks on the Internet. I give you an FTP tour later, too.

In fact, FTP is not just a good idea, it's the law, more or less. It does a high-speed file transfer from the remote computer to your Internet host. That process lets the other high-speed traffic pass you on the information superhighway. You can then get the file from your host to your Mac in your own quiet, modem-based slow lane. Most sites expect you to do your file transfers with FTP.

First You Search, and Then You FTP

A nice bunch of people at McGill University in Canada set up a computer that maintains lists of the files on a huge assortment of Internet networks. Instead of telnetting to computers one at a time and poking through the files, go to the computer at McGill. The computer is called an *Archie server* because it maintains archives and lots of people can use it at the same time.

Archie in action

Other places, mostly universities, soon installed their own Archie servers. Figure 5-4 shows a sample search. As a demonstration, I looked for files with the name "MacTCP" in them. I did the search on an Archie server in Finland at 4 a.m. Finnish time. There are only 4 million people in Finland, and even Finns have to sleep sometime, so I figured that there would be room on the system for me. The Finns were snoring, all right — I was doing the only search on the system.

You can see the first part of the search results near the bottom of the figure. In 23 seconds, as advertised by the FUNET system, Archie found 200 sites with files on MacTCP (the other sites take 20 pages).

Figure 5-4 demonstrates two key points. Once again, you get into another network with telnet. (You see what I mean when I say that telnet is really the fundamental Internet trick?) The second point is that Archie by itself is a bit cryptic. It can manage all kinds of fancy searches, but it's not easy to use. Therefore, I'm going to tell you about Gopher.

```
OK : telnet archie.funet.fi
Trying 128.214.6.102 ...
Connected to archie.funet.fi.
Escape character is '^]'.

SunOS UNIX (archie.funet.fi)
        Finnish University and Research Network FUNET
                Information Service
Select service (gopher/www/wais/archie/exit) ? archie
Starting Archie ..

archie> set search sub
archie> prog MacTCP
# Search type: sub.
# Estimated time for completion: 23 seconds.

Host ftp.univ-rennes1.fr   (129.20.128.34)
Last updated 03:30  4 Mar 1994

  Location: /pub/Macintosh
    FILE   -rw-r--r--   51769 bytes  14:46  4 Feb 1994 MacTCP_2.0.2_->_2.0.x
    FILE   -rw-r--r--   68246 bytes  14:47  4 Feb 1994 MacTCP_Guide.sea.hqx
    FILE   -rw-r--r--   87986 bytes  14:47  4 Feb 1994 MacTCP_Watcher_1.1.0x
```

Figure 5-4:
Archie goes
to Europe,
looking for
Mac
utilities.

CyberRodents, InfoBurrows, HyperMice, TeleDogs, InterCats . . .

AAAAAGGHH! Excuse me, please. I really dislike words with capital letters in the middle. And I hate cute names for programs. The one exception is Gopher (as in TurboGopher for the Mac), which is so useful that they could have called it Mucus and it would still be one of my favorites.

Going pher it

Gopher is a menu system that directs searches at different Archie servers. You connect to a Gopher server and make choices from the menus. That's it.

In the background, Gopher furiously telnets to different Archie servers, formulates searches, hauls the results back, and presents them to you. All Gophers are connected to other Gophers, presumably with tunnels dug right through the earth. The Big Gopher in Minnesota is connected to all of them. If you have to start a search somewhere, telnet to

consultant.micro.umn.edu

and log in as "gopher."

In Figure 5-5, I connected to my own Internet host and then telnetted to a Gopher site, this time in Australia. At this point, you need to know only how to type what you want without misspelling it. In this sense, doing a Gopher search is better than using Archie directly. Not only does it require less planning from you, but it gets in and out of its own Archie connections thousands of times faster than you can, conserving Net resources.

```
OK : telnet info.anu.edu.au
Trying 150.203.84.20 ...
Connected to info.anu.edu.au.
|
|                    |Welcome to ELISA
|
| Welcome to the wonderful world of Gopher!
           Search Gopherspace: Jughead & Veronica

 --> 1. Search GopherSpace: Veronica (AARNet, Australia) <?>
     2. Scope of AARNet Australian Veronica Server.
     3. Search GopherSpace: Veronica & Jughead (Other Servers)/
     4. About using the Veronica databases.
     5. About using the Jughead databases.
     6. FAQ: Frequently-Asked Questions about veronica (1993-08-23).
     7. Archie (searching anonymous ftp sites) Via Texas A&M/
     8. How to Compose Veronica Queries.

+-------------Search GopherSpace: Veronica (AARNet, Australia)-------------+
|
| Words to search for  MacTCP
|
|                     [Cancel ^G] [Accept - Enter]
|
+-------------------------------------------------------------------------+
```

Figure 5-5:
The friendly, albeit text-based, world of standard Gopher.

Too much fun?

What, you inquire sweetly, was I doing in Australia for this search? On the day I did it, I couldn't get into the Big Gopher, as it was too busy, or the Gopher at infopath.ucsd.edu (my dear old alma mater, in fact). Neither could I reach the Gopher at scilibx.ucsc.edu, where you log in as "infoslug" (the sports teams at UC Santa Cruz are inspirationally named after the banana slug — no kidding). The Internet is getting to be a crowded place.

But think of the snoring Finns and remember that it's always 4 a.m. somewhere, and the main users of a given network are still the locals. Pick a good time, and then get in and out before they wake up!

FTP — Fetch This Phile!

Using Gopher, you can find all sorts of files on the Internet. Now you have to get them back to your Macintosh. That's when you use FTP.

Figure 5-6 shows a typical FTP session. There's really not much to it. You issue the FTP command followed by the name of the Internet host that contains the files. Doing so connects you because, like practically every other Internet function, FTP has its own built-in analog of telnet. On some systems, it's more typical to sign on with this sequence:

```
OK: ftp
ftp> open
(to) archive.wherever.com
```

but your Internet host is supposed to tell you all that.

```
OK: ftp mac.archive.umich.edu
Connected to mac.archive.umich.edu.
220 pogue.admin.lsa.umich.edu FTP server (ULTRIX Version 4.1 Tue Mar 19 00:38:1.

Name (mac.archive.umich.edu:chseiter): anonymous
331 Guest login ok, send ident as password.
Password:

230 Guest login ok, access restrictions apply.
ftp> get 00readme.txt
200 PORT command successful.
150 Opening data connection for 00readme.txt (198.93.4.10,52382) (5999 bytes).
226 Transfer complete.
local: 00readme.txt remote: 00readme.txt
6122 bytes received in 0.4 seconds (15 Kbytes/s)

ftp> bye
```

Figure 5-6:
This FTP session takes me to a big archive in Michigan.

In this case, I already knew that a plain text file called 00readme.txt was waiting at the Internet host in the main directory. If you don't know which file you will be looking for in advance, read the sidebar about FTP tips and traps and then look at Figure 5-7. Such screens are the main reason why this edition of *The Internet For Macs For Dummies* is an extended plea for using national on-line services to get the 500 most popular Mac files. Right now, you are the Internet equivalent of a guy with a free airline pass flying to Sydney to buy a Coke. Think globally, act locally (or at least act on your local network, if possible).

```
OK: ftp wuarchive.wustl.edu
Connected to wuarchive.wustl.edu.
220 wuarchive.wustl.edu FTP server (Version wu-2.3(1) Fri Apr 8 14:26:26 CDT
19.
Name (wuarchive.wustl.edu:chseiter): anonymous

530-Sorry, there are too many anonymous FTP users using the system at this
530-time.  Please try again in a few minutes.
530-
530-There is currently a limit of 200 anonymous users.  Yes, there REALLY are
530-that many users on wuarchive -- this message is not the result of a bug.

530 User anonymous access denied.
Login failed.
```

Figure 5-7:
Uh-oh. Internet logjam spotted!

TECHNICAL STUFF

FTP tips and traps

Using a standard UNIX interface to navigate at an FTP site is a bit of a pain. Here's what you should know:

1. The good files usually aren't in the first directory you see (the top directory). At the ftp> prompt, type **dir**.

   You see a listing that contains two kinds of entries, such as the following:

   ```
   -rw-r--r— 1 5193    31        5999
      Apr 1 16:27 00readme.txt
   drwxr-xr-x   3 5193    31
      2048 Feb 3 15:59 internet
   ```

   You can get the entry that starts with -r — it's just a file. In this listing, the letter *d* on the second line means that `internet` is a directory (the Mac equivalent is a folder). You have to type

   ```
   ftp>cd internet
   ftp>dir
   ```

   to see what's in the `internet` directory.

2. When you see the listing in this directory, you should be aware that most large files are compressed. You see file types like .sea (*self-extracting archive*), .sit (compressed with the application StuffIt), and .hqx (stored in a format called binhex) or .bin (a binary file). Sometimes file transfer works whatever the type, but to be safe, you should type

   ```
   ftp>binary
   ```

   before you get the file. Then type

   ```
   ftp> get <filename>
   ```

   and type **bye** when you're done.

   Files of the type .sea uncompress themselves, and .sit files require UnStuffIt, available free from your own Internet host. For unpacking .hqx files, I recommend a shareware program called HQXer.

3. Unless you have a direct connection, you have now transferred the file to your own directory on your Internet host, not to your Mac's hard drive. Call up your own host help file to find out how to download by using your communications software. At this point, having Microphone or ZTerm really helps.

Digging Deeper

REMEMBER

Of course, there's more to life than finding and retrieving files. Hey, even *I* think so, and file-hunting is about all I've done for the past six months. You may want some information and not have much of an idea about where it is stored. The information you want may be stored under a funny filename that doesn't tell much about what's in the file.

As the Internet has expanded to the point where it's barely searchable even by a Gopher, two new tools (described in the following sections) have emerged from the laboratories of various advanced thinkers. Actually, this business is very important — the tools are a model for retrieving electronically stored information in general. In the next few decades, that will mean practically all information.

Info from everywhere with WAIS

The first tool is WAIS, or *wide area information server*. A WAIS database is an index of keywords in the text of its files, so you can search what's *inside* those files. Figure 5-8 shows an edited transcript of a plain-text WAIS search — the main point is that the search turns up lots of sources of information in which the keywords turn up in the *description* of the files as well as in the filenames. When you call up a Gopher server, you usually see a WAIS option (my Australian adventure included one). Using WAIS requires no special skills, so if you find yourself with access to a WAIS server, just jump in and start answering the prompts.

```
OK: telnet quake.think.com
Trying 192.31.181.1 ...
Connected to quake.think.com.

login: wais
Welcome to swais.

SWAIS                        Source Selection              Sources:  1
   #            Server                    Source                    Cost
001: * [     quake.think.com] directory-of-servers           Free
Keywords: bootstrap  statistics
Found 13 items.
SWAIS                        Search Results                Items: 13
   #   Score    Source                    Title              Lines
~~~~~~~~~~~~
006:   [ 858] (directory-of-se)  bit.listserv.cdromlan            22
007:   [ 858] (directory-of-se)  cool                           108
008:   [ 858] (directory-of-se)  queueing-literature-database   157
009:   [ 858] (directory-of-se)  sas-archive                     14
010:   [ 858] (directory-of-se)  spss-archive                    15
011:   [ 858] (directory-of-se)  statfaqs                        17
~~~~~~~~~~~~
```

Figure 5-8: WAIS gets the inside information on file sources.

Hyperactivity: WWW

The very ambitious project called WWW, or *World Wide Web*, uses another search technology. WWW is essentially a database that's made of linked hypertext documents. You call up a starting screen, and some of the words on-screen are highlighted or underlined. Select a word (in the clunky plain-text version, you do so with arrow keys), press Return, and you get a new screen. Of course, to the poor old Netheads who have been using UNIX for years, this technology seems pretty futuristic. It's harder to be impressed by the interface in plain WWW if you're a longtime Mac user.

Just a few months ago, there weren't many WWW servers, and WWW information also leaned toward academic topics. Then businesses recognized that you could make a pretty good on-line catalog in hypertext if you could add pictures. That resulted in a WWW explosion, with Mosaic as the most prominent example of a WWW browser. Because the Mac version of Mosaic (and its competitors MacWeb and NetScape) is worth its own section, I'll do some Mosaic demonstrations later in this chapter.

Of course, no one would let a resource this cool exist without a cool interface for long, so WWW has two of the coolest: Mosaic and Mac Web. You'll see these in Chapter 13, where the topic is direct Internet connection. For now you should simply be encouraged that there is a choice of real-Mac interfaces for the rapidly expanding WWW.

Back to the Mac

So far, I've been using the Mac as if it were just a VT-102 terminal. No Finder, no folders, no icons, no menus, no mouse — you may as well be computing in 1975.

Here is a short preview of Internet navigation with real Macintosh software. Right now, the problem is that you need some kind of direct connection to the Internet to use Mac software: either you're directly wired to an Internet host at work or at school, or you have a SLIP account with a service provider.

This access situation will change during the next year. Merry elves at the major national on-line services are diligently copying the best features of these Mac products, and you're going to be able to get most of the cool real-Mac features of the programs described here just by signing up with a service. If you're a student at the University of Minnesota, it won't matter much, but if you're an individual Mac user in Dayton, Ohio, it's big news. Meanwhile, compare a few of these screens to what you've seen earlier in this chapter.

Archie? How about Anarchie instead?

Figure 5-9 shows an Archie search, using the brilliant shareware program Anarchie. Send a nice e-mail message to

```
peter.lewis@info.curtin.edu.au
```

and ask him for his current mailing address; be sure to send him $10 if you download Anarchie.

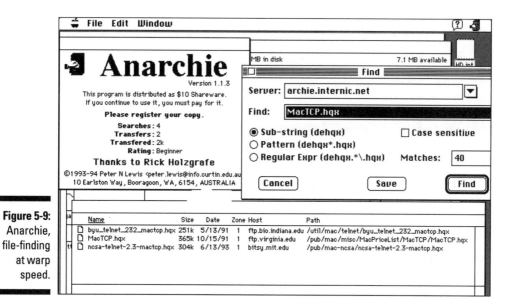

Figure 5-9:
Anarchie,
file-finding
at warp
speed.

To use Anarchie: Type your search terms and then click Find. You get a lovely, completely specified list of matching files. Anarchie still uses UNIX search terminology, but it's so fast (and has built-in search limiting) that you can experiment until you get the hang of it.

TurboGopher, the runnin' rodent

This program from the University of Minnesota practically turns the rest of the world into one big directory. It's preloaded with the most useful Mac software sites, so it knows the right places to look as soon as you start it.

As Figure 5-10 demonstrates, you can operate this program if you know how to open a folder on your own Mac. When it's working, a hilarious cartoon of a Gopher scampers along on-screen.

Fetch, the super retriever

Fetch, from Dartmouth University, is a Mac replacement for FTP (see Figure 5-11). That's an understatement. If you've been stuck poking your way through UNIX directories on remote machines, Fetch will knock you flat — it brings back everything but a Frisbee. Like TurboGopher, it already knows where to look, so it doesn't have to nose through sites with hundreds of UNIX utilities that you'll never need. You click Get File, and you get the file. It was supposed to be that way all along.

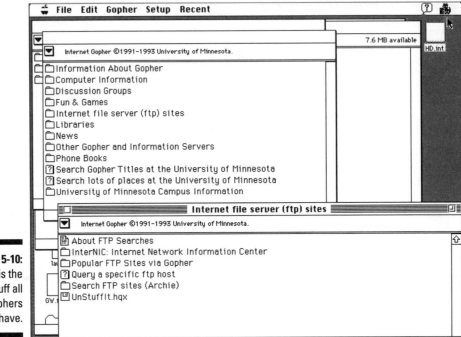

Figure 5-10:
This is the
stuff all
Gophers
should have.

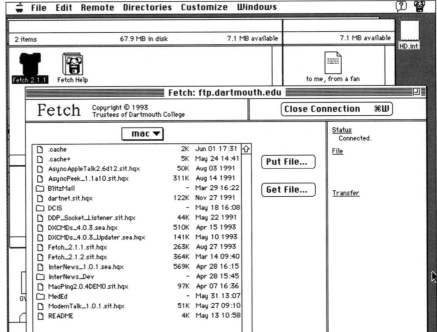

Figure 5-11:
Fetch.
This dog
will hunt.

Easy WAIS to do it

WAIS, even standard WAIS, is pretty easy because all you do is follow menus. MacWAIS, shown in Figure 5-12, requires that you 1) double-click the MacWAIS icons and 2) type your search terms in the dialog box and click the Ask button. This little gem of a program logs itself onto the appropriate host, finds everything, and reports back to you in a few seconds.

Because MacWAIS is a shareware product, you can send some e-mail to

```
mac-shareware@einet.net
```

for the latest information. If you're really interested in WAIS searches, you'll want this program.

Figure 5-12:
MacWAIS
delivers the
goods.

Something for Everyone

The hottest Internet topic these days is, without question, the World Wide Web browser called *Mosaic*, available free from most national on-line services or by FTP from `ncsa.uiuc.edu`, which is the National Center for Supercomputing Applications. The NCSA has also licensed commercial development of this software, so Mosaic variants are popping up, but the original is still available and is probably the greatest piece of free software ever released.

The point is, it's just ridiculously easy to use once you have a working SLIP connection (for details, check out Chapter 13). Make a connection to your service provider, double-click the Mosaic icon, and you see the glorious vista of Figure 5-13.

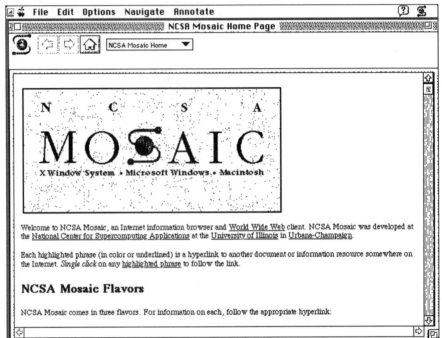

Figure 5-13:
The Mosaic
home page
at NCSA.

Where do you go from here? I recommend scrolling down this page to the What's New section (as shown in Figure 5-14), because the WWW has more genuinely new stuff every week than, say, all the national TV networks have produced since the day you were born. I've been following Internet developments since the whole thing was called ARPANET, and I can tell you there's just nothing like the Mosaic/WWW phenomenon.

Roaming around on the Web

To navigate, you use the list in the little box next to the Home icon at the top of the page. You can also use the -> and <- arrows at the top of the page, or get back to Home and start over by clicking the Home icon. When you do this yourself, you will be relieved to find that Mosaic has "cached" or stored enough material to show you something right away. Because some Web documents are

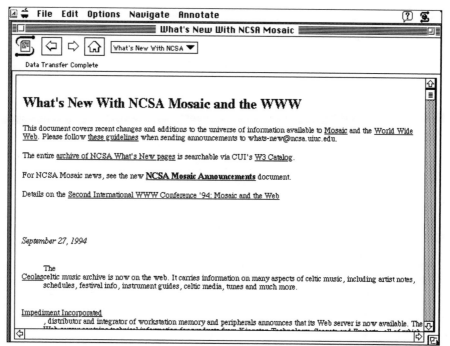

Figure 5-14:
What's New
(a lot!).

not just lengthy but are full of graphics, it can take a long time, even at 14.4 Kps, to get results. Rather than just scroll through new topics (although doing so can entertain you for days), you may want to check the whole W3 catalog (W3 is equivalent to WWW). This catalog (see Figure 5-15), which will have more than 10,000 entries by the time you get to it, is typical of the hefty files lumbering around the Web — the recent changes link is a 250K download.

One of the first things you'll find, dipping into the CUI W3 catalog, is We Are Not Alone. Living in North America, a giant land mass with thousands of miles of cold salt water at either side, it's easy to forget the reality of the rest of the planet. On the WWW, the rest of the planet jumps right down your modem wire and splashes on your screen. Look at the first entries in the new part of the catalog (see Figure 5-16) — they're postings from math departments at universities in Portugal and Germany. That's because the WWW is rapidly supplanting traditional research journals as a means of distributing papers. All sorts of transnational scientific collaboration is now possible through the Internet.

Although a lot of this international material is provided in the originating languages (I have a friend who has managed to learn rudimentary written Finnish simply from logging on the FUNET server for a year), services looking for wider audiences offer translations.

Figure 5-15:
The giant
WWW
catalog.

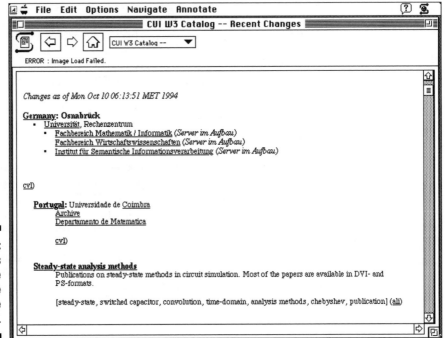

Figure 5-16:
Universities
are
everywhere
on the
WWW.

WWW . . . fun, fun, fun

I suspect, although I cannot prove, that most readers of this book are not fired up about Mosaic solely because it will give them access to Portuguese language math papers from the University of Coimbra (which, by the way, is one of the oldest universities in Europe, and Coimbra is an amazing medieval town).

You probably had something a little lighter in mind. How about the official Web site for the world's most profitable geriatric rock collective? There they are, costing you about five extra minutes on-line (see Figure 5-17) to download all those little tongues and other icons. (I can't tell if they are demons or if it's just Keith Richards in his seldom-seen Bozo the Clown haircut.)

Another item worthy of your consideration is the Paris home page (available in French through a click on the tiny language version link). How did I find this? (How did I find the Stones, for that matter?) They were all back on the original What's New page at NCSA, and I just scrolled down with the scroll box to find them.

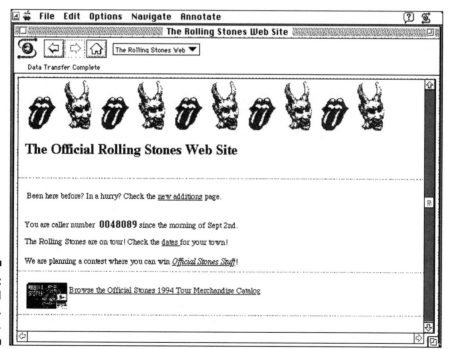

Figure 5-17: Ladies and gentlemen, the Stones.

The Paris site has complete, gorgeous, full-color tours, along with tons of other more standard informational material. This site is a real *tour de force*, as I believe Parisians themselves used to say, in the pages of American high-school textbooks. If the Paris resource were the only site available on the Web, it would be worth getting a copy of Mosaic just to look at it.

Other Ways to the Web

As fine a product as Mosaic is, perfectly good alternatives exist. Mosaic was the first graphic Web browser, and its developers deserve a world of credit, but it's not going to be the final word on the WWW.

I particularly like MacWeb, available from `ftp.galaxy.einet.net` and from every national on-line service's software libraries. MacWeb is fast, efficient, compact, and has one impressive advantage — it starts up from a home page (see Figure 5-18) at `galaxy.einet.net` that never seems to be crowded.

What will be happening in 1995 and 1996? National on-line services will be trying to make their own software look more like Mosaic and MacWeb — and some will even offer Web access with a custom browser. The examples in this chapter have been just a glimpse of what will be a nearly universal way to access information in the next few years.

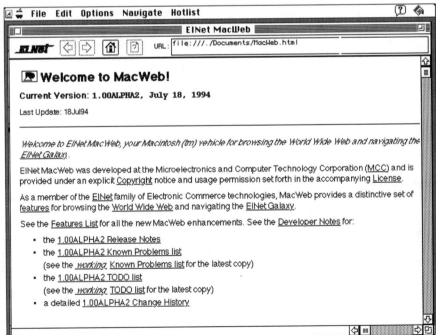

Figure 5-18:
Arrows, a little house, a URL window — *deja vu*!

Part II
Internet via National On-Line Services

The 5th Wave — By Rich Tennant

"I'M SORRY, BUT MR. HALLORAN IS BEING CHASED BY SIX MIDGETS WITH POISON BOOMERANGS THROUGH A MAZE IN THE DUNGEON OF A CASTLE. IF HE FINDS HIS WAY OUT AND GETS PAST THE MINOTAUR, HE'LL CALL YOU RIGHT BACK."

In this part...

All the big national on-line services have figured out that they aren't viable without any more good Internet connections. So, they're scrambling as fast as they can to offer Internet services with a friendly Mac face to lure you on-line.

In this part, I'll compare the services from the point of view of their own content and their Internet readiness. This area is rapidly evolving, but it's possible to see what's going to happen. Think of this part as a shopping tour for your Internet connection.

Chapter 6
Internet from America Online

● ●

In This Chapter

▶ AOL puts a Mac face on the Internet

▶ Easy mail links to the whole planet

▶ Here Comes Everybody — AOL and newsgroups

▶ Watch Gopher burrow through the on-line universe

▶ Finally, FTP and "real" Internet

● ●

They Said They'd Do It, and They Did It (Almost)

In 1993, reading the handwriting on the wall, not to mention the hype in the Wall Street Journal, America Online decided to begin moving into Internet service. Through the first part of 1994 Internet e-mail service was introduced, and then a "toy" version of Gopher, and then a few newsgroups, and by June 1994 America Online users had access to thousands of newsgroups as the system operators gradually added to the list.

In the America Online Internet user group area, the AOL operators have promised telnet and ftp capabilities for many months, and have endured heaps of abuse about delays. FTP finally arrived; it's as easy to use as AOL's other services. It takes these people a while, but they do keep their promises. In fairness to AOL, software development for a large on-line service is not a trivial task. And the oldest rule in computing is: software always ships late (the software for *this book* shipped late).

One last service to be added is an AOL equivalent of Mosaic. Until AOL gets lots and lots of 14.4 kbps service signed up, there's not much point in perfecting a graphical Web browser. But the inside scoop is that an AOL World Wide Web service will probably be appearing by early 1995, at which point AOL will have a pretty impressive "Internet for Beginners" package.

AOL as an Internet Tool

Yes, the Internet is cool. The Internet contains a huge amount of information and allows easy communication with millions of people. But the fact is *every* large on-line service provides lots of the same features.

What I'm proposing is this: The Internet is wonderful, and you and I can keep it wonderful by using it for real Internet tasks. Only you can prevent forest fires, and only you can keep the Internet from becoming an unusable electronic trash heap. If you want stock quotes, if you want to chat in real-time with people in Chicago, or if you want to download finance templates to use with a spreadsheet, simply use AOL.

From the standard archives at Stanford and elsewhere, the service has already retrieved nearly all the Mac-specific shareware you could want (see Figure 6-1). The stock quotes are up to the minute. You can tap into brilliant and idiotic opinions of users who happen to be logged onto the network at the same time as you are. So if you're looking for a job as a historian, by all means use the Internet to look up the academic jobs database at the University of Kansas [listserv@ukanvm.cc. ukans.edu]. But if you're just in a mood to flame about bugs in Microsoft Word 6.0, do it on AOL instead.

Figure 6-1:
Most good Mac shareware is available directly from AOL.

Just Do It!

America Online has the best Macintosh interface of any of the national services currently operating. Place a call to America Online customer service at 800-827-6364, and a few days later you will get in the mail a disk with instructions. Every few months, you will find an introductory offer for AOL with some free on-line time bundled with a copy of *Macworld*, too. In either case, insert the disk, double-click the installer icon, and you get a screen like the one in Figure 6-2.

Figure 6-2:
If the AOL installer works, you see this folder.

What AOL Is Like: A Personal Tour

After you type in your password, the software, which has been configured to run your modem at the highest speed available, connects you automatically to AOL. AOL provides you with a local phone number for calls. It took AOL a while to get 9600 bps local access numbers available in most areas, and it will probably take until late 1994 for 14.4 Kbps or 19.2 Kbps service to appear. (Kbps means a thousand bps, so 14.4 Kbps is 14,400 bps, as described in Chapter 3.)

When you sign on, you see the screen in Figure 6-3. As a newcomer, you should check the icons on the right and at the lower left of the screen. By double-clicking on the Discover AOL icon, you can guide yourself through a tutorial. By double-clicking on the letter icon (which is the No mail icon in Figure 6-3), you can enter a sophisticated e-mail system that can access Internet mail. The icons at the right are usually topics that AOL management thinks are newsworthy. Right now, I'm displaying this screen so that you can admire the amazingly clean design.

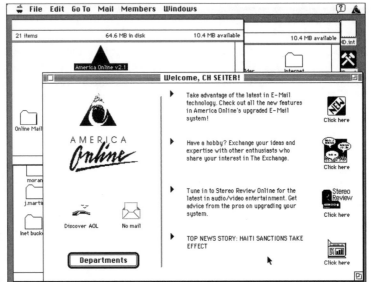

Figure 6-3: In AOL, most navigation is done just with mouse clicks.

AOL has a real Mac interface

In most on-line services, you have to perform a significant amount of idiotic grunt labor, calling up menus and answering questions. Often you find yourself arguing with the service menus as different commands become available or unavailable, depending on the last menu you were shown. This problem is in direct contradiction to the style of all the other Mac software you use in daily life. If the services want my money, they gotta do better than that!

So AOL did better. Instead of expecting thousands of on-line users to pound away at their keyboards and scroll through menus, trying to work around the deficiencies built into an interface, AOL hired a handful of programmers to code a proper point-and-click, Apple-interface-guidelines front end for AOL services. There is great efficiency — which saves *you* precious time — in the AOL on-line screen design. At any point, you can figure out your next move just by inspecting the icons or scrolling the lists presented to you on-screen. You think this would have occurred to some-body else, but it didn't.

Too much fun!

Even in its currently incomplete form, AOL is one of the few ways to get going on the information superhighway without getting lost in traffic. This list covers some top points in support of AOL:

- The people at AOL know you're lazy — and they *like* it that way.
- AOL e-mail is easier than licking stamps.
- You can use a screen name, such as Zorro or Bambi.
- AOL people don't censor your flames.
- AOL's Internet administrator has the patience of Mother Teresa.
- The AOL Gopher is so cute that you just have to click him.
- AOL runs thousands of Usenet groups, even the strange ones!

The icons speak

The first thing you hear is a voice announcing that you have mail. AOL packs some amusing sound files into the interface program it sends you on disk. The message itself isn't sent through your modem — a flag in the sign-on data plays the sound at your end of the connection. At this point, you can read the latest headlines or double-click on some new service — but you're going straight to the Internet.

You can get to the Internet area by clicking the Departments button and then picking your way through more icons, but it's faster to pull down the Go To menu, pick Keyword from the choices, and type **internet** in the Enter keyword text box in the Go to Keyword dialog box. The screen then changes to the glorious vista presented in Figure 6-4.

Keyword: Internet

The list at the left of the Internet Center window in Figure 6-4 contains an amazing amount of material. For example, it contains Zen and the Art of the Internet, Brendan Kehoe's admirable information file, arranged in searchable form. If you don't like my explanations, you can try one of his, although the file is mostly a guide to old-style UNIX telecommunications.

If you double-click on About the Internet Center, you get AOL's own explanation of its services. Double-clicking the Mac Communications Forum gets you into the Apple Professional Exchange, a legal group, and "nomadic" computing discussions.

Another interesting bunch in this forum is the Electronic Frontier Foundation, an organization that's trying its best to keep information transfer free and unmonitored. At present, the U.S. government is desperately trying to maintain its right to "wire-tap" e-mail when it thinks it's necessary, and the EFF doesn't like this invasion of privacy, to put it mildly.

Figure 6-4:
Welcome to
the big time.
There's
enough real
Internet here
to keep you
busy.

The Internet Center Message Board, shown in Figure 6-5, is where you see announcements of new services. It's also where you see AOL management being mercilessly slagged by impatient users. To AOL's credit, it doesn't censor any of its on-line criticism. These AOL people get flamed plenty.

Figure 6-5:
The Internet
message
board is full
of tips, quips,
and
complaints.

AOL Mail Gateway

I now leave the flames, change out of my fire-resistant pajamas (decorated, in fact, with little appliqués of gophers), and put on a business suit. I click back through the main Internet Center window (a fast way to do so is to give the Keyword command Internet) and click the Mail Gateway icon, which gets me to the window in Figure 6-6.

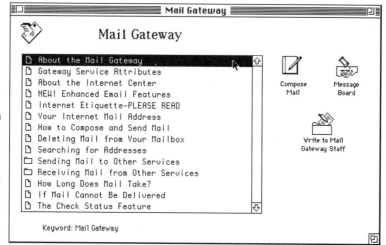

Figure 6-6:
Read the
etiquette
note about
mail before
you start
posting.

```
Mail Gateway

     Mail Gateway

  About the Mail Gateway
  Gateway Service Attributes          Compose    Message
  About the Internet Center             Mail       Board
  NEW! Enhanced Email Features
  Internet Etiquette-PLEASE READ
  Your Internet Mail Address          Write to Mail
  How to Compose and Send Mail       Gateway Staff
  Deleting Mail from Your Mailbox
  Searching for Addresses
  Sending Mail to Other Services
  Receiving Mail from Other Services
  How Long Does Mail Take?
  If Mail Cannot Be Delivered
  The Check Status Feature

  Keyword: Mail Gateway
```

While you're in the Mail Gateway window, read the Internet Etiquette message. *Etiquette,* in this sense, doesn't really have much to do with Miss Manners; instead, it refers to being careful about addressing messages so that they don't clog up the wrong e-mail mailboxes.

Next, read the document called Your Internet Mail Address. Check this out! You now have your own Internet address, even though you did nothing more than follow a few Mac menus. Sending and receiving mail are handled automatically by AOL, and you can put your new Internet address on your business cards.

If you click the Compose Mail icon, you get a screen like the one in Figure 6-7. Because the America Online software is a real Mac application, you can actually compose your letters in a Macintosh word processor and simply cut and paste text into the message area. Similarly, you can cut sections of messages you receive and paste them into standard documents in other applications. In the To box, at the top of the form, you can list an Internet address in the same way you list an AOL internal address (a screen name, in AOL lingo).

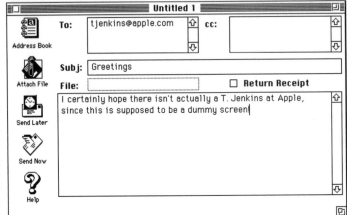

Figure 6-7:
An AOL
message in
the mail
system can
hold 32K.

It's hard to see how AOL could be much easier than this. But there are still two problems with AOL Internet mail as it stands today. First, messages are currently limited to 32K. If the system could handle longer text messages, people could send you files with a sort of trick called FTP mail, in which a text file is sent to you as a mail message.

Second, the nifty Attach File feature — very useful for sending files of pictures or sound or bits of database to other AOL users — doesn't work for messages to other services.

Despite these problems, AOL's e-mail messaging system is convenient and inexpensive (you get ten on-line hours per month for your monthly fee). Later in this book (see Chapter 13), I show you what e-mail is like in a traditional UNIX-based system — the comparison is a shocking argument for AOL.

Newsgroups on AOL

E-mail is certainly useful. It offers a major justification for getting an Internet connection. But it's not all that entertaining, and just using e-mail doesn't make you a "real Internet" user. So it's time to get cool. Close the Mail Gateway window and you're back at the Internet Center. If you click the Newsgroups icon in the Internet Center window, you get a personal gateway to the thousands of newsgroups on Usenet, BITNET, and WhatNotNet (OK, I made up the last one). Figure 6-8 shows what these newsgroups look like on-screen.

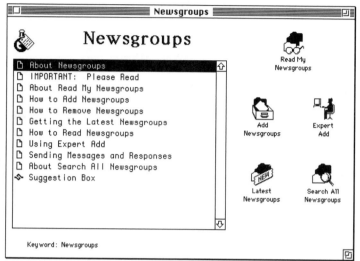

Figure 6-8:
The world's
simplest
newsgroup
connection.

The list of groups is so huge that AOL doesn't even offer to show you the whole list. Instead, you pick topics of interest and search for newsgroups that match. When you first start the AOL service, "your" newsgroups are a short list of six or seven newsgroups that AOL thinks may be of general interest.

To add to this list, you can find newsgroups by searching or by using the Expert Add icon. To add a newsgroup with Expert Add, you need the exact name of the newsgroup you're joining. I list some groups in Appendix D, and you can join the group news.lists to see the whole list. Actually, using AOL's search procedure is the easiest way.

A key point to watch is the sheer number of messages that crop up in an active group. The group Alt-Tv-Mst3k, for example, discusses Mystery Science Theater 3000, a show that appears on the Comedy Channel, and it picks up nearly a hundred messages a day! (A lesson from the Internet: The world is big — one percent of a million people is a lot of people.) You're not going to get around to reading most of the messages unless you feel like spending hours every night on-line and making AOL ridiculously rich.

Fortunately, AOL shows you the subjects (see Figure 6-9), so you can scan them and pick out a few favorites. Then click the icon that says "Mark As Read." Otherwise, you would drown in a week, even with a rigorously austere list.

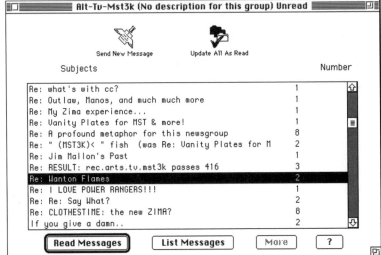

Figure 6-9: A modest sample from an "alternative" newsgroup.

All these newsgroup correspondences are conducted in plain text. However, you're going to need to know just a bit of Internet code, such as BTW and IMHO, to read and respond to newsgroup messages. A standard set of abbreviations has been developed over the years; Table 6-1 provides a minimal list of these abbreviations so that you know what's going on when you see them. To convey some sort of accent to the text, symbols that look like cartoon faces soon appeared, too; Table 6-2 contains a smattering of these symbols, called *smileys*, and their interpretations.

I predict that within three years, Mac Internet interfaces will have improved to the point that you can annotate messages with sounds and pictures for impact — a sort of smileys-on-steroids. But for now, these abbreviations and smileys are standards. If you poke around in the AOL communications forums, you can find whole dictionaries of smileys (various jokers have concocted about 500), which may interest you for cultural anthropological reasons.

Table 6-1	Short Takes
Code	*It Stands For*
IMHO	In my humble opinion
BTW	By the way
FYI	For your information
LOL	Laughing out loud
GMTA	Great minds think alike
RTFM	Read the f*&^% manual

Table 6-2	Keep On Smilin'
On the Keyboard	*What It Says*
:)	Smile
;)	Wink
:*	Kiss
:(	Bummer!
:>	Fiendish grin

Getting Listed

Mailing lists are just collections of Internet e-mail addresses. The mailing list system evolved mainly as a way for researchers at widely separated institutions to keep in touch. The biggest set of mailing lists, in fact, evolved separately from the Internet on BITNET, although there's considerable crossover.

The window in Figure 6-10 shows some mailing lists turned up by clicking on Search and entering the word *politics* in the text box (when you click the mailbox icon in the Internet Center window, search is one of your options). In AOL, you can sign up to join any of these discussion groups just by adding your name to the list, and you can quit a group just as easily.

Figure 6-10: AOL has set up an Internet mailing list search.

These lists are amazingly interesting and entertaining, but there are a few precautions you should be aware of. The first is that when you join a list, you should probably monitor it every day for the first few days to get an idea of the traffic volume. When anyone on your list sends a message to the rest of the list, it appears in your mailbox. If you sign up for lots of active lists, you will find that your AOL mailbox limit (550 messages) can be reached quite rapidly.

The other precaution is that you should read the messages for a week or so to determine whether you really have a contribution to make to the other list members. The Internet gives you, in effect, an introduction to most of the research and special-interest groups in the world. I don't want to sound like too much of an old grump on this point, but please think about whether you'll be wasting your own time and someone else's time by getting involved in an endless series of messages.

Having pointed out the precautions, I still want you to believe that mailing lists are a fantastic way to keep in touch with individuals who share your interests. Somewhere out there in Flatville, Illinois, there's probably someone who's fascinated with Minoan archaeology, and now she can read daily reports from researchers doing field work in Crete. That's wonderful!

Finding Stuff in the Internet Jungle: Gopher and WAIS

There's so much information available on the Internet that special sets of searching tools (I describe them in Chapter 5) have evolved. One standard tool is Gopher (named for the mascot of the University of Minnesota, home of the Golden Gophers and a pioneer Internet software site). There are hundreds of Gopher sites all over the planet, and they maintain menus of files available on different topics. You give a Gopher some possible file titles of interest, and the Gopher tells you what's available. WAIS, for *w*ide *a*rea *i*nformation *s*erver, searches the contents of files rather than just file titles.

In "full" Internet access, you could connect to any Gopher server (a server is just a computer, generally big and fast, set up as a central resource for "client" computers, like yours). To connect to another Gopher server, you find a Gopher list for yourself and Gopher Internet addresses. On AOL, none of these procedures and details really matters.

AOL hides the search details

AOL has done something a bit different. First, it evaluated dozens of Gopher sites for reliability. Most of these are noncommercial sites maintained as a public service, and some of them are as flaky as a basket of crescent rolls. AOL then wrote an interface in which you, the end user, can't always tell whether you're getting information from a Gopher site or a WAIS server. You get the information — you don't get the search path or the Internet details. Unless you're an experienced on-line searcher, you get better results the AOL way than you get poking around on your own.

From the Internet Center screen, just click the Gopher & WAIS databases icon. Figure 6-11 shows some of the available topics, and in AOL, you can click in these folders to carry out a search. At present, AOL has loaded a large array of topics into what appears to be its own site so that searches are fast and don't usually connect you to other computers.

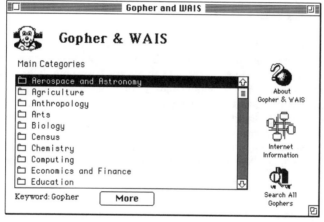

Figure 6-11: Gopher, the lovable rodent, burrowing for data through the front lawns of the Internet.

Searching absolutely everything

To find specific subjects, you can also perform a Veronica search over all available Gophers. Just click on the Search All Gophers icon in the Gopher and WAIS window, and you'll see a window like the one in Figure 6-12. I searched on the word *analytical* because I design analytical equipment for biochemistry, so I used this keyword to tell AOL how much material to access. (By the way, I did this search because I already knew what was available from doing searches with full access to all known Gophers and WAIS databases.) At present, my guess is that AOL databases probably have between 20 and 30 percent of all text files on this topic that are available worldwide, but the list is expanding fairly quickly as AOL adds behind-the-scenes access to more Gophers.

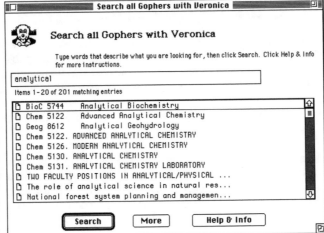

Figure 6-12:
A Veronica
search pulls
out the
details.

Gossip Hot Line!

To learn more about the direction the Internet is taking, including new kinds of searching systems, you can click back to the main Gopher screen and then click on the Internet Information icon. Figure 6-13 shows the fairly complete set of AOL Internet informational files, including material on InterNIC, a prime resource on Internet operations. At this point, if you want to impress your friends with your totally cool, leading-edge status among Internauts, go and read the items in the Heard on the Net Electronic Newsletter. Even though you haven't spent more than a minute suffering through "real Internet" commands, you'll have all the gossip just as if you were a lifelong UNIX communications hacker. Seems like cheating, doesn't it?

Figure 6-13:
Spend some
time
browsing
these
information
sources.

Whimsy in cyberspace

Archie is a program that lets you search over files that you can find on the Internet and is basically an index of archived software, hence the name. Later, a more powerful search program was named Veronica, for *very easy rodent-oriented netwide index to computerized archives. Rodent-oriented* means that the program works with Gophers, but the name Veronica was cooked up as a reference to Archie and Veronica comic books. There is also a program for Archie-searching called Jughead, meaning that a program called Betty can't be too far away. I explain these programs merely because many Internauts are probably too young to have seen any of these harmless relics of a bygone comic-book age (the age cutoff seems to be about 21).

As Long As You're Here

AOL has mountains of non-Internet material. I'll just show you a few choice bits, and you may find that a lot of what you've been told is out there on the Net is already on AOL.

Buy something

AOL is a commercial service. There is no squeamishness about serving businesses on-line. The only point you may need to investigate is whether your interests qualify as mere shopping or whether they constitute a lifestyle. If you want to buy airline tickets or roses, for example, you're just an AOL shopper (see Figure 6-14).

If you are fascinated by gadgets, on the other hand, that's a lifestyle (Figure 6-15). It's no trouble to find what you want on AOL (you can usually do with a keyword), but the logic of classification is sometimes quite amusing. I'm sorry to say that nearly everything I do is apparently part of a lifestyle, a humiliating bit of stereotype because I live in the Wine Country in California and remember the ratings of every Chardonnay for the last 20 years. They've got my number, I'm afraid.

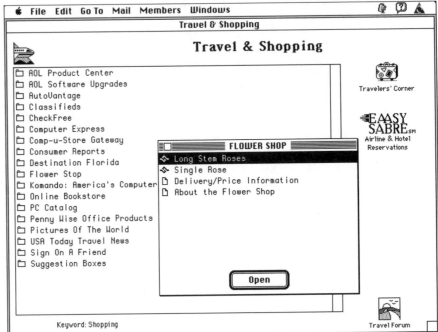

Figure 6-14:
Send
somebody
roses.
Really, it's
always a
good idea.

Figure 6-15:
The gadget
lifestyle on
AOL.
Let's talk
breadmakers.

Get mellow

Fans of the Grateful Dead have always been one of the best-organized groups, electronically (see figure 6-16). The brilliant journalist Mary Eisenhart (editor of *MicroTimes*), for example, used to maintain an electronic bulletin board for Deadheads, following them to every conference appearance with a laptop. And she was doing this 12 years ago, when there probably weren't more than a handful of musicians who could identify a modem. The AOL Grateful Dead Forum is a real little hot spot — and a whole universe for fans.

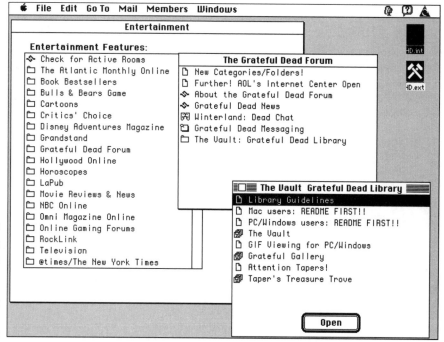

Figure 6-16: Like just the other day I was thinking about Pigpen....

Stay informed

Figure 6-17 shows the huge list of on-line magazines available on AOL. As soon as you start cruising this area, you'll discover that on-line magazines are better as a way to find specific topics than as a way to browse. There are no ads, and the information is stunningly fresh — I usually see the final version of my own *Macworld* reviews here three weeks before I get the magazine in my mailbox.

Figure 6-17:
Of course,
you'll miss all
the lovely
advertising
reading
these
on-line
magazines.

FTP, the Latest and Greatest

In response to incessant demand, AOL got its version of FTP up and running in October 1994. Although FTP will be integrated into the Internet keyword area soon, in the Preview version it has its own keyword (Figure 6-18).

In the FTP area you get a screen with some choices of explanation of the service and icons for action. The explanations are important, since for many AOL users this will be the first glimpse of FTP.

In Figure 6-19 you also see a bit of AOL cleverness. Rather than telling you to learn Archie and locate files before starting your FTP, AOL has built in a proprietary search system, and I'll bet it runs on an index maintained on AOL's own computers. Technically this means AOL is its own Archie server and it uses a custom front end. All you have to know is that it's easier than the traditional way.

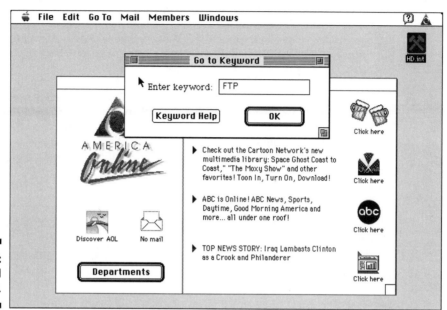

Figure 6-18:
Keyword
FTP, at last.

Figure 6-19:
AOL has its
own search
system for
FTP.

AOL has pre-loaded its Gopher service with a bunch of starting points, and the same is true for FTP (Figure 6-20). By the way, the note in the previous figure strongly encouraging off-peak-time usage of FTP is serious business — AOL users could bring the poor old VAX at Dartmouth to its little electronic knees if they all started jamming on 2:00 PM on the same day.

Just for fun, try the White House site. You'll find all sorts of briefing papers, the President's daily schedule (with enough detail to give a Secret Service agent security nightmares) and pieces of the wit and wisdom of Al Gore. Think about it — you can get up every morning and download the President's schedule into your own electronic Day-Timer. Pseudo-interactive fantasy adventures like this are a big part of the fascination of the Internet!

Figure 6-20:
Internet
starting
points for
FTP.

Chapter 7

Internet from CompuServe

● ●

In This Chapter

▶ That old-time connection

▶ Mail is the answer

▶ Finding Mac stuff in the libraries

▶ Real Internet? Not yet, but at least there's Navigator

● ●

CompuServe has been around for a long time. At a point when the only people with Macintoshes were personal friends of Guy Kawasaki or Steve Jobs, CompuServe was taking care of business at 300 bps for users connected to primitive character-oriented computers.

This gives CompuServe some advantages and disadvantages for Mac users. Its collection of files you may want to download, for example, is quite impressive. (It should be impressive because CompuServe has been collecting them since the dawn of time, at least in computer terms.) A big disadvantage is that lots of things on CompuServe are done in a particular way because that's the way they have always been done. The menu-system design choices were made back in the days of slow computers and even slower networks, and they don't represent the state-of-the-art choices as compared to newer services, such as America Online.

Its relative antiquity means that CompuServe is a big service with more than a million subscribers (nearly two million at press time). CompuServe has also had the time to work out arrangements with the companies (SprintNet, TymNet) that give you local access numbers in a huge variety of cities.

Getting into CIS

My CompuServe name is a five-digit number plus a three-digit number. Numbers aren't very exciting — even bulletin boards that are run with freeware on someone's old Mac II in a basement let you log in with a cool name like ZIPPY or AlexBell. But at CIS (CompuServe *I*nformation *S*ervices), you have a number that's faintly reminiscent of the number card under your chin when you're being booked for disturbing the peace.

The passwords assigned to you, however, are almost poetic. I've had six CompuServe passwords over the years, all of them two-word passwords with the words apparently chosen at random. Someone out there probably has the password *free spirit* and relishes every day the irony of having a beautiful password but a number instead of a name.

Managing information

In traditional CIS-land, you did most of your navigating by picking numbers. The system presented you with a numbered menu, and you responded with the number of your choice. These days, most CompuServe access is bundled with CompuServe *I*nformation *M*anager (CIM), part of the starter kit you buy in computer stores. If your current CompuServe setup doesn't include CIM, you can buy it on-line, or you can download it (at present, you have to pay extra either way).

CIM is worth getting because it makes CompuServe look like a Macintosh service. If you're not good at menu manipulation, a record of your on-line session could go on for twenty pages with the same menus appearing over and over again as you step around in the hierarchy. CompuServe should really include CIM at no additional charge, not just as part of the starter kit, and perhaps soon it will. I used CIM for the illustrations for this chapter because, quite frankly, the standard CompuServe interface was driving me crazy.

Figure 7-1 shows the Browse window in the CIM welcome screen. All you do at this point is click the Go icon, and the program connects you. Now, where do you suppose the Internet Forum is — under Computers, Communications, or Forums in the Browse window? It's not obvious. The fastest way to find the Internet Forum is to choose the GO option under the Services menu and then type **inetforum**. These steps get you to the promising Internet Forum screen in Figure 7-2.

This screen looks promising because Internet is prominently mentioned. But where do you go from here? You have four choices:

- ✔ You can read messages.
- ✔ You can scan the libraries.
- ✔ You can join a conference.
- ✔ You can go back up to another menu.

In the preceding list, the fourth choice lets you leave the Internet Forum and go to a different forum.

But I'm not leaving the CompuServe Internet Forum now because I have to tell you about CompuServe's unique approach to Internet service. Remarkably, CompuServe has the same goodies as other services, and it started offering them only since April 1994.

Figure 7-1:
The Browse window in gateway to the world of CompuServe.

Figure 7-2:
Setting the Internet stage with the Internet Forum.

The Big Mailbox

What you have on CompuServe boils down to mailboxes and libraries (collections) of files. There isn't a real Internet connection yet, and CIS has not (since the summer of 1994) presented much in the way of plans for offering Internet stuff. The Internet file libraries are good and very complete (see Figure 7-3), but it is frustrating to be able to collect all this expert advice and neat shareware and have no way to use most of it, yet.

Figure 7-3:
Lots of info,
lots of files,
not much
connection
yet.

| | File | Edit | Services | Messages | Libraries | Conference | Special | | | | |

Library Files

| | Info | Abstract | Mark | View | Retrieve | Delete |

View Topics

Messages since Sat, Jun | Browsing "FTP & File Transfer [6] "

Section		Filename	Title	Submitted	Size	Accesses
General Information		MACFTP.TXT	Mac-FTP-list Version 3.8.6	6/1/94	39.5K	158
Getting Started [2]		WNCODE.ZIP	Windows UUEncode & Decode	5/1/94	55.5K	828
Internet Access [3]		CD.TXT	INTERNET VIRUS	5/1/94	2179	1088
Directory Services [		WNCOD2.ZIP	Wincode V2.3	4/26/94	251.5K	546
Electronic Mail [5]		GZIPLH.EXE	gzip 1.1 for .z & .gz & .Z files. UNCO...	4/9/94	48.5K	622
FTP & File Transfer		WEIRDI.ZIP	Weird Sites on the Internet	3/20/94	43K	1809
Newsgroups/Usenet [		COMPRS.ZIP	File Compression FAQ	3/2/94	72K	498
Mailing Lists [8]		AUDIOF.ZIP	Audio File Formats FAQ	3/2/94	37K	259
Gopher / WAIS / WW		NCFTP.DOC	Info on ncftp, an alternative to ftp	2/28/94	38K	218
International [10]		FTPLOC.ZIP	Anonymous FTP Site Listing	2/22/94	99.5K	3005
Resources–Academic		FTPFAQ.ZIP	Anonymous FTP FAQ	2/22/94	10K	1685
Resources–Business		FTPDOS.ZIP	Recommended MS-DOS shareware/fr...	2/22/94	26K	2601
Resources–Communi		FTPNET.ZIP	Anonymous ftp from the Internet via ...	2/21/94	101.5K	2837
Resources–Govt. [14		FTPHOW.TXT	How to use anonymous FTP (Internet ...	2/18/94	26.5K	2923
Resources–Technical						
Resources–Personal						
Resources–Mac [17]						

The files-by-mail gimmick

You can't do Archie or FTP directly on CompuServe, yet. There is, however, a classic Internet trick known as Internet-by-mail, and it works very well on CompuServe. You send an e-mail message to a remote computer that's been specially set up as an Internet server, and the remote computer acts on your commands and sends a file back to you as an e-mail message. This technique has been used for years for Archie and FTP services.

Gopher-by-mail is a newer possibility. It works better on CompuServe than on other services that are obliged to resort to this hack because CIS can handle

Godzilla-size e-mail files. Even if an FTP server wants to send you the whole 1.02MB of Mosaic 2.0, CIS can handle it — at least in chunks. Every other on-line service that uses this by-mail stuff as a patch until the operators work out real Internet access has a terrible problem with file size (eWorld has an 8K limit; AOL's limit is 32K; Prodigy has special problems). Even breaking up the file into pieces gives you too many pieces. On CompuServe, this system works pretty well most of the time, so let's take a look at how to set up Archie and FTP as Gopher-by-mail.

Archie

Archie-by-mail is still a hack, a kludge, a fix-up — you wouldn't use it if you had real Archie. I predict that all the services, including CompuServe, will have a substitute for this trick within a year. In the meantime, here's how it goes.

Let's say you're looking for a file called pixie. Someone told you it's a cool new shareware program that's better than Photoshop, and you just have to have it. To get the file, you send an e-mail message just like this:

```
To: INTERNET:archie@archie.sura.net
Subject:
prog pixie
.
```

You put nothing in the subject line, do the second line just as it appears, and put a period *by itself* on the last line.

There are lots of Archie tricks, but you won't need them here. If you want to learn how to do fancy Archie searches, send an e-mail message to the following address:

```
archie-l@cs.mcgill.ca
```

Then politely request the file archie.man.txt. Better yet, look for this file in CompuServe's own Internet libraries.

It may take a few days before you get your Archie file back by return mail. If you don't hear from poor old overworked sura.net, try a different Archie server (there's a list in Chapter 5). If you haven't asked for something very specific (don't try prog mac, for example), the file will be huge. But the results will tell you where to find the file.

FTP

Suppose that the Archie search said that pixie.hqx can be found at ftp.univxyz.edu, and it's 150K in size. Now send the following e-mail message:

```
TO:INTERNET:ftp.univxyz.edu
Subject:pixie.hqx
reply five.three@compuserve.com
connect ftp.univxyz.edu
chunksize 49000
get pixie.hqx
quit
```

The expression `five.three` means your CompuServe number with a period instead of a comma, such as 70781.234. `Chunksize` makes the file segments acceptable to CIS. Here's what you do: Download the e-mail files to your own Mac through CompuServe mail. You have to take each e-mail message into a word processor and take off the mailing information. You also have to add the chunks together to have one big file of gibberish lines with lots of ASCII punctuation marks and no spaces between the lines. You then uncook this omelet by using StuffIt Lite, which gives you a real working Mac program called `pixie` (all you do is select Expand from the File menu). This whole procedure sounds like a hassle, and it is.

Some files require special treatment. If you're serious about FTP-by-mail, go into the CompuServe Internet Forum libraries and simply download everything you can find about FTP and read it off-line. There's plenty of Internet material that will call for processing with the program uuencode. Don't worry if you don't feel like going through this bit of postgraduate education in Internetica. Someone back at CIS headquarters is going to find a way to make this process easier. These people want your business.

ID: 73452,203

Because Internet e-mail is the main CompuServe Internet function implemented so far, here are the rules for e-mail.

1. Incoming

Other people will need your CompuServe ID numbers to send you mail on the Internet. Inside CIS, the numbers are always written with a comma between them; for communication over the Internet, you must replace the comma with a period.

If you had the ID in this section heading, your Internet address would be

```
73452.203@compuserve.com
```

2. Outbound

You can send e-mail to your pals at other Internet e-mail addresses simply by putting `INTERNET:` as the first part of the address, as in

```
INTERNET:chseiter@crl.com
```

in response to the address prompt in CompuServe mail. You can also get messages out to people who are technically on BITNET or other services, at the expense of a little more typing, as in

```
INTERNET:SteveM@EDUWXY.BITNET
```

So, Where's the Internet?

It's not here. Not at CompuServe. Not yet. But a visit to the Internet area under construction shows that CIS users will probably get some real services by late 1994. Then all this doing-it-by-e-mail stuff will be a fond memory, such as inkwells on school desks or phone switchboards answered by humans.

If you type **libraries** at the prompt you get after you typed **inetforum** (that's how you get to the Internet Forum), you get the promising assortment of topics shown in Figure 7-4. Hey, looks like it's all starting to happen!

```
Libraries Menu
  1 General Information
  2 Getting Started
  3 Internet Access
  4 Directory Services
  5 Electronic Mail
  6 FTP & File Transfer
  7 Newsgroups/Usenet
  8 Mailing Lists
  9 Gopher / WAIS / WWW
 10 International
 11 Resources-Academic
 12 Resources-Business
 13 Resources-Community
 14 Resources-Govt.
 15 Resources-Technical
 16 Resources-Personal
 17 Resources-Mac
```

Figure 7-4:
CIS Internet
Libraries
menu.

But the reality is this: You have access to all these Internet-related programs and informative text files — and they're quite up-to-date — but you can't actually *do* anything with them on CompuServe yet.

You can find good explanations of the Archie and FTP e-mail tricks, special-purpose communications programs, and on-line guides to the Internet. In the CompuServe messages area for Internet access, you can exchange opinions with disgruntled CompuServe users who are impatient about lack of real Internet, and you can receive faintly superior messages from the lucky few who have Internet connection from another service.

Navigating in Style

So, you may ask, why is CIS even in this book? It's here because some day soon you will check into INETFORUM, and telnet and FTP will appear on the menu. And when this happens, CompuServe Navigator will be even more valuable. CompuServe Navigator is sold separately by CIS. You can order it on-line, and CIS will bill your credit card. Navigator (see Figure 7-5) is designed to log you on, do your work, and log you off quickly and automatically. Navigator started as shareware years ago, and it has been through lots of optimization (everyone else's software in this category is a first attempt).

Figure 7-5:
Navigator
gives you a
choice of
areas to
visit.

Easy on

What really eats up connection time is sitting at the computer, staring at the on-line-service screen, and trying to decide what to do next. A typical half-hour session can consist of 2 minutes of download and 28 minutes of interactive head-scratching.

With Navigator, however, you do your planning off-line because the program has a database of all the contents of CompuServe. When you choose Run from the Session menu, it logs on by using its own script (see Figure 7-6). It cruises all the choices you made, including visiting forums, finding messages for you (see Figure 7-7), and sending messages to other people.

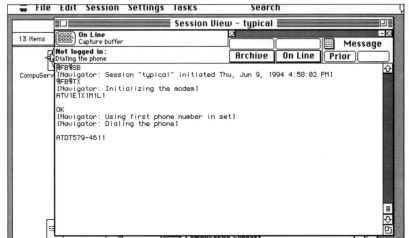

Figure 7-6:
Navigator
handles the
telecom
details.

Figure 7-7:
Collecting
messages in
a forum.
Fast.

Easy off

And then Navigator clears out without a second thought. There's no way you could do all this stuff yourself at anything like this speed. If you want, you can also interrupt this high-speed automated action and insert yourself in the loop, but after you find where the goodies are on CompuServe, you can set Navigator to find anything new. The procedure is always the same, and it's always pretty simple. You check the areas you want to visit in Navigator's CompuServe session window, and Navigator looks for new material in those areas when it connects.

Do you remember all that talk about doing Archie and FTP by e-mail? Navigator actually makes it a reasonable form of access (see Figure 7-8). You simply prepare your Archie and FTP requests off-line, and then a day later you send Navigator out to CompuServe to fetch the results. It's not interactive; it's sure not netsurfing; but it makes thrifty use of Internet resources and produces tiny on-line charges at CIS. When the real Internet options get installed on CompuServe, Navigator will still be an excellent way to do FTP transfers and Gopher searches.

Figure 7-8:
Navigator
handles
Internet e-
mail for you.

Towards Real Internet

In an effort to bring some "real" Internet to its millions of users, CompuServe now offers USENET newsgroups. Newsgroup access in CompuServe is pretty effortless. Follow these simple steps in CompuServe Information Manager, and you're connected!

1. **Choose Go under the Services menu, as seen in Figure 7-9, and type** USENET.

2. **Look at sample newsgroups to get a feeling for how this works (see Figure 7-10).**

3. **After you're in a listing of newsgroups, you can pick a group, and CompuServe automatically pulls up the first article for you to read (see Figure 7-11).**

Figure 7-9:
Basic
newsgroup
choices.

Figure 7-10:
CompuServe
shows you
some recent
articles.

```
USENET News

Choices
 1 REPLY
 2 REPLY with Quotation
 3 MAIL
 4 CREATE an article
 5 CANCEL article

 6 REREAD this article
 7 HOLD this article
 8 NEXT article
 9 NEXT THREAD
10 PARENT article

11 CLEAR articles in this newsgroup
12 IGNORE
13 DOWNLOAD this article


Enter choice !
```

Figure 7-11:
CompuServe
gives you
another
menu for
actions
inside a
newsgroup.

As Long As You're Here

CompuServe has accumulated some unique on-line information resources over the years, many of which replace standard household or library reference books. For example, rather than buy a copy of the Physician's Desk Reference every year, you can look up background information on your prescriptions in CompuServe's drug database.

Assuming that you are the sort of person who plans vacations carefully, you can use CompuServe to find yourself golf courses everywhere you go. This service would be more helpful if you could download color pictures of difficult holes, along with weather reports, but you can't have everything (at least not yet). It would be nice if this database pointed out, for example, which of the California courses shown here are flat as a billiard table and 115° F most of the summer.

The golf course database may be missing some crucial notations, but you can't complain about CompuServe's movie reviews. I had the system search on "Peter O'Toole" and it popped up Roger Ebert's reviews of the celebrated Irish thespian's greatest hits.

I regard it as a public service that CompuServe doesn't carry reviews of some of Mr. O'Toole's less fortunate outings (*The Seventh Coin, Foxtrot*) although the lack of a review of *The Stuntman* is an odd omission. In any case, these examples just scratch the surface of the CompuServe databases. A large fraction of what people expect to find on the Internet is here on CIS already.

Chapter 8
Internet from Prodigy

- -

In This Chapter

▶ Managing Prodigy like a mini-Internet

▶ Not your usual e-mail

▶ Meeting your Net friends

▶ No telnet, no promises

- -

It will be clear to you in a page or two that I don't think Prodigy is a top choice for Macintosh Internet access. Nonetheless, it's a very distinctive type of service. If you like Prodigy, I can tell you right now that there is no substitute for it. It is the only source of Prodigy-type stuff, that's for sure.

Three Good Things about Prodigy

In an effort to be positive, I will enumerate Prodigy's virtues first and then examine the downside of this service, particularly as an Internet source.

Prodigy is big

Prodigy has more than two million users — about as big as the Internet was itself a few years ago. Most of these users have computers at work and computers in a home office as well, meaning that they are chosen from the same general demographic as the readership of this book.

Actually, if you discount all the people at government research labs, UNIX wireheads at universities, and physicists in Sweden, there probably aren't more than four or five million people on the Internet even now who are merely individual users motivated by curiosity. Prodigy is big enough to generate its own discussion groups on herpetology or coin collecting, and its designers put lots of work into reaching the home market. All you do is double-click the Prodigy icon (on the software Prodigy sends you) to get to the screen in Figure 8-1.

Figure 8-1:
Prodigy is
designed for
easy use.

Prodigy means business

The Internet is noncommercial. You're not supposed to send advertising or business messages over the NSF-sponsored high-speed network that makes the Internet work. In fact, please don't.

Hey, but every now and then you *want* to shop. On Prodigy, you can't avoid it. There are ads and promotions at the bottom of nearly every screen on the system (see Figure 8-2). I, for example, have had an out-of-control fountain-pen-buying problem for years. In making up the Internet screens for this book, I found myself wandering off through the menus and ordering a pen from a dealer in Los Angeles.

You may find yourself ordering discount airline tickets to Hawaii! This, of course, is the aspect of the information superhighway that has all the businesses drooling. You will either love or hate this aspect of Prodigy, but it's a fact of life.

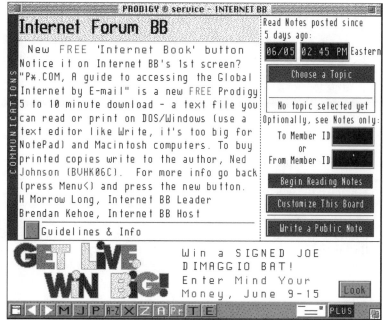

Internet Forum BB

New FREE 'Internet Book' button
Notice it on Internet BB's 1st screen?
"P*.COM, A guide to accessing the Global
Internet by E-mail" is a new FREE Prodigy
5 to 10 minute download - a text file you
can read or print on DOS/Windows (use a
text editor like Write, it's too big for
NotePad) and Macintosh computers. To buy
printed copies write to the author, Ned
Johnson (BVHK06C). For more info go back
(press Menu<) and press the new button.
H Morrow Long, Internet BB Leader
Brendan Kehoe, Internet BB Host

Guidelines & Info

Read Notes posted since
5 days ago:
06/05 02:45 PM Eastern

Choose a Topic

No topic selected yet
Optionally, see Notes only:
To Member ID
or
From Member ID

Begin Reading Notes

Customize This Board

Write a Public Note

GET LIVE, WiN BiG!

Win a SIGNED JOE
DIMAGGIO BAT!
Enter Mind Your
Money, June 9-15

Look

Figure 8-2:
Internet
meets
advertising
on Prodigy.

Prodigy has Brendan Kehoe

Brendan Kehoe is the Internet bulletin board host on Prodigy. Mr. Kehoe wrote
a work called *Zen and the Art of the Internet*, which has been distributed for free
at thousands of locations on the Net. This has made him one of the Internet's
early heroes, and he is indeed one of the good guys.

There are more good things about Prodigy (see the section "As Long As You're
Here" at the end of this chapter), but these features are particularly important.

Three Bad Things about Prodigy

Now I am obliged to give you the bad news.

Prodigy is slow

Every time you pick a menu item, Prodigy has to write you a new full-color
screen. Even at 9600 baud, it takes a long time to ship these big files. It's too bad
that you can't see the vivid (close to garish, actually) color interface in this
book. Text files move fast; black-and-white graphics move reasonably fast; but
color takes forever.

Prodigy is not a Mac-oriented system

Prodigy has a nice mail-manager program, for example, but it's only for PC users. Everywhere you turn on Prodigy, you encounter PC-specific pitches — an ad for a low-cost PC-specific modem has been a feature of the sign-off screen for months. Everyone also can get a special deal on this cool high-speed modem, everyone, that is, except Mac users. Prodigy is a joint venture of Sears and IBM, and you can confidently predict that Apple's latest gyrations don't loom large in Prodigy's planning.

Another example of non-Macness is the e-mail system. For on-line message entry, you use the little pencil icon as the text insertion point (see Figure 8-3). You have to click to get to the next screen when you have a few hundred characters in this frame (it doesn't scroll), and you can see for yourself that the fonts are pretty stringy by Mac standards. Prodigy is designing a new Mac interface in which a single click and a double click will work in the same way as they usually do in Mac software, but they had years to make this change already. I also haven't had much luck with customer support on Mac questions.

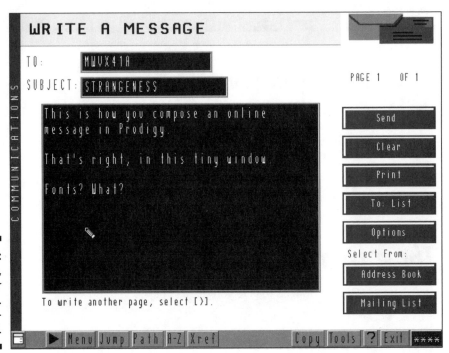

Figure 8-3: Weird fonts, 40-character lines . . . Prodigy e-mail.

Prodigy is not Internet-friendly

Prodigy is the most controlled on-line environment on the planet. The Internet is, by contrast, for all practical purposes not controlled at all. Prodigy was notorious a few years back for censoring complaints on its bulletin boards — not just complaints about Prodigy service but about all IBM products. Most networking pioneers believe in free information exchange. They found this censorship despicable and flamed Prodigy to the point where you might have expected IBM to develop fireproof pin-striped suits for its Prodigy staff.

Consider, for example, the warning in Figure 8-4. Prodigy not only advises you that your privacy on the Internet can't be guaranteed (this from a service with a record of filtering posted messages) but also has more warnings about the possibility of children gaining access to the raunchy side of the Internet (see the next sidebar). Oddly enough, the Internet forum on Prodigy itself is starting to accumulate some postings about adult parties and so forth (Figure 8-5).

Figure 8-4:
Internet Alert! Prodigy warns you of lurking dangers.

Figure 8-5:
Funny
business for
Prodigy
Internauts.

Blue moves

As long as Prodigy has raised the subject in its warning to parents, I want to make a few reluctant points here as a public service. First, there is text material flying around on the Internet, particularly in Internet Relay Chat, that qualifies easily as "beyond adult." The fellows who wrote the First Amendment probably weren't thinking about this stuff explicitly, but these messages are, I guess, made up of Constitutionally-protected electrons.

The second point, for the curious, is that the Internet is not generally a viable source of pornographic pictures. There are, by all accounts, not many of these pictures out there, and those that are out there are not very spectacular. The hardcore graphics files are all on bulletin boards, which you can look up in local computer publications. The fancier grade of this material is found on commercial CD-ROMs. Do yourself a favor by not trying to find color graphics files like this to download from the Internet. The data transmission rate involved in buying a copy of *Penthouse* or *Playgirl* is multiple gigabytes of graphics over the counter in a few seconds. That's better than the fastest modems on the drawing board, and it's the appropriate technology for the job. (If you're into that sort of thing.)

Internet by E-Mail, Again

There is, as you would expect, e-mail connection to the Internet, and you can compose messages off-line for uploading (see Figure 8-6). Prodigy doesn't offer telnet, Archie, FTP, or any other direct Internet services yet, but it has plenty of files (see Figure 8-7). If you take the time to read through the material Prodigy provides, you will have a thorough education not only in Prodigy Internet access but in the aspects of Internet service you can't get now on Prodigy.

Figure 8-6: Words of encouragement for an Internet-hungry public.

Prodigy has a whole 50-page on-line book about doing Archie and FTP by e-mail. The book is specifically geared toward the Prodigy user — a nice touch. Unfortunately, the book is also geared toward the PC user, not the Mac user, and is full of references to file types and programs you're not likely to know. If you've used a PC, you know what it means to PKUNZIP a file and get to an .EXE file; however, the reason you have a Macintosh is to avoid this information!

Figure 8-7:
The Prodigy
Internet
library, a
browser's
dream.

Archie-by-mail

Archie-by-mail from Prodigy is straightforward. Just click the Mail button in the sign-on window. You send an e-mail message like this:

```
To: archie@archie.sura.net
Subject:
prog <insert name of file you want>
.
```

You put nothing in the subject line, do the second line just as it appears, and put a period as the last line. The archie server will send you back an e-mail message that tells you where to find the file you requested. For more details on Archie searches, send an e-mail message to the following address:

```
archie-l@cs.mcgill.ca
```

and request the file `archie.man.txt`. Prodigy's own on-line book has more information, too.

It may take a few days before you get your Archie file back by return mail. If it is `sura.net`, try a different Archie server from the list in Chapter 5. If you haven't asked for something very specific (don't try `prog mac`, for example), the file will be huge. But the results will tell you where to find the file.

Suppose that the Archie search said that <filename> can be found at
ftp.world.com, and it's 120K in size. Now send the following e-mail message:

```
TO:ftp.world.com
Subject:<filename>

reply <yourID>@prodigy.com
connect ftp.world.com
chunksize 59000
get <filename>
quit
```

The expression <yourID> means your Prodigy identifier (four letters, two
numbers, a letter). The Chunksize command makes the file segments fit into
the Prodigy mail system. When you get sent the file (in pieces), you download
the files to your own Mac through Prodigy mail. You will have to take each e-
mail message into a word processor and take off the mailing information, and
you will have to consult the Prodigy on-line book PCOMM.TXT for details on
knitting the file together and processing it so that you can use it on a Mac.

This will usually involve putting the chunks together to have one big file of
gibberish lines with lots of ASCII punctuation marks and no spaces between the
lines. You then can try to expand this file using StuffIt Lite. If you're lucky, this
will work. If you're not lucky, send the name of the file you want to one of the
Internet Forum operators — the amazing Mr. Kehoe for example — and politely
ask that the file be fetched and put in a Prodigy library.

The mail audit trail

Another more primitive objection, besides the complication, to using Prodigy
as your Internet e-mail gateway — even with its carefully explained access to
FTP services and so forth — is that Prodigy has a schedule of small but annoy-
ing fees for mail services (see Figure 8-8). Instead of a monthly flat rate or a
monthly rate and per-hour charges, there's a bean-counter's delirium of
charges for messages and parts of messages. Master FTP-by-mail on this service
at your own risk.

Figure 8-8:
A
disincentive
plan for big
file transfers.

Prodigy and Newsgroups

Gearing up for the demand for real Internet service, Prodigy has done a commendable job of adding USENET facilities. In the new Mac interface (introduced in late 1994), you can Jump directly to Internet and click the USENET button, which produces a screen like the one in Figure 8-9 :

Figure 8-9:
Welcome to
Prodigy
newsgroups.

If you click the Access Control button, you see a manifestation of Prodigy's concern for family orientation. Nonetheless, you can access most USENET newsgroups once you've given yourself access permission just by clicking the appropriate self-explanatory buttons.

Figure 8-10: Prodigy wants to keep some news off-limits, with good reason.

As Long As You're Here

Prodigy is the biggest as-long-as-you're-here on-line service, even if it's taking a long time to get real Internet service. It's a complete, if somewhat carefully edited, universe of its own. Its news services collect everthing instantly, reformat it into Prodigy style (Figure 8-11), and put it on-line. I have it on good authority that the font in this picture is the exact font used on the equipment found in disabled alien spacecraft. That's why you, as a Mac user, probably can't identify it— the font is called Zartron, after the home planet of the big aliens (who control the little aliens most often pictured with big black insect-like eyes). OK, I made that up. But it might be true anyway.

Figure 8-11:
Hello,
sports fans.

Similarly, there is a distinctive twist on other information services. Prodigy has the same Grolier's Encyclopedia (Figure 8-12) as the other services (in retrospect, making an on-line version of this encyclopedia must look like a good business decision), but it's got that Prodigy look (compare it to the same encyclopedia on eWorld (Chapter 11).

Figure 8-12:
On-line
encyclopedia,
in Prodigy
format.

Prodigy's graphics orientation gives it an edge in many areas. Games, for example, appear in full color (Figure 8-13). I should tell you that the vast majority of Internet games are still text-oriented role-playing games, which are apparently highly involving if you have some imagination (I don't). Besides looking halfway decent onscreen, Prodigy games are also abundant— it's the biggest game collection I've found.

Figure 8-13:
At least it's not: "You find yourself in a garden."

Figure 8-14:
Be your own travel agent on Prodigy.

Figure 8-13:
Looks like
Edina,
Minnesota,
is the right
place for a
tan.

In other words, the Internet has more uncensored materials, and certainly more high-level academic information, but Prodigy has everything else pretty well covered. (Refer to Figure 8-14 and Figure 8-15.) It still isn't a Macintosh hotspot, but Prodigy keeps working on interface issues, and it has the resources to get it all right some day soon.

Chapter 9
Internet from Delphi

• •

• •

*E*very now and then — probably because of our pressing national shortage of marketing MBAs (just kidding, just kidding) — an organization runs advertisements that accurately represent the organization's services. Yes, this honesty in advertising does actually happen.

For more than a year, Delphi has been filling the back covers of computer magazines with an offer of a free, five-hour Explore The Internet! service. Remarkably — given that Delphi operates in a world where Internet access in an ad can often mean a badly designed e-mail interface and nothing more — Delphi delivers the goods. Jolly good show, Delphi!

Complete Internet Service

Delphi is, of course, not the only longtime full-service Internet provider. Plenty of places have offered shell accounts for several years. With a *shell account*, you have a user name, a password, and the right to dial in as a terminal on (typically) a UNIX network. If you're happy with UNIX commands, you'll like the shell game. You should then also buy a copy of the original *The Internet For Dummies* and see a psychologist about reconciling your left-brain UNIX personality with your right-brain Mac side.

Ordering from the menu

Delphi has gone far beyond shell account service. Walt Howe, Delphi's Internet system operator, has designed a menu-driven front end for the Internet service so that all you have to do is be able to type out responses to menu prompts. Look at the password procedure in Figure 9-1, for example. Think you can handle it? You bet you can. And the rest of Delphi is just that easy.

Figure 9-1:
As easy as
1-2-3.
Actually,
easier than
Lotus 1-2-3.

```
Greetings, and welcome to the DELPHI Guided Tour.

Before using DELPHI the first time, you should select a new password.  Your new
personal password should be different from the one you were initially assigned
and have just used to log on.  Your new password should consist of six or more
letters and numbers and should be somewhat cryptic;  your name, nickname, or
other obvious information is not appropriate as it may be possible for someone
else to happen upon it.

You will first be asked for your old password (the password you just used when
you logged on) and then your new password.  When prompted for the verification
of your new password, type the same new password again.

Old Password:

New Password:
```

Asking Howe to do things

Normally, in the Dummies universe, all relevant questions can be answered by reference to another . . . *For Dummies* book. I have every confidence that IDG will publish a *Genetic-Algorithm Software Design For Dummies* book by the year 2000. *Home Brain Surgery For Dummies*, another example, is actually under contract right now and should be ready soon.

In the matter of Mr. Howe, we have a special case. If you have signed up for Delphi, you can order, on-line, a Delphi-specific, Internet-specific manual by Walt Howe and Steve Lambert that runs to 480 pages. You'll be a happy little Delphi camper with that document, I can promise you, because if there's anything in the book you don't understand, you can e-mail a question to Walt (see Figure 9-2).

For reasons of page allotment and preservation of sanity, this chapter covers the principal highlights of Delphi Internet. For horrible, niggling little what-went-wrong-here questions, ask Walt.

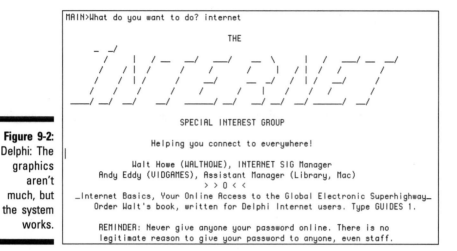

```
MAIN>What do you want to do? internet
                          THE
         _ _/
        / |  |  _/  _/  _/   \  |  |  _/ _/ _/
       / / \ | _/  _/  _/  _ \ | _/  _/ / / /
      / _/ \ |  _/  _/   \ _/ _/  _/ _/ / /
     / / / | / / _/  _/  _ \ / _/ _/ / / /
   __/ _/ _/ _/ ___/ _/ __/ _/ _/ _/ ___/ _/

              SPECIAL INTEREST GROUP

           Helping you connect to everywhere!

        Walt Howe (WALTHOWE), INTERNET SIG Manager
     Andy Eddy (VIDGAMES), Assistant Manager (Library, Mac)
                      > > 0 < <
   _Internet Basics, Your Online Access to the Global Electronic Superhighway_
       Order Walt's book, written for Delphi Internet users. Type GUIDES 1.

       REMINDER: Never give anyone your password online. There is no
         legitimate reason to give your password to anyone, even staff.
```

Figure 9-2: Delphi: The graphics aren't much, but the system works.

Plain Text

The only downside to Delphi Internet service is that these people don't mean the same thing by *menu* that you or I or the folks at Apple mean. Delphi is strictly a text-oriented service. No color pictures. Just characters. You press Control-C to stop. Nothing on-screen looks right (or, at least, looks like the screen shots in this chapter) unless you display all your text in the Monaco font, where all letters have the same width.

An advantage of this text-oriented service is that you can use any old communications software to reach Delphi. A disadvantage is that all the way-cool Macintosh software I was showing off in Chapter 5 can't be used here. To use this fancy software, you need a separate *serial-line-interface-protocol* (SLIP) account on another service. There is also no indication that Delphi intends to "iconize" its interface, probably because Macintosh users are a small minority on Delphi.

Later in this chapter, I'll describe a partial fix-up, called D-Lite, for this deplorable situation. There are rumors that a real Mac interface will be available soon. But for now, it's just as my third-grade teacher told me, "Charles, you simply can't have everything your own way!"

Delphi: The Real Thing

How do you find the Internet service on Delphi? You can't miss it. I have highlighted it in Figure 9-3, just for emphasis. You can't highlight words on-line in this graphically pitiful terminal-style system, so italic and bold are indicated by underscores that are located before and after the word(s) to be highlighted, such as in the following example: _drama_. Dramatic, no? To get to the Internet, type **internet** at the prompt, and you get to the special Internet menu.

Figure 9-3:
Go ahead.
Pick one
from
Column A.

```
MAIN Menu:

Business and Finance        News, Weather, and Sports
Computing Groups            Reference and Education
Conference                  Shopping
Entertainment and Games     Travel and Leisure
Groups and Clubs            Using DELPHI
Internet Services           Workspace
Mail                        HELP
Member Directory            EXIT
```

The menu in Figure 9-4 is full of possibilities. It contains not only every Internet buzzword I have mentioned so far in this book, but it also contains a convenient menu to back up each buzzword. It's the whole Internet, fresh off the high-speed national fiber-optic link.

Figure 9-4:
Yep, looks
like it's all
there, all
right.

```
Internet SIG Menu:



About the Internet      Help
Conference              Exit
Databases (Files)
EMail                   FTP
Forum (Messages)        Gopher
Guides (Books)          IRC-Internet Relay Chat
Register/Cancel         Telnet
Who's Here              Utilities (finger, traceroute, ping)
Workspace               Usenet Newsgroups
```

Unfiltered

Delphi doesn't censor on-line material. In fact, Delphi offers so much material that it couldn't possibly censor it. A case in point is Internet Relay Chat, a kind of global Internet conference call in which a virtual "roomful" of people type their comments on a topic in a running dialogue.

Some of these chat groups are, um, remarkable (see accompanying figure). Some are amateur radio operators trading tips on upgrading equipment. Some of them are "adult" chat groups — with a variety of specialty interests — describing activities that I'm pretty sure no one could actually do (hey, after all, you can't see anyone in a plain-text interface). I have a friend who spent years in the Navy seeking out the least elegant entertainment imaginable near every U.S. Navy base in the Far East, and he turned pale and left the room after looking over my shoulder while I let a particular chat group scroll past.

Uncensored adult entertainment is one of the aspects of the Internet that gives fun-for-the-whole-family services, such as America Online and Prodigy, fits. Family services just *can't* let the kiddies point and click their way into some of these discussions. Wouldn't work. No way.

```
***     #malang:      4  Cangkruk dul, Jagongan Dul!

***     #DogWorld:    1  Cats: enter at your own risk!
***     #aposoc:      6  Alpha Phi Omega National Co-ed Svc Fraternity
***     #dementia:    2  Weird Al, Dr D., Tom Lehrer, and other demented music!!!
*** #Demon's_L*       1  What evil lies in the hearts of Men? The DemoN knows!
***     #kun:         1  Welcome to the KUN: Katholieke Universiteit Nijmegen

*** #Doom(201):       2  ANYONE IN 201 AREA WANNA PLAY D O O M ?

***     #freenet:    14  Freenet Finland

***     #math:        5  what is mathematics?
***     #BotFree:     2  IRC Astrology /sign (your sign here)
*** #machscafe:       5  Marry me and be my Love for always!
***     #anime!:     16  Japanese Animation and Comics (manga)
***     #vampires:   |7  If you are going to be offended by the exchange of ideas,
                                IRC isn't for you
*** #macintosh:      11  http://disserv.stu.umn.edu/~thingles/macintosh.html
***     #depeche:     7  THE DEPECHE MODE CHANNEL
***     #nippon:     15  kokoh nihonjin ryuugakuseitachi no tamariba
```

Telnet, if you must

Telnet is the most basic Internet function. Therefore, you should, in my humble opinion, use telnet only when it's the only way to do the job. If, for example, you have been assigned a real user account at a remote computer and you want to run UNIX programs on that computer for some reason (this happens all the time in science), you have to use telnet. If you just want to poke around on a remote site to see what may be there, you will use up everyone's resources and patience scrolling through the directories.

Here's how to do your homework before setting out with telnet. Instead of going directly to the Internet conference, type **computing** at the opening menu and then type **mac**.

This set of commands gets you to the choices in Figure 9-5. Delphi usually has 99 percent of the files, fonts, and information a Mac user will want right here in the Macintosh group. Usually, you can save yourself plenty of time and frustration by looking through this section before sailing out into the vastness of the Net. Remember my Uncle George's proverb: "Just because you have a swimming pool doesn't mean you have to practice holding your breath."

Figure 9-5:
These Delphi areas have tons of interesting material.

```
APP - Applications Sig      ENT - Entertainment Sig

DAT - ICONtact Files        COM - Communications Sig

DEV - Developer's Sig       FOR - ICONtact Forum

UTI - Utilities Sig         INT - Mac Internet GOPHER

USE - USENET Groups
```

At this point, the INT command gets you the deliriously detailed menu in Figure 9-6. And thar she blows, mateys, at number 11. These are the sites, all right. If you fetch the site list by recording the on-line session in your communications software, you can review it on paper and make yourself a little telnet guide with all the current Mac sites. This, in fact, is probably the only telnet plan that will work by mid-1995 because sites pop on and off the Internet with alarming regularity. Another Delphi source of telnet information is HytelNet, a hypercard stack with a catalog of sites (it's in the TOOLS&UTILITIES area of DATABASES in the Mac interest group).

Figure 9-6:
Bingo! You've landed on Delphi's Macintosh treasure barge.

```
Macintosh ICONtact Gopher
Page 1 of 1

1    PERSONAL FAVORITES                      Menu
2    A DIRECT FTP INTERNET CONNECTION        Menu
3    ABOUT DELPHI'S GOPHER SERVICE           Text
4    ARCHIVES OF MAC FILES                   Menu
5    DOCUMENTATION, ETC FOR MACS             Menu
6    FAQ'S, MAC INFO, HELP FOR YOUR MAC      Menu
7    FONTS FOR THE MAC                       Menu
8    GRAPHICS OF ALL FLAVORS                 Menu
9    INTERNET SEARCH UTILITIES               Menu
10   MAC BBS'S ON INTERNET                   Menu
11   MACINTOSH TELNET SITES                  Menu
12   MISC. FILES FOR THE MAC                 Menu
13   PRODUCT INFO ON MACS                    Menu
14   TOOLS FOR YOUR MAC                      Menu
15   UTILITIES FOR YOUR MAC                  Menu
16   WEATHER INFORMATION                     Menu
17   DELPHI'S MAIN GOPHER (INTERNET SIG)     Menu
```

Delphi — being pretty much a model of good Internet service and the only other service that's as Mac-friendly as America Online — has collected everything you may want in this fantastic Gopher menu. There's enough stuff here to keep you busy for weeks.

When you launch telnet from Delphi, Delphi provides you with a set of useful definitions and commands right after the prompt. In most communications software, you can scroll back to these commands if you get lost or need further advice. This ability to go back to the commands is helpful because plenty of the telnet sites have only primitive or nonexistent help. Again, I think that for souvenir collecting and such, telnet is actually the last resource you should use (Gopher is more efficient), but Delphi at least makes it as easy as possible to use it when you must.

FTP, if you like

There is also a menu item for FTP in Figure 9-6. If you have a file in mind that hasn't already been downloaded to some area on Delphi, you can get it with FTP. This is *real* FTP, of course, not the FTP-by-mail operation required at some other services.

Figure 9-7 shows an FTP session (the commands I typed in are highlighted in bold — you can do the same). I logged onto the giant Mac collection at Stanford, and I'm ashamed to say I did it in broad daylight because I was in a hurry. It's usually better to try a less popular "mirror" site (a copy of the original collection) as a point of netiquette, but your chances of getting into the Stanford sumex-aim site during the day are about as good as your chances of getting admitted to Stanford's freshman class as a high-school dropout.

Figure 9-7:
Straight
FTP, with a
little Delphi
hand-
holding.

```
Internet SIG>Enter your selection: ftp
Enter destination INTERNET address: sumex-aim.stanford.edu
Enter username (default: anonymous): anonymous

To get a binary file, type:  BINARY and then GET "remote filename" myfilename
To get a text file, type:    ASCII  and then GET "remote filename" myfilename
  Upper and lower case ARE significant; use the "quotes" shown above.
To get a directory, use DIR.
To type a short text file, use TT for myfilename
To get out, type EXIT or Control-Z.

Enter password [XXYYZZ@DELPHI.COM]: XXYYZZ@DELPHI.COM
220 SUMEX-AIM FTP server (Version 4.223 Thu Jun 24 16:42:58 PST 1994) ready.
331 Guest login ok, send mail address (user@host) as password.
230 Guest connection accepted. Restrictions apply.
FTP> ls

200 PORT command successful.
150 Opening ASCII mode data connection for /bin/ls.
info-mac
226 Transfer complete.
```

Watch out for file extensions

Again, as in the telnet example, you can scroll back to look at Delphi's hints about commands. Most sites that have interesting material have a combination of binary files and ASCII text files, so pay attention to the file extension (.BIN and .SIT are binary; .TXT and .HQX are ASCII).

You're not quite home yet

The file you request in an FTP transfer to Delphi leaves the remote computer and lands on Delphi's computer. You don't have it yet on your Mac. It's in your *workspace*. There's a WORKSPACE command available at the Internet menu. Just type **workspace** and then get your bearings in workspace-land by typing **help**.

If you look at the directory of your workspace, you should see whatever files you have FTP'd to Delphi. Just type the download command and follow the instructions to receive the file on your own computer.

Gopher, the right way to go

The world of the Internet is a world of choices. You can find them all by telneting to one site after another. In one perspective, this is "surfing the Net," and it has some entertainment value for people who want to feel like they're hacking. The problem, of course, is that if enough people decide to explore the Internet in this way, the situation will have more in common with a logjam on a river in British Columbia than surfing on Maui.

Fortunately, all sorts of diligent, kindly, and clever people have set up Gophers for you. Gophers are simply-structured menus that have all the resources of the Internet neatly classified. Just pick your way through all those remote computers by selecting menu choices. At the end of the menu trail, you usually get down to text files or programs. By using Gopher instead of FTP, you will notice a prompt asking you if you want to download the material — the Gopher already knows whether the file is binary or ASCII.

Just look at the lovely Gopher menu in Figure 9-8. How about the choice ALL THE WORLD'S GOPHERS? Is that good enough for you? It's your assurance that if you are willing to work in Gopherspace, you are going to find essentially everything that's out there.

```
Internet SIG>Enter your selection: gopher

Internet SIG Gopher
Page 1 of 1

1    PERSONAL FAVORITES                                       Menu
2    "ABOUT DELPHI'S GOPHER SERVICE"                          Text
3    *** FAQ: FREQUENTLY ASKED QUESTIONS *** (REVISED 5/25)   Menu
4    ALL THE WORLD'S GOPHERS                                  Menu
5    BUSINESS AND ECONOMICS                                   Menu
6    COMPUTERS                                                Menu
7    FREE-NETS AND COMMUNITY ACCESS                           Menu
8    FTP: DOWNLOADABLE PROGRAMS, IMAGES, SOUNDS               Menu
9    GAMES AND MUDS, MUSHES, MUSES, AND MOOS                  Menu
10   GOVERNMENT AND POLITICS                                  Menu
11   HEALTH AND MEDICINE                                      Menu
12   INTERNET INFORMATION                                     Menu
13   LAW                                                      Menu
14   LIBRARIES AND RESEARCH GUIDES                            Menu
15   SCHOOLHOUSE (K-12)                                       Menu
16   SEARCH UTILITIES (INCLUDING WORLD WIDE WEB)              Menu
17   SUBJECT MATTER MENUS                                     Menu
18   THE GRAB BAG (WITH WHAT'S NEW 6/21)                      Menu
```

Figure 9-8:
Gophers to
everywhere
and
everything!

I know I have this paragraph labeled with a Tip icon, but this remark is a tip the way "Do unto others . . ." is a tip. It's really a plea, an approach to things, a way to *be*. I realize that Archie (also available on Delphi), FTP, and telnet are honorable Internet commands of long standing and are greatly beloved by the UNIX guys who put the Internet together. Using them with suitable ingenuity, you can do all sorts of neat things on the Internet. However, *you should always try Gopher first. It's powerful and easy to use, and it's designed to conserve Net resources.*

I know there is always a temptation to stray away from the tour group and start exploring directly on your own, but if you're new to the Net, you're going to get better results with Gopher. If you need anything — from aerospace engineering files to multiuser dungeon on-line games — this Gopher will lead you to the right place. It's true that it takes all the mystique out of the Internet, but you don't have to tell anyone you use it. Do your searching with Gopher and *pretend* you have hundreds of telnet site addresses memorized along with scads of UNIX commands.

E-mail, of Course

If using the Gopher on Delphi is that simple, can you imagine what e-mail is like? Well, you're right again. There's almost nothing to be said about it, as you'll find out if you accept Delphi's free trial offer. To use Delphi e-mail, you just pick MAIL from the main menu and follow the directions. To send Internet mail, you put INTERNET first in the address. People will send you e-mail at [yourname]@delphi.com. That's it.

Because Delphi is real-thing Internet, you don't have to bootleg services through e-mail. You used to have to manage Usenet newsgroup access through Delphi e-mail, but there's a gloriously effective NEWSGROUP choice now in the Internet menu.

D-Lite: It's Mac and It's Fast

Nothing you have seen so far, although it may have been first-rate Internet access, looks much like real Mac software. However, there is a third-party Delphi interface for the Macintosh called D-Lite (see Figure 9-9), a semi-mandatory-payment shareware product that costs $29 to register and is worth considerably more.

D-Lite is a Delphi equivalent of CompuServe Navigator. D-Lite is designed to let you run a Delphi session faster than you can possibly type by logging requests in advance and then playing them into the service. It logs on, does everything you want at blinding speed, and then logs off. For sessions of any level of complexity at all, it's ten times faster than you are.

In D-Lite, you can prepare all your outgoing e-mail messages off-line (see Figure 9-10). You can write them in your favorite word processor and just paste them in the message space. D-Lite signs on Delphi, collects your mail, jams your messages into the system, and then ends the session. You can set it to collect all the new messages in your interest groups; you can assign it to scan your newsgroups; and it can manage an automated FTP session. It's very, very good.

Figure 9-9:
D-Lite, a
bright idea
for Delphi
users.

```
  ⚏  File  Edit
 ┌─────────────────────────────────────────────────────────────┐
 │To:    │ me@aol.com      │ Delivery:│        │ Status: Pending │
 │       │                 │          │        │     (Send)      │
 │Subj:  │ D-Lite|         │          │        │(Cancel) (Import)│
 │                                                               │
 │  ┌──────────────────── New Message ──────────────────────┐   │
 │  │This is a pretty cool product.                      ⇧  │   │
 │  │                                                       │   │
 │  │                                                       │   │
 │  │                                                       │   │
 │  │                                                       │   │
 │  │                                                       │   │
 │  │                                                    ⇩  │   │
 │  └───────────────────────────────────────────────────▫──┘   │
 └─────────────────────────────────────────────────────────────┘
```

Figure 9-10:
The D-Lite
e-mail
system
saves loads
of time.

D-Lite is not as cool as the America Online interface, in which all you need to do is point and click, but it certainly enhances Delphi for the average Mac user. In this book, I've been making a big point of efficient use of Internet resources, and D-Lite is a key program for efficiency. It's like windsurfing the Net with a 60 mph wind.

Delphi Does It All

To write this book, I signed onto every kind of Internet access and on-line service. I have monthly on-line charges on my credit card that look like Hono-lulu mortgage payments. A few months after publication, I'll be cutting back a bit.

But I won't cut Delphi. This service is a keeper. It's simply more useful for most Mac users than a shell account, and the Macintosh is a big part of Delphi rather than an afterthought. Hey, it's got to be worth a five-hour free trial!

As Long As You're Here

For a nice practical thing to do with a text-based interface, try this little mortgage calculator (Figure 9-11) in the Business forum available from the main menu.

Delphi also has some unusual options because it's a relatively highbrow service compared to the rest. The Dictionary of Cultural Literacy (Figure 9-12) is available on-line under the Reference menu, reminding you of the basics (in my opinion, this dictionary has some shocking non-Western omissions).

Figure 9-11:
A sample mortgage calculation, with optimistic numbers.

```
BUSINESS>Which service? MORTGAGE

This program does mortgage, loan or lease calculations.  Default entries are
shown in brackets like [this].  Enter Control-Z to exit.

What would you like this program to calculate?

Term, Interest, Principal, or Payment (? for help) [PAYMENT] ?PAYMENT

Will compute PAYMENT.

Term of loan, in years [15] ?20
Interest rate, in percent [10] ?8.5
Principal (amount borrowed) [10000] ?125000

Term of loan         20.00 years.
Interest Rate         8.500% per year.
Principal        125,000.00
Monthly Payment    1,084.78
```

Figure 9-12:
This dictionary is strong on Western Civ basics.

```
The Dictionary of Cultural Literacy
Copyright (c) 1988 by Houghton Mifflin Company
All rights reserved.

Search for: AESCHYLUS

1  AESCHYLUS

(ES-kuh-luhs, EES-kuh-luhs)

An ancient Greek poet, often considered the founder of TRAGEDY. He was
the first of the three great Greek authors of tragedies, preceding
SOPHOCLES and |EURIPIDES.

References for AESCHYLUS
--------
    1   EURIPIDES
    2   SOPHOCLES
    3   TRAGEDY
```

The collaborative novel project (Figure 9-13), in the Writer's forum, is another Delphi intellectual adventure (uh-oh, Toto, something tells me we're not in Prodigy anymore). You pick a novel and make a contribution. This figure shows just a few choices out of several hundred in progress. This activity is strongly addictive, though a pretty demonstrable waste of time.

Figure 9-13:
The collaborative novel project lets you create without dealing with editors.

```
WRITERS Menu:

Announcements            Poll
Collaborative Novel      Set Preferences
Conference               Topic Descriptions
Databases (Files)        Who's Here
Entry Log                Workspace
Forum (Messages)         Classified Ads
Member Directory         Help
MAIL                     Exit

WRITERS>What do you want to do? COLLABORATIVE

List of novels:

PLANET TONUCISH
BILLY
ALL THINGS EARTHLY
FAIRYTALES FROM A BROKEN HEART
A WEEKEND AT CEDARWOOD
GILLIAN'S ISLAND: A TV SCRIPT
MUFFY AND THE SKINHEADS
```

The 5th Wave — By Rich Tennant

Wendle finds that his mail reader is automatically displaying all the GIF files from alt.erotica.

Chapter 10

Internet from GEnie

· ·

· ·

*G*Enie is a national on-line service that can call on the rather deep pockets of General Electric to finance its expansion. For most of the 1980s, GE managed networks for large corporations — Apple's own AppleLink was operated by General Electric Information Services. Now GEnie is what those "in the know" call a major player in the struggle for the hearts and minds of America's computing public. GEnie has local access numbers all over and a growing list of features. One of the new features, under development in the summer of 1994, is a decent Macintosh version of the service, at long last.

A Mild Complaint

Before I launch into the story of GEnie's many virtues — and indeed they are many — I am going to complain about the way this service has been presented to Mac users. *Macworld*, my own magazine, has been running advertisements in which America Online and CompuServe are represented by pairs of broken nerd-glasses held together by tape. GEnie is then described against a colorful mock generation-X graphic with the slogan, "The most fun you can have with your computer on!"

Ahem. First, the most fun you can have with your computer on is to find a mood-enhancing screen-saver, turn off the other lights in the room, and do something amusing on the floor. Everybody already knows this.

Second, please inspect the screen in Figure 10-1. *That's* what you see when you sign on to GEnie. Think you can handle it? Got the blood-pressure medication ready? There's nothing particularly wrong with the opening screen, but it's hard to make a case that it's anything but the same-old by-the-numbers menu system available not just from CompuServe but from half the local computer bulletin boards in North America. To make it more insulting yet, my local access number is still 2400 bps, and my ID and password would embarrass a Martian.

```
CONNECT 2400
HHH
U#=XKY24249,SFKTRMBX

GEnie Logon at: 00:41 PDT on: 940518
Last Access at: 01:01 PDT on: 940317
      GEnie Announcements

  1. Uncle Yog's Storytime; coming soon to the.................SFRT1
  2. Author LYNN KERSTAN on blending humor & emotion in writing..ROMANCE
  3. The glory of the Gladiatorial Games, this weekend in.......GEMSTONE
  4. KNITTING Machines are humming in..........................NEEDLE
  5. LAST NIGHT to register for CA$H and time tournament prizes..CHESS
  6. Deja vu - INTERNET MTS Transcript available from Menu on....GENIEUS
  7. Venez pratiquer votre francais au.........................CANADA
  8. Writing Astrological software 5/18 10pm - ASTROLOGY RT in...PROGRAMMING
  9. Refunding Premiums GREAT Gifts at a GREAT Price............COLLECT
 10. Hug a KOALA May 17 --- Ride the EUROPEAN RAILS May 18.......TRAVEL
 11. The boss is on vacation - It's PARTY Time and it's FREE in..EAST
 12. Online Class on HOW TO MAKE ASCII ART, Sunday at 9pm EDT....FAMILY
```

Figure 10-1:
Wild fun,
thrills, and
chills.

And to belabor the point just a bit: When you follow the menu choices all the way down into the lists of available files, as shown in Figure 10-2, things aren't much different here from what you find elsewhere, either.

```
1159 NEWS090.ZIP          X NEWSLETTER   940515   19328   109   8
     Desc: ZIPped version of NEWSLTR.090
1158 NEWSLTR.090          X NEWSLETTER   940515   62592   105   8
     Desc: GEnie Online Newsletter, Issue #90!
1155 CYBRSIGN.TXT         X PROF.MARK    940510   50176   116   1
     Desc: Explains emoticons & abbreviations
1153 NEWUSER.TXT          X JEB          940506   25728   281   5
     Desc: A quick guide to GEnie for new users
1152 CHEAPER.GE           X BOMBADIL     940506   34944   259   5
     Desc: Guide to saving time & money online.
1151 GENIEUS.LIB          X PROF.MARK    940503   67584   119   3
     Desc: The GENIEus Software Library.
1149 INTERNET.MTS         X PROF.MARK    940502   51968   126   7
     Desc: The Internet Meet the SysOps RTC!
1148 NEWS089.ZIP          X NEWSLETTER   940430   17536   121   8
     Desc: ZIPped version of NEWSLTR.089
1147 NEWSLTR.089          X NEWSLETTER   940430   56448   106   8
     Desc: GEnie Online Newsletter, Issue #89!
1145 TCAROL.GIF           X T.CAROL      940427  184576   101  10
     Desc: A picture of me on my Motorcycle.
```

Figure 10-2:
GEnie files:
meat and
potatoes, no
radicchio.

Internet by Request

But bless its electric corporate heart — GEnie has done the One Big Thing all the other on-line services should have done: It has hired people to process your Internet requests. GEnie has provided a great service while offering the interim solution to the big Internet question, "What do we give them while we figure out what to do?"

You can use e-mail on CompuServe for Archie and FTP access, but this process is something you wouldn't do if you had a better alternative. Direct Archie and FTP is one better alternative. Even better than this alternative — especially if you're just starting out on the Net — is using someone with lots of experience to do your searching for you.

Help!

If you are a GEnie user and you're interested in an Internet topic or topics, you can send an e-mail message to the GE system operators of the Internet RoundTable (RoundTable is GEnie-speak for forum or conference). In the Mac front end, there's always a cute little mailbox icon you can click to do this; in the text-interface, mail is always available as an option.

The system operators do whatever Internet searching is required in Archie or fetch some files for you with FTP and send you the whole package. If you like, you can ask them to forward the search transcript so that you can see how the search was formulated. After you collect a dozen or so of these search transcripts to inspect, you'll see how to do the search for yourself.

GEnie people are really smart

You can send a message to the sysops (*system operators*) at GEnie. Even if your message contains typos, outright misspellings (horrors!), or fairly vague descriptions of what you want, you'll get something useful back. That's because people are pretty good at divining your intentions from a few remarks.

If you try this at the standard interface on a UNIX-based Internet server, however, you're likely to get error messages you can't even read. UNIX requires that you get your commands exactly right the first time, and it won't second-guess your intentions.

Placing an experienced Internet user between new users and the machines on the Net reduces the frustration level for everyone. Even a user with two weeks hands-on experience is smarter than the best interface that an artificial-intelligence design can produce. That's why GEnie uses trained searchers to find files for you. GEnie provides you with people who are the equivalent of reference librarians in a standard book-library— this experience will make things easier down the road when you do your own searches. This Internet-access program has been so successful thus far that GEnie is hiring full-time Internet reference specialists to assist the system operators.

A Solution For Internet Crowding

In 1993, about ten Internet books appeared in bookstores across the land. In aggregate, they probably sold nearly a million copies. Every one of the books tells you to try an Archie search at the same server at the University of Maryland. If 0.01 percent of the people who bought these books actually try this at any given time, the server won't be able to generate anything but the Internet equivalent of busy signals.

Channeling requests to sysops who can access the Internet at odd hours (GEnie pays them to do this) greatly relieves traffic problems. Instead of GEnie putting 100 newbies on the Net at 4:00 in the afternoon, the whole GEnie network generates managed bursts of access late at night. You make your requests any time you like (actually, this approach is thrifty with your own connect time as well), and GEnie processes the requests during low-traffic time.

The GEnie Internet RoundTable

Direct FTP and telnet, and presumably a special GEnie Gopher, will be available by early 1995. By that time, GEnie users who have been participating in the Internet RoundTable (see Figure 10-3) will be able to use these tools effectively because the users will have had on-line question-and-answer access to a talented group of systems people.

Figure 10-3:
Start here
for an
Internet
education.

```
                     Internet RoundTable

     1.   Internet Bulletin Board
     2.   Internet Conference Room
     3.   Internet Library of Files
     4.   About the Internet RoundTable
     5.   RoundTable News (940216)
     6.   Send Mail to RoundTable Staff
     7.   Internet Mail
     8.   Download Sysop's Pick File
     9.   Unix RoundTable
    10.   Search the Internet for a file
    11.   Request a file from the Internet
    12.   What is my Internet Address
    13.   Virus/Computer Security RoundTable
```

GEnie is the only national on-line service that seems to have understood that there's a demand not just for Internet access but for something approximating training. Yes, yes, yes! I know that there are plenty of people who want full Internet access, and they want it right now. And once you get the hang of it, navigating the Internet isn't that hard. For a gentle introduction where you never see ACCESS DENIED flashing at you, this GEnie system has lots to recommend it.

E-Mail Basics

Like all other national services, you can send and receive Internet e-mail at GEnie. Using GEnie for e-mail is just a bit different from what you might expect.

Incoming

Tell your pals to send you mail at the following address:

```
yourname@genie.geis.com
```

The geis part is essential because General Electric manages more than one network. Sending a message to genie.com doesn't work.

Outgoing

In keeping with this last little delicately nuanced bit of weirdness, the mail you send has a funny address inside GEnie, too. To reach my old mailbox at another Internet host, for example, I would address the mail like so:

```
TO:chseiter@crl.com@INET#
```

That's right, we're talking about nearly the only scheme on earth with two @ symbols in the address. It works, though. Just follow the usual Internet address by @INET# and it will get to the right place on the Net.

GEnie Joins the Revolution

GEnie is working on a beautiful new Macintosh interface for the system, as shown in Figure 10-4. Now you don't have to crawl through endless numbered menus to get where you're going.

Figure 10-4
The magic
lamp
beckons.

In the new look, the standard-issue-geek's-delight sign-on screen is replaced with a list of options preceded by icons that look like open books (see Figure 10-5) because different sections of GEnie are cataloged as pages. The Internet RoundTable also has a new look, with neatly organized libraries (see Figure 10-6) and easy mail contact with the ever-helpful sysops.

Figure 10-5:
The easy
way to
cruise GEnie
topics.

Figure 10-6:
The whole
Internet,
arranged in
little folders.

Finally, if you have any other problems, all you have to do in GEnie's new look is get the Help Window from the Windows menu and click your way to a state of clarity (Figure 10-7). This Help system is a pretty admirable piece of work.

Figure 10-7:
The new
GEnie Help
system is
the best in
the on-line
world.

A Snapshot in Time

Fortunately, GEnie produced a working prerelease of its new Macintosh software in time for this book. The software is still rough in spots, but if GEnie can combine its program of providing sysop assistance for new Internet users with direct Internet access and this real-Mac front end, it will be the red-hot service its advertising describes by early 1995. As this was being written, GEnie was working to develop an icon-based access system to the full range of Internet features.

As Long As You're Here

GEnie has piled up an assortment of interesting reference and shopping services. One of the most impressive is the DIALOG service, a collection of professional databases on technical topics (Figure 10-8). DIALOG use invokes extra hourly charges beyond the monthly and hourly GEnie fees, but from astronomy to zoology it's the definitive reference. I found over the last few months, working for a consulting client on a patent in polymer surface treatment, that I can use DIALOG as a replacement for the chemical engineering libraries at Stanford and UC Berkeley. That's right — you guessed it — when I'm not writing computer books, I'm the kind of guy who knows how to have fun in a library. And now I can have all that fun at home!

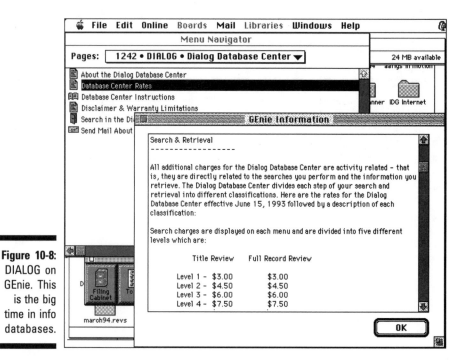

Figure 10-8: DIALOG on GEnie. This is the big time in info databases.

Another GEnie professional initiative is education. Figure 10-9 just hints at one of the things to come, which is the development of degree programs and other kinds of professional credentialling through on-line services. In the 1990s, not only are jobs disappearing and then appearing elsewhere at a terrifying rate, but your set of professional skills are being made obsolete almost monthly. There's going to be plenty of technical education flying around on the Net.

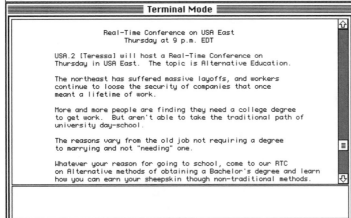

Figure 10-9:
The Internet
will start to
replace
schools for
coursework.

And once you get your information, collect your degree, and start bringing home the big bucks, GEnie will stand ready and able to help you lighten your pockets. The Mall on GEnie is a prototype for shopping services that will probably appear elsewhere on the Internet. Frankly, the main attraction of these services is quick ordering of products you already know. On-line book-stores, for example, tend to be very good, since they have better selection and prices than the local mall chain-bookstore. But it's hard to picture buying sporting goods or clothes from this sort of arrangement, since transfer of decent color pictures still takes too long even with a fast modem. Just wait and see (I probably shouldn't propose this) . . . some genius will figure a way to send you color pictures as a background activity when you're just looking at the screen trying to decode the menus.

Chapter 11

Internet from eWorld

● ●

In This Chapter

▶ Real Macintosh service at last

▶ Apple sends you its best

▶ Using the simplest e-mail on earth

▶ Into the future with eWorld

● ●

*I*n Apple's eWorld on-line service, started in the summer of 1994, you can see the most extreme contrast between the old world of character-oriented computing and the new world based on the Macintosh graphical interface.

In the traditional Internet, tiny little packets of characters went zinging down the wires of the networks. If you wanted to make the Internet do anything for you, you had to master a large set of commands. If you wanted to connect with any interesting place, you had to get a list somehow and know where you were going in advance. If you made a typing mistake in a command, you were out of luck. Of course, the old Internet was very thrifty with computing resources: you could sign on by using only a terminal program (some as small as 20K!), and the text file you were likely to download was still small compared to a run-of-the-mill color picture or sound file.

The World's Friendliest Interface

The Macintosh interface arrived in 1984; by 1994, it had taken over the world. It may appear in parts of the world in the form of Microsoft Windows, a rather clumsy copy of the Mac interface, but there's no denying that the Mac way is now *the* way, even on non-Mac machines.

Flying over the net

Look at the little screen in Figure 11-1, which is rendered in the real application in lovely pastels instead of the dull grays of book publishing (users frequently ask why the eWorld images of people look like bowling pins wearing overcoats). You get to this screen by clicking on a Connect button in the program Apple sets up for you. Within 20 seconds or so, you're in eWorld (Figure 11-2), a mythical electronic on-line paradise, with an interface that looks like the map they give you on the way into Disney World. In eWorld, you click on the buildings (that's right, the buildings!) to get where you're going. This seems very far away from the electronic network universe of commands, such as

```
%telnet  archie.techno.whatzis.org
```

It's not really. In the Macintosh-style graphical interface, every time you click on some spot on-screen, the program looks up the location that you clicked, finds the piece of code that corresponds to that spot, and sends the code to another part of the program that translates it to Mac instructions. If you click on the Computer Center building shown in Figure 11-2, the program translates the click into a Mac instruction to open the window in Figure 11-3.

Figure 11-1:
Apple's
strange little
man in the
overcoat
represents
you.

Pictures Take Time

One way or another, you pay for convenience most of the time, and eWorld is no exception. In this case, you pay for the program's size and speed. The early version of eWorld that I used for these figures contains 6MB of color graphic files to present these attractive screens. On an older Mac, the screen shuffling with these big files is noticeably slower.

Figure 11-2:
Knock on any door in this eTown.

Figure 11-3:
eWorld has tons of goodies for Mac owners.

Apple has designed this service to be a jump or two ahead of the other on-line services, and it has landed itself a jump ahead of the current-state telecommunications, too. 9600 bps is the minimum modem speed for using eWorld conveniently, and a higher speed than this would be lots better. During the beta phase of eWorld development, it frequently took *two hours* to download the latest version of the program. And following the Iron Law of Software, programs never get smaller.

eWorld: Stocked with Goodies

If you've made it this far in the book, you've seen me make the following point at least five times in earlier chapters. But who knows, maybe you skipped right to this chapter. So I'll say it again because the very future of the Internet depends on it (ahem). *Use the Internet for files and services you can get only from the Internet.*

Get other files and services elsewhere. Some of the most famous Internet sites were already starting to clog up by mid-1994 just because most of the first-generation Internet books recommended the same handful of sites, over and over, as places to collect the coolest stuff.

Imagine giving everyone in the U.S. a free airline pass. Now picture yourself at O'Hare International Airport in Chicago on Christmas Eve. See what I mean? Don't call up the Internet file server at poor old Stanford just to see if it has a blackjack game for you. Absolutely every national on-line service has a choice of blackjack games, including the same games they have at Stanford.

Time out for games

eWorld so far is doing a very good job of finding the most-accessed files and posting them right. In the fabulous Arts and Leisure Pavilion, shown in Figure 11-4, you can find a selection of games that is about as good as it gets (the eWorld staff has weeded out the duds). Besides standard computer games (see the list in Figure 11-5), eWorld has on-line interactive multiplayer games that are a giant improvement on the plain-text dungeon games of the traditional Internet. And because eWorld members tend to be "into this kind of stuff," the level of play is great.

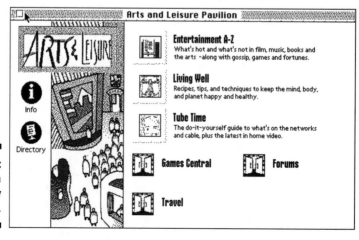

Figure 11-4:
eWorld in a
leisurely
mood.

Easy files

There's another advantage to using a cozy Apple-based service for collecting programs and files. Out on the Internet, it's pretty typical to find files both compressed and then *binhexed* — converted from a binary to an ASCII (character) file. After you find a file, you get to rewash it with the program HQXer or the equivalent and then uncompress it with another program. This process is a hassle. In even worse cases, the file would be processed with a UNIX utility first so that you have to have a copy of UUTool or one of the ghastly and confusing programs for dealing with .tar and .z files (check the Glossary for the lowdown on these beasts).

Because all the files on eWorld were put there by Apple, getting a file on this service is easy. When you see the file you want, click on the Download button, and eWorld does the rest. After you sign off, eWorld automatically uncompresses the file (if it was compressed). All you do is pick the file, and it appears on your Macintosh in working order. That, folks, is how it should be. It's supposed to be someone else's job to do file manipulations.

So in terms of my glorious self-appointed mission to keep the Internet open for real Internet jobs, I would encourage you to look on eWorld first if you've heard of a hot file. Honest, it's easier.

E-Mail for the Rest of Us

If you can't use the eMail Center, shown in Figure 11-6, you probably can't operate stamps either. Everything means just what it says. There are, however, a few wrinkles that may not be obvious.

Figure 11-6:
Welcome to the eMail Center.

Time-delayed transfers

When you use the Files to Get option, you can mark files to get later. Simply find the files you like, mark them all, leave your computer and modem on overnight, and set eWorld to download them all at 4:15 a.m. (when, presumably, you are otherwise engaged). Using the Automatic Courier option works in a similar way — you can choose times to send and deliver mail and files.

These options are important features because even shareware and freeware programs are gigantic these days. And the king of gigantic files in eWorld is eWorld itself. At 9600 bps, updating your version of this program takes nearly an hour and a half to download. Downloading this program is best done while you're snoozing.

Getting from eWorld to reality

eWorld is still small enough at this point that you will be sending lots of e-mail on the Internet to people outside of eWorld. Communicating outside of eWorld is easy. Click on the eMail Center icon and you get to the standard eWorld e-mail window. As you can see in Figure 11-7, you just type out a standard Internet address in the address space (click the little Internet button in the mail window to get this message).

Figure 11-7:
eWorld
connects to
the
Internet.

Because of the ease of connecting to the Internet, you may think that you can use all sorts of Internet e-mail services, such as Archie and FTP by e-mail. As it stands now, however, eWorld e-mail was originally set up to accommodate both Macintoshes and Newtons. Files bigger than 8K tend to blow the Newton's tiny hand-held mind. This means that in the first issue of eWorld, there is a file size limitation of 8 Kbytes. This, in turn, means that unless you are willing to put yourself through all sorts of contortions (stitching together binhexed 8K file fragments by hand and using a text editor), you can't collect much useful stuff through the old e-mail tricks. eWorld needs to get the rest of its Internet act together.

Internet Forum: Gripes 'R Us

Technically, eWorld has the weakest set of Internet facilities of the national on-line services, but it also has a very high level of awareness about what is missing. In the first round of eWorld users, faithful correspondents of the Internet interests discussions (see Figure 11-8) are mostly cutting-edge techno-hipsters who know what they want.

Before eWorld went on-line, it was tested for four months, and the beta testers patiently explained to Apple in the Internet interests area that without some equivalent of FTP or telnet, eWorld wouldn't be able to compete in the big leagues (see Figure 11-9). Apple probably knew this all along, but it can't hurt that eWorld users are unanimous in pointing out the missing parts of the service.

```
┌─────────────────────────────────────────────────────────────┐
│ ▤□▤▤▤▤▤▤▤▤▤▤▤▤      The Discussions      ▤▤▤▤▤▤▤▤▤▤ 回▤ │
├─────────────────────────────────────────────────────────────┤
│  ┌──┐   ⊘     ┌ Find Since... ┐       ┌ Add Topic... ┐  ┌ Open Topic ┐│
│  │  │  Help   └ Show New ─────┘       └──────────────┘  └────────────┘│
│                                                               │
│  │ Discuss your opinions, impressions & aspirations for eWorld with each│
│  │ other and Mr.Beta, your host.                             │
│                                                               │
│  Topic                               Msgs  Topic Started  Last Message │
│  📁 The "catch-all" area             205   03/24/94      06/07/94  ⇧│
│  📁 Internet interests               114   03/24/94      05/28/94   │
│  📁 Talk Amongst Yourselves          107   03/24/94      06/06/94   │
│  📁 Bugs & Other Crawly Things       211   03/17/94      06/07/94   │
│  📁 Ask Mr. Beta!                    147   03/10/94      06/07/94   │
│  📁 Interface Enhancements           255   03/09/94      06/07/94   │
│  📁 Content Enhancements             154   03/09/94      06/03/94  ⇩│
└─────────────────────────────────────────────────────────────┘
```

Figure 11-8: eWorld gets plenty of constructive criticism.

```
┌─────────────────────────────────────────────────────────────┐
│ ▤□▤▤▤▤▤▤▤▤▤▤▤▤      Internet interests      ▤▤▤▤▤▤▤ 回▤ │
├─────────────────────────────────────────────────────────────┤
│  ┌──┐   ┌ Find Since... ┐  ┌ Add Message... ┐  ┌ List Replies ┐ ┌ Read Message ┐│
│  │  │   └ Show New ─────┘  └────────────────┘  └──────────────┘ └──────────────┘│
│                                                               │
│  │ eWorld and the Internet - services, mail, connectivity, and the like.│
│                                                               │
│  Message                        Author      Replies  Last Reply │
│  What and where to post here    Mr. Beta         4   05/07/94 ⇧│
│  Internet Mail Gateway          Mr. Beta         9   05/22/94  │
│  Internet Mail Attachments      Mr. Beta        11   05/02/94  │
│  Internet Services              Mr. Beta        56   04/30/94  │
│  Delegation to the Internet     Mr. Beta         8   05/19/94  │
│  Incoming mail - small segments MaryC            4   05/11/94  │
│  Forwarding Internet Mail to eW ScottP          2   04/18/94  │
│  Where is the Internet area?    BobS             1   05/28/94  │
│  Faxing with PPC 8100/80AV      MacPPC           1   04/25/94  │
│  Outgoing mail identification   Lor              1   05/06/94  │
│  TCP Connection for eWorld?     Bounce           6   05/21/94  │
│  Internet Addresses?            Hilm             0   05/12/94 ⇩│
│  * Message has an official reply.                             │
└─────────────────────────────────────────────────────────────┘
```

Figure 11-9: eWorld's users tell Apple what to do next.

Full Service?

As this book went to press, Apple was officially keeping quiet about its plans for eWorld's future. Nonetheless, some of the developers working on the project were willing to blurt out a few choice remarks off the record.

There is almost certainly going to be, by late 1994, some form of "managed" real Internet access. In this scheme, you forward Archie, Gopher, or FTP requests to an Internet center, and the service processes the order in a few hours. The next time you sign on, the information you wanted is there in your mailbox. This improvement is easier for a service to manage than direct telnet for all users because the service can design a program to handle all the requests automatically at high-speed during nonpeak hours. In the meantime, eWorld is busily building up its file libraries so that it can offer the most-requested files and information itself. eWorld is easy, it's fun, and although it's not really Internet-ready yet, it's worth a look.

As Long As You're Here

Although eWorld's connection to the late Pleistocene UNIX systems that make up the Internet is still under development, there's plenty to do in Apple's jolly little on-line playground. In the figures that follow, note the number of construction-style hard hats that appear in the screens. Apple is furiously loading content into eWorld, but there's plenty left to do.

About money

You can make money, you can spend it, and eWorld will help you do both. Figure 11-10 shows the stock-quotation system, one of the most sophisticated on-line systems available, that's built into eWorld. I used it to track Microsoft stock while Microsoft lost its court decision over hard-drive file compression to Stac Software. If you like to believe that crime doesn't pay, this was not an encouraging spectacle. When Microsoft was convicted of stealing intellectual property from a much smaller company, the stock price was *up* within a few days.

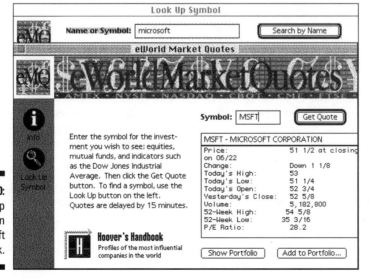

Figure 11-10: Checking up on Microsoft stock.

Now that you realize you've made money in your speculations, you may as well spend it, upgrading your Mac (I mean, really, what other use is there for money?) Figure 11-11 shows the screen for the on-line version of MacZone, one of the largest Macintosh discount mail-order houses. These guys are very hard to beat for price or delivery, and while writing this, I found myself absent-mindedly ordering more memory for my rapidly aging Quadra. What I really need is a source of snap-in memory modules for my own head — as far as I can tell, the Quadra's doing better than I am.

Figure 11-11:
Click-based
eWorld
shopping.

About information

Speaking of my once-fine mind disintegrating under the impact of reading too many press releases from Apple, eWorld lets you take intellectual decay further or attempt to reverse it. It's your choice.

For example, if you want to see an application of technology at its finest, you can join a discussion group about the TV show "Melrose Place." It's really quite remarkable — think of Shockley inventing the transistor, and the brilliant work of Turing and von Neumann on computers, and Apple's pioneering computer interface developments — 40 years of dazzling technical ingenuity making it possible to discuss Heather Locklear on-line (Figure 11-12). Kind of makes you wonder what Virtual Reality products will really emerge some day.

On a more elevated intellectual plane, eWorld has libraries stocked with electronic equivalents of magazines, newspapers, and encyclopedias.

Figure 11-12:
Of course,
"Melrose
Place" is
Shakespeare
compared
to "Bay
Watch."

To avoid a transition shock upon leaving Melrose Place, I could start by leafing through the on-line edition of *USA Today*, sometimes nastily characterized as the paper for people who don't have the time for TV news (Figure 11-13). Actually, this is a sort of business edition of *USA Today*, and the news is about eight hours ahead of anything you can find in print.

Figure 11-13:
eWorld
features a
USA Today
business
hot line.

eWorld also has some of the standard on-line magazines (computer and business magazines, mostly), but the encyclopedia feature in eWorld is a standout. When you search for a term in the eWorld Grolier's, you get an easy-to-use file of related topics (see Figure 11-14). This makes the eWorld encyclopedia much more like a paper version, in which you often find things that are more interesting than your original topic. The only problem is that on-line encyclopedias don't offer nearly as many illustrations as the print variety (Figure 11-15).

Figure 11-14:
Grolier's via
eWorld:
simply the
best.

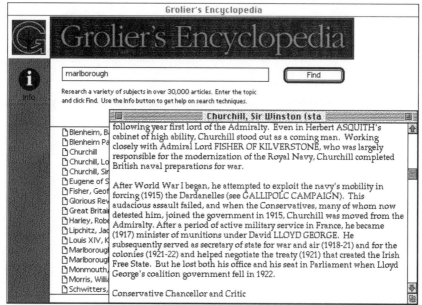

Figure 11-15:
Hey, how
about a
picture?

The image shows a Grolier's Encyclopedia window with a search field containing "marlborough" and a Find button, with text reading "Research a variety of subjects in over 30,000 articles. Enter the topic and click Find. Use the Info button to get help on search techniques." A list of entries including Blenheim, Churchill, Eugene, Fisher, Glorious Rev, Great Britain, Harley, Lipchitz, Louis XIV, Marlborough, Monmouth, Morris, Schwitters. An article window titled "Churchill, Sir Winston (sta" contains the following text:

following year first lord of the Admiralty. Even in Herbert ASQUITH's cabinet of high ability, Churchill stood out as a coming man. Working closely with Admiral Lord FISHER OF KILVERSTONE, who was largely responsible for the modernization of the Royal Navy, Churchill completed British naval preparations for war.

After World War I began, he attempted to exploit the navy's mobility in forcing (1915) the Dardanelles (see GALLIPOLC CAMPAIGN). This audacious assault failed, and when the Conservatives, many of whom now detested him, joined the government in 1915, Churchill was moved from the Admiralty. After a period of active military service in France, he became (1917) minister of munitions under David LLOYD GEORGE. He subsequently served as secretary of state for war and air (1918-21) and for the colonies (1921-22) and helped negotiate the treaty (1921) that created the Irish Free State. But he lost both his office and his seat in Parliament when Lloyd George's coalition government fell in 1922.

Conservative Chancellor and Critic

Junior-high-school confidential

This on-line stuff looks like the answer for every research assignment you could have in ninth grade. It's good, but it's not the last word. Here are some points for concerned students and worried parents.

1. The dog CAN'T eat your homework any more. It's on-line in Cupertino and you can download it again.

2. You've GOT to use more than one source. The teacher has already seen everything you can find on eWorld.

3. With a little cut-and-paste and a thesaurus on the big words, you can make an encyclopedia entry sound like your own work.

4. The class can chip in and pay someone's older sister to do all the on-line searching.

5. You can't meet your friends at the eWorld library, so you may actually learn something.

6. "The dog ate my modem" may work as an excuse. "Dad reformatted my floppy by accident" could also fly.

Part III
Do-It-Yourself Internet

The 5th Wave   By Rich Tennant

"WE'D LIKE TO TALK TO YOU BOYS ABOUT COMMERCIALIZING YOUR INTERNET FREEWARE APPLICATION."

In this part...

*1*f you're an adventurous spirit, you may want to strike out and get your own Internet connection, rather than use a national on-line service.

Frankly, a roll-your-own connection is harder to do, but this book still brings it within the reach of Dummies. I'll tell you all about the dazzling Mac software you can use to surf the Net.

Chapter 13, my personal favorite, is the only guide to SLIP connection for your Mac that gets down to the real what-next details of a direct-connect SLIP Internet account.

Chapter 12

Bulletin Boards — The Local Electronic Community

· ·

In This Chapter

▶ Finding bulletin boards for everything from astronomy to zebras

▶ Discovering ten reasons to use bulletin boards

▶ Getting everything you could want, except icons, from the WELL

▶ Learning how Internet technology invades your local library

· ·

*A*nyone who can afford to leave a computer running all the time can operate a *bulletin board,* or its grander cousin, a *conferencing system*. Both terms really just mean a computer with incoming lines and a filing system for messages. A national on-line service like Delphi, for example, consists of big computers that carry hundreds of specialized message areas and thousands of files. A bulletin board may consist of a single Mac with only one or two incoming lines. But in both cases, you get to rummage around the files and see what's there, post messages, or join a discussion group.

The biggest urban bulletin boards can have tens of thousands of paying members and carry all the latest Mac files — some big boards are, in effect, mini-Delphis. Other smaller boards flourish by specialization. Specialty bulletin boards cater to people interested in steam locomotives, 18th-century antiques, phenomenally kinky sex, multiuser on-line games, chess, astronomy, and any other topic you can — or can't — imagine. The big boards are quite stable (the WELL in San Francisco was operating before most national services), whereas small ones require monthly reading of *Boardwatch Magazine* just to see who's still there and who's not.

In the past, bulletin boards rarely had Internet connections, but now it's becoming common. A board that is free (or charges a few dollars a month), has an Internet connection, and is a local call for your modem is the cheapest connection you're likely to get. Unless, of course, you're a Stanford student, where your $20,000-per-year tuition includes absolutely *free* access to sumex-aim.stanford.edu (I vaguely remember some proverb about free lunches . . .). In this chapter, I give you a couple examples of bulletin board access to the Internet and then send you out looking for these local on-ramps to the information highway. All you need is a modem to dial the service and a willingness to use a text-based interface.

Ten reasons to use bulletin boards

1. If you find a date, you both live in the same area code.

2. You can find cheap used Macs.

3. You're a hard-core nerd (EMS 301-924-3594 voice).

4. You're a Buddhist (Mt. Kailas 617-252-9988 modem).

5. You hunt elk (Vacation Source 800-868-7555 modem).

6. You hunt dragons (ONIX 215-879-6616 modem).

7. You're gay (Eye Contact 415-703-8200 modem).

8. You want to join Throbnet, Kinknet, and Wildnet (I'm not making this up! Blues Cafe 214-638-1186 modem).

9. All your credit cards are maxed out and Prodigy won't let you on.

10. You believe that the national on-line services are simply fronts for a giant market-research firm (I'm not sure that I don't believe this myself).

The WELL: It's Swell

Almost every big city has a bulletin board that's been a hangout for Macintosh fans for a decade now, and most of these boards are now Internet-ready. Some states have their own statewide boards: in Hawaii it's Hawaii FYI, in Montana it's Big Sky Telegraph, and in Michigan it's NovaLink.

Deluxe hand-holding

The San Francisco area's WELL (Internet name is well.sf.ca.us, voice phone 415-332-4335) is an excellent example of a community bulletin board. The name stands for Whole Earth 'Lectronic Link, as this bulletin board was founded by the crew of jolly futurist pirates who published the wildly successful "Whole Earth Catalog," a mild dose of counterculture during the 1980s. They took the profits from the catalog and used some of the money to start the bulletin board. With its foundation as a nonprofit, electronic-freedom pioneer, the WELL is similar to many other bulletin boards from a computing point of view, but it has a rather high-minded internal Net culture.

Figure 12-1 shows you what happens when the wireheads meet the hippies. The WELL is a UNIX system, but instead of leaving you with a one-character prompt, it gives you chatty little menus and live on-line help.

```
UNIX(r) System V Release 4.0 (well)

This is the WELL

Type    newuser   to sign up.
Type    trouble   if you are having trouble logging in.
Type    guest     to learn about the WELL.


login: chseiter
Password:

    May 17   Intermediate Tutorial (g wellcome ; s 93)          <== TOMORROW!
    May 20   WELL Office Party #92 (g news ; s 1541)            <== Friday
    Jul 23   Annual WELL Picnic (g news ; s 1515)

              Welcome to The WELLcome Conference!

Gotta question? Ask away over in topic 118: type    s 118 nor    then type    r
Introduce yourself in topic 119:              type    s 119 nor    then type    r
For immediate help from a real person:        type    helpers
For the WELLcome Conference menu:             type    wellcome
```

Figure 12-1: Wherever you go, there you are — WELL help covers it.

I don't know how they do it, but they have people around to answer your questions at 4:17 a.m. The whole system is as friendly as a Yorkshire terrier snoozing in your lap.

Real Internet, plus Help

But, you may ask, where's the Internet? It's all here, and for a text-based system, it's pretty spectacular. You type

```
g inet
```

and you're in the Internet conference. Then type

```
netmenu
```

and you see the choices shown in Figure 12-2. On the WELL, you don't really need to know these commands because you can ask for options or help at any point and the system gives you your choices.

```
OK (type a command or type  opt  for Options): netmenu

        The   Internet   Conference   Menu
type  1  for Introductory Readings

type  2  for Rules and Regulations on the use of the Internet from the WELL

type  3  for Cheat-sheets on how to use Internet tools

type  4  for Information on Libraries online

type  5  for Information on FTP (File transfer protocol)

type  6  for Information on Internet Services

type  7  to look for an Internet site near you

type  8  for the Miscellaneous files
```

Figure 12-2:
Detailed
WELL
menus start
you on the
Internet.

Gopher on the Well

You get on-line cheat sheets for help with Archie, FTP, and telnet and also on-line versions of the standard Internet beginner's documents. Where this bulletin board really passes up the competition, however, is in its own Gopher, called, appropriately, wellgopher (see Figure 12-3). Because it's a real Gopher, this menu lets you automatically sail out into all the other computers on the Net, searching for the elusive wonder-file. And because it's the WELL, "Cyberpunk and Postmodern Culture" is one of the busiest topics.

Going down a more sedate wellgopher hole (Figure 12-4), you find yourself ready to scan the latest from the Advanced X-ray Astrophysics facility. (If this facility is advanced, is there a Beginner's X-ray Astrophysics site in a high school somewhere?) The wellgopher keeps telnetting to other Gophers until you're satisfied.

Fun and games

Some day, weary at last of advanced X-ray astrophysics, you may want to play an on-line game. The people at the WELL are so concerned for your happiness that they not only equip this bulletin board with plenty of interactive games, but they also include tip files (see Figure 12-5) so that you don't wander into a simulation as a "clueless newbie" and get killed off in 12 seconds. A bulletin board that defends you against your own cluelessness is a treasure indeed.

```
OK (type a command or type  opt  for Options): wellgopher
Welcome to the wonderful world of Gopher!
Press ? for Help, q to Quit
Root gopher server: gopher.well.sf.ca.us

  --> 1.  About this gopherspace (including a quick "How To" guide)/
      2.  See the latest additions to this gopherspace/
      3.  Search all menus on the WELLgopher <?>
      4.  Internet Outbound (*New!*)/
      5.  Art, Music, Film, Cultural works, etc/
      6.  Authors, Books, Periodicals, Zines (Factsheet Five lives here!)/
      7.  Business in Cyberspace: Commercial Ventures on the Matrix/
      8.  Communications and Media/
      9.  Community/
     10.  Cyberpunk and Postmodern Culture/
     11.  Environmental Issues and Ideas/
     12.  Hacking/
     13.  K-12 Education/
     14.  The Matrix (information about the global networks)/
     15.  The Military, its People, Policies, and Practices/
     16.  Politics/
     17.  Science/
     18.  The WELL itself/
```

Figure 12-3:
Do you feel
lucky,
cyberpunk?

```
           Internet Gopher Information Client 2.0 pl11

                  SCIENCE, MATH, STATISTICS

    1.  ASCinfo (Info. relating to Advanced XRay Astrophy. Facility) <TEL>

    2.  E-Math (Am. Math. Soc. bbs w/ software and reviews) <TEL>

    3.  Math Gopher (Math archives (software, teaching materials, other go../

    4.  Nuclear Data Center (National nuclear data) <TEL>

    5.  Particle Information (Lookup information on any particle!) <TEL>

    6.  Periodic Table (electronic periodic table of elements) <TEL>

   >7.  STIS (Science & Technology Information System) <TEL>

    8.  The Scientist (Biweekly paper targeted at science professionals)/
```

Figure 12-4:
Serious
information
from around
the globe.

```
People gather treasure, slay monsters (and each other), gain experience
points, and thereby become wizards, with powers that are useful in
playing the game. In a variety of MUD known as a Muse (Multi User
Simulation Environment), communication and education and worldbuilding
are the goal of the exercise, rather than gaining points in a game.

Some MUDs can be brutal. If other players can gain points by killing
off "clueless newbies" (which is what you will be until you learn the
ropes), you might find that the first action someone in a new world
takes is to slash at you with a virtual broadsword.

Other MUDs are entirely nonviolent. One good example is Cyberion City.
You can get there by telnetting (see topic #7 in the Internet
conference) to michael.ai.mit.edu, registering as guest, and connecting
as guest. If you decide that you want to get a character, follow the
instructions in the guest login screen.
```

Figure 12-5:
Tip files
keep your
cluelessness
from making
you lose
games too
quickly.

Power to the Public

The WELL is a private, nonprofit bulletin board that charges a monthly fee (basic fee is $12.50 a month). There are also private, for-profit bulletin boards, some of which justify their membership fees by providing harder-core stuff than the Internet, and some of which are very specialized and charge something just to make sure that you're really interested.

The Internet invades the library

Yet another type of bulletin board with Internet connection has appeared lately — the community information service. Typically, this service is organized by a library network, because once a library commits to the horrendous expense of replacing card catalogs with an on-line system with a big computer and terminals, the extra effort of joining the Net is negligible.

Library networks tend to have limited message systems and limited or no e-mail. After all, the library is supposed to serve up information for you, not run your errands. Figure 12-6 shows a typical sign-on screen from the local branch of a countywide library system. I can tell you with confidence that a community information service is coming to your town, if it's not there already, because the vendors have all the parts in place and are lobbying the librarians like crazy.

Moving out of the stacks

So there's the usual stuff you expect from a library, and then there's choice 13 on the menu in Figure 12-6, which is your gateway to the Internet. What the system does when you pick number 13 is fairly simple. A script behind the choice telnets you to a bigger computer — in this case, the main library at Sonoma State University (see Figure 12-7). Then *that* computer presents you with a menu that telnets you to other sites if necessary (refer to Figure 12-8).

Once you get out onto the Net, the choices keep expanding. The library system, you may have noticed, is really just a specialized Gopher in which all the other Gopher Internet sites happen to be libraries or on-line databases. Nonetheless, in the next few years, this system will be offering a large portion of the print material stored in traditional libraries.

Figure 12-6:
The library
on the
corner gets
wired to the
universe.

```
16 JUNE 94              Healdsburg Library              10:45pm
                  PUBLIC ACCESS (402 , ttyd4p6)

                  Welcome to the online catalog.
         Please type the number and press the key labeled RETURN.

              1.  TITLE
              2.  AUTHOR
              3.  SUBJECT
              4.  MAIN WORDS IN TITLE
              5.  MAIN WORDS IN SUBJECT
              6.  SERIES
              7.  CONTENTS (Plays, short stories, etc.)
              8.  COMMUNITY RESOURCES
              9.  PERIODICAL INDEXES
             10.  Search Your Holds and Fines
             11.  Bulletin Board
             12.  Print Saved Bibliography
             13.  Other Searches (INTERNET)
             14.  Logoff
```

Figure 12-7:
If the book
you want is
not at the
local library,
you can
check the
nearest
college.

```
Connecting to ADMVAX.SONOMA.EDU on account OPAC -- PLEASE
WAIT
Password:
     SONOMA STATE UNIVERSITY      RUBEN SALAZAR LIBRARY      MERLIN SYSTEM

                         == MAIN MENU ==

     1   SSU Catalog -- Books, Media, Gov. Doc., Other Index/Full Text...

     2   SSU Library Information; Reserve Book Room; Tips on Using This System;
         Suggestion Box, etc...

     3   Indexes, Abstracts & Full-Text Databases--periodicals, encyclopedias,
         book reviews, company profiles, etc...  (Password Required)

     4   Additional Libraries and Online Information Services...

     5   Quick Access to All Resources

     6   Exit
```

```
SONOMA STATE UNIVERSITY   RUBEN SALAZAR LIBRARY   MERLIN SYSTEM

                      === RESOURCE MENU ===

    RESOURCES REQUIRING PASSWORD:        PUBLIC ACCESS RESOURCES:
      11 CARL (CL)                         21 CTP (CTP)
      12 Chronicle of higher educ. (CH)    22 LIBS (LIBS)
      13 Dow Jones info service (DJ)       23 LOCIS (LC)
      14 DowQuest (DQ)                     24 MELVYL (MVL)
      15 Eureka (EU)                       25 Sonoma Co Lib (SCL)
      16 InfoTrac (IT)                     26 SRJC Lib (JC)
      17 Lexis/Nexis (LN)                  27 Open Access CARL (OAC)
      18 CD-RomNet (CD)

    TRIAL PRODUCTS:
      31 Eureka (TEU)
      32 Full Text CARL (TCL)
      33 SSU OPAC (SSU)
```

Figure 12-8:
Casting the
info-net
even wider.

The Internet in Your Backyard

People in my small town are often startled to discover that the Internet they've been reading about in the newspapers is the same Internet they can reach from terminals in the library. Our library system lets you dial it from home as well. It's worth checking in your town — if a system is in place, you can practice Internet navigating on the library system before you start shelling out $2 per hour on-line to get lost.

You should also make an effort to find local computer publications — you can usually find them in big-city newsracks. Not only do new private and public bulletin boards appear all the time, but lately, an amazing number of boards have decided to stop charging fees. An Internet-connected board with a decent system operator is as good an introduction to the Net as you're likely to find.

Chapter 13
Really Wired — Direct Connection

- -

In This Chapter

▶ Connecting yourself

▶ Using TCP and SLIP the easy way

▶ Fulfilling all your info needs with Fetch and Gopher

▶ Relating Mosaic to the future

- -

*1*f you have read this far, I'm assuming you haven't been completely seduced by the comforts of America Online or Delphi. Instead, you want to become a real, roll-your-own, big-time Internet "site." Now, instead of being just a user, you'll have your own number address (such as 121.113.8.214) and can even maintain files for other Internet users to access.

Now, here's a way to tell whether getting your own address is easy or not. Look up every book on the Internet you can find in your local library. (Remember, you're supposed to *buy* IDG books, but you're allowed to read the other ones for free if necessary.) Look up the section on MacTCP, if the book has one.

You will find that every last one of the authors says something like "Um, when you get to the part where you actually have to install the Internet connection, you better find a hotshot Mac guru to do it for you." Or "Find a net buddy." Or "Talk to your system administrator." That's not encouraging.

I'll tell you exactly how to get your own Internet connection. It's not exactly going to be summer beach reading, but it's no worse than learning to use a spreadsheet with *Excel For Dummies*. And while it may not be the good old Dummies song-and-dance exactly, it's the most detailed (and demystifying) explanation of SLIP connection you're going to see in print.

Getting on the Internet

There are a few different ways to get an Internet account that lets you use Mac software. If you already have a Macintosh at a university that is directly connected to a network or you have a Mac on an office network, read the next chapter, not this one. This discussion is for individuals who are willing to find a service provider that offers SLIP accounts and who will be contacting the service with a modem. That's a *dial-up SLIP account*, in case your friends ask you. Back in Chapter 5, I told you that SLIP means *Serial Line Interface Protocol* without giving many technical details. Here come the details.

Step one: Collecting the tools

Don't take any of the following steps as your introduction to the Internet. Instead, take one of the free introductory offers from a national on-line service. In the five to ten hours of connect time you get free, you can not only orient yourself, but you can also get some software and files that you need.

Go to the Internet forum, conference, or bulletin board of your service. Search the software libraries for InterSLIP and download it to your Mac. Also search for any information files on MacTCP and get them, too. If you don't know how to search for files, just send an e-mail message on the service to the system operator. The system operator is almost always identified by name as soon as you get to the Internet area of the service.

I wish I could tell you that you can collect a free copy of MacTCP, but right now, that's not clear. MacTCP comes from Apple, and at the moment, Apple expects you to buy it from APDA, the Apple Programmers and Developers Association (800-282-2732) for $60.

However, MacTCP can be found in many university archives, although strictly speaking you're not supposed to download it unless you're enrolled or working at the university. All this distribution hassel is soon to disappear, however, as MacTCP is simply included as part of Apple's System 7.5. Meanwhile, you're stuck getting MacTCP any way you can (check a Mac user's group in your area) because its required for direct connection to the Internet.

On a more cheerful note, you can get the programs Fetch, Anarchie, TurboGopher, Mosaic, and MacWeb from the software libraries on any national on-line service. They are the best free (or nearly free) software on earth.

Step two: Call a SLIP provider

How do you find a SLIP account provider? The service runs ads that have the word *SLIP* in them. You can also look in Chapter 19 for services that say *SLIP* in the description. Alternatively, find *Boardwatch Magazine* or *Online Access* and leaf through the ads because new players appear in this game almost weekly. A local version (different cities produce different editions) of the tabloid computer monthly *Microtimes* is another good place to look because you can find it for free at newsstands in big cities.

Expect a setup fee and monthly fees between $15 and $25, but it's also typical not to have a per-hour charge. In the conversation about getting an account, ask for the customer-support number. Call the number and ask the person you reach at customer support if he or she is familiar with MacTCP and InterSLIP. Some services do ten Mac setups a day, and some can't be bothered. You want one that will bother. And get a fax number because you'll need it in a bit.

Step three: Setting up

After you get MacTCP, you put it in the Control Panels folder of your System folder. InterSLIP has a Control Panel too, called InterSLIP Control, and it goes in your System folder too. When you drag the icons for the MacTCP and InterSLIP Control panels to your System folder, the System itself will ask you if you want to put them inside the Control Panels folder.

Now take this book to a photocopier and make copies of Figures 13-1, 13-2, 13-3, and 13-4. I'm serious about this step. You should do the following tasks to save yourself and the customer support at the service untold agony:

- ✔ Fax these figures to customer support at the service.
- ✔ Tell support to fill in the right numbers in the blank spaces.
- ✔ Ask the support people to show you where to set the little slider for Subnet Mask setting in Figure 13-2.
- ✔ Have the support people fax the whole set of figures back to you with all this information marked on the faxes.

With this information, you'll be in great shape. I don't know why, but it's typical for Internet service providers to have their own forms, developed a few years ago, that are almost uniquely confusing. Insist that the service show you what to enter in these software screens. You're paying a setup charge to get a SLIP account, and any service worth having will be glad to consider this step as part of the setup.

Figure 13-1:
The
MacTCP
Control
Panel.

Figure 13-2:
MacTCP
Setup data
page.

Countdown before Launch

I want to make sure you're all checked out before you press the InterSLIP
Connect button, shown in Figure 11-3. Watch for the following points.

MacTCP

Find Control Panels under the Apple menu and select it to open it. Find the
MacTCP icon and double-click on it. If your screen doesn't show an InterSLIP
icon like the one in Figure 13-1, you haven't put the InterSLIP parts (Control
Panel and Extension) in the right places. Fix this problem now (get the InterSLIP
Control Panel in the Control Panels folder and the InterSLIP Extension into the
Extensions folder), and then come back and type the IP Address.

Figure 13-3:
InterSLIP
Setup
application.

Figure 13-4:
InterSLIP
Setup data
page.

More MacTCP

Double-click on the More button in the MacTCP window. Fill in the information the service gave you for Figure 13-2. Make sure that you have the Obtain Address radio button set properly according to the fax from your service; move the Subnet Mask slider to the position the service recommended; fill in the Domain Name Server data at the lower-right of the window; and pick the default.

SLIP

You may have downloaded a version of SLIP that shows nothing in the scrolling list area in the InterSLIP window yet. To enter the information about your SLIP service provider, just pick New from the File menu and fill in a name in the dialog box. When you're done, click back to the window in Figure 13-3, double-click on your new filename, and you get to a screen that looks like Figure 13-4.

And more SLIP

In the Gateway option on the wonder window, choose Simple UNIX/Telebit because you're not a direct connection. In the Dial Script option, choose Hayes and pick your modem's speed. Every other bit of information should be on the fax of Figure 13-4 that you receive from the support people.

Launch!

When you have filled in every last scrap of data provided to you, double-click on the InterSLIP Setup icon (in the InterSLIP folder) to get to an InterSLIP window like the one in Figure 13-3. Click on the Connect button, and InterSLIP makes your connection.

Watch the top of the window. You see the message change from `Idle`, to `Dialing`, to `Signing In`, to `Connected`. Sometimes you'll see it pop back to `Idle`.

It's a good idea to check the Speaker on while dialing box in Figure 13-4 so that you can hear whether your dial-up number is busy or whether (as often happens) there just isn't a line. If you have problems for more than two days, call customer support. You'd be amazed at how often the service itself has made setup mistakes that it needs to fix (your password is wrong, for example).

The Big Payoff

I know this has been a tiresome section, but hey, if you think this is tiresome, you ought to try figuring out TCP/IP setups from scratch. I couldn't think of any other way to give you enough information to make this connection work. It was a slow news day on `rec.humor.funny` when I wrote this, too.

Your reward for being patient is that if you get a dial-up SLIP connection, you can use Fetch, TurboGopher, and Mosaic. There are other amazing Mac programs, and now that you can use Fetch, you can find them all in a few days, but these three are worth mastering.

Fetch

You've seen the rest; now try the best. For FTP, at least, this is a reasonable statement about Fetch, the lovable mascot from Dartmouth. Fetch is the premiere Macintosh utility for Internet file retrieval.

When the message in the InterSLIP window says you're connected, double-click on the Fetch icon. The wonder-pooch leaps into action, and you see the equivalent of Figure 13-5. I've clicked the little black triangle next to Shortcuts in the Open Connection window, and this action lets me pick any of the top Mac sites.

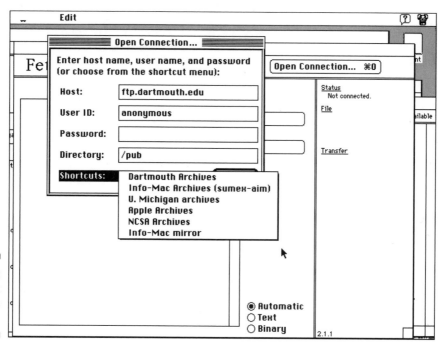

Figure 13-5:
You want it;
Fetch gets
it.

As a good citizen, you should fill in an assortment of Mac software collection sites (see The Part of Tens for ten good examples) in the shortcuts. You can, of course, just type any site in the world you may want to visit anyway. Fetch logs you onto the site, and you can look through the available files just as if you were connected directly to a big hard drive. When you see a file you like, click the file to highlight it and click Fetch's Get button.

TurboGopher

Unless you get a commercial product called SLIPper ($95, Sysnet Corp., 800-683-5515), you can only run one of these programs at a time. Quit Fetch and double-click on TurboGopher. If you're calling at a nonpeak time, you'll usually find yourself connected to the Gopher server faster than you were connected to your service provider. That's because TurboGopher works with one computer direct-connecting to another over a fast network, instead of a modem connecting to a computer.

Good old TurboGopher. This animal has saved me from certain doom many times. The diligent creature has links to all the other Gophers in the world, so if you're looking simply to explore, this is an excellent place to start. Figure 13-6 shows an exploration of the archive at Stanford (I needed a Greek-language font) that took about three minutes from sign-on to sign-off.

```
 File   Edit   Gopher   Setup   Recent                          ?

    ▼  Internet Gopher ©1991–1993 University of Minnesota.

 ☐POPmail for Macintosh
 ☐TurboGopher Distribution
 ☐Info-Mac Archives (sumex-aim.stanford.edu)

        ▼  Internet Gopher ©1991–1993 University of Minnesota.

     ☐info-mac

                                    info-mac
                ▼  Internet Gopher ©1991–1993 University of Minnesota.

             ☐00readme.txt [ 3May94, 2kb]
             ☐00readme.txt [ 3May94, 2kb]
             ☐Application
             ☐Communication
             ☐Compress-Translate
             ☐Configuration
             ☐Development
             ☐Disk-File
             ☐Font
             ☐Game
             ☐Graphic
             ☐Help
             ☐Hypercard
```

Figure 13-6:
An exploration of the archive at Stanford.

All you do is open these folders as if they were folders on your own Macintosh, and you can highlight files and tell Gopher to download them. The difference between Fetch and TurboGopher is that TurboGopher lets you search for files by title rather than having to page through the files yourself.

Mosaic

The future of the Internet for Mac users looks like it includes a program called Mosaic. A new, free Macintosh version (2.0) of Mosaic was introduced in the summer of 1994, and two different projects are under way to produce special commercial versions (Spyglass, Inc. and Mosaic Corp.) The reason Mosaic is important is that it's a point-and-click interface to the giant World Wide Web (see Chapter 5) project, which itself is an effort to produce hypertext-linked databases of all the information on the Net.

The sequence of Figures 13-7 to 13-10 was produced simply by double-clicking the icon for Mosaic 2.0 (in the downloaded Mosaic folder) and then clicking on the underlined expressions in the screens. That's about all there is to navigating in Mosaic. You can find a huge assortment of files simply by reading the screens and clicking on selections.

One reason I say that Mosaic is the future of Macintosh Internet access is that it's not exactly the present, because it's annoyingly slow even at 14.4 Kbps dial-up access. But modems will get faster, SLIP connection will get easier, and everyone will want this product by late 1995. It's one of the few truly great pieces of software ever written, since it will let absolute Internet beginners navigate the vast collection of information that's available.

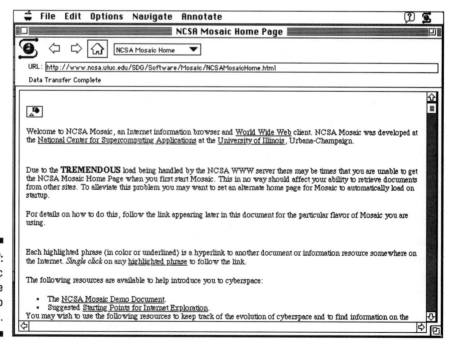

Figure 13-7: The Mosaic Home Page tells how to use Mosaic.

Figure 13-8:
Mosaic is
based on
World Wide
Web.

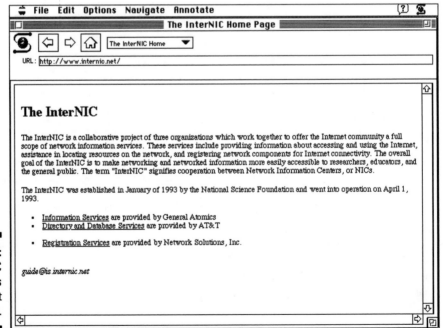

Figure 13-9:
InterNIC
maintains
Internet
databases.

Figure 13-10:
This "page"
leads to info
on neural-
net models.

What about e-mail?

A dial-up SLIP account can, in principle, be used for e-mail. In the software libraries of the national on-line services, you can find early versions of Eudora (now a commercial program) and LeeMail, a very nice shareware program.

A dial-up SLIP account has a problem in the way it gets to e-mail, however. You are now your own Internet address (a number). If you're not connected, your mailbox is not available. Some service providers have a mail-forwarding plan worked out, in which they take your mail on a big computer that is connected 24 hours each day and then notifies you when you dial up with your SLIP connection. Other providers don't provide this service. The convenience of e-mail on a big system is one reason the national on-line services are so popular. I get mail at America Online and Delphi, and I have a SLIP account from CR Laboratories (see Chapter 19). This combination lets me pick the best way to accomplish any given on-line task.

Being Cool

TIP

A dial-up SLIP account will probably cost you more than an account at a national on-line service. But SLIP gives you direct access to some of the best Mac software available, so if you're serious about the Internet, it's worth the trouble and expense.

There's an exciting alternative to Mosaic, called MacWeb. This product is still under development by the same people who developed MacWAIS. In the fall of 1994, an alpha version was circulating on the Net. The finished "shipping" version will likely appear in early 1995. A look at Figure 13-11 shows a screen that, at first glance, looks pretty much like a Mosaic page. There are little arrows and a home Icon in the upper-left corner, there are icons for images, and hyperlinks are highlighted and underlined.

MacWeb has a few advantages over Mosaic. The standard Mac version of MacWeb only takes 408K, compared to more than a megabyte for Mosaic 2.0. It's also fast. But one of the nicest features of MacWeb is that it's all set to connect to `galaxy.einet.net` with a single click, and `einet.net` is one of the few World Wide Web sites that appears to be open at all hours of day and night. When everyone else is crowded, give Galaxy a shot.

Figure 13-11:
MacWeb
and the
WWW
server at
EINet.

Chapter 14

Internet in the Workplace

· ·

· ·

*I*f you are associated with any sort of large organization, you probably have a computer that's part of a network already. Everything I've said so far about Internet access strategies needs to be modified a bit for the workplace.

The difference between single-user and network solutions for Internet access is that on a network you have to get consent from other people. In this chapter, I look at the options available for network-user access to the Internet, but instead of running out and implementing them right away, you'd better speak to the Authorities first.

Network Administrators Are Your Friends

Most of the time, an administrator — you know, that person at whose picture everyone throws darts in the lunchroom — tells you what you can't do. On a computer network, however, an administrator is an absolute necessity. If individual users run different versions of the same application, it's often enough to crash the whole network. If no one assumes the responsibility of watching out for viruses, the whole system can pick up a virus in no time. Besides, someone simply has to know what to do when problems arise. Even if you buy only a *three-user* license for the Macintosh database 4th Dimension, you have to name one of the three users as the administrator.

TIP

If you have a computer account at a university, you're almost certainly in great shape for Internet access. Not only should there be great stacks of Internet reading material at your computer center, the university probably offers short classes about the Internet in general and tutorials for Fetch, Mosaic, TurboGopher, and other Mac software. And you have a direct connection instead of working through a bulletin board or cobbling together a SLIP link through an outside provider. The direct connection lets software like Mosaic really fly, making it the general solution for all Internet access.

Of course, the people in higher education have all this Internet stuff wired (pun only partially intended). They *invented* it. And universities tend to be heavy-duty Mac sites, so you're covered on that point, too.

WARNING!

In business, things aren't necessarily that nice. Your Mac may be a minority member of a network crowded with PCs. Your system administrator's hands may be full just in managing the upgrade to WordPerfect 3.0. Your company's management may be concerned that one unhappy employee could blow a hundred company secrets onto the whole Internet by e-mail in a 15-minute fit of temper. I give you some notes here on business Internet access — it's up to you to call a meeting and present your case for getting your office wired.

TECHNICAL STUFF

NetBits

This section provides a little digression into terminology. If you have to discuss Mac Internet possibilities with the higher-ups at work, you don't want to sound like a dummy.

A *gateway* lets you connect two different kinds of networks. Typical Macintosh networks run along rules specified by the AppleTalk standard, and the Internet uses, appropriately, Internet protocol (IP). You need software to translate messages designed for one network into messages that the other network can read properly. That's a gateway.

A *bridge* is typically hardware and software that connects two local networks of the same kind.

You may have two different AppleTalk networks in different parts of a building or in different departments. If you want the two networks to look like one big network to the users, you have to buy a bridge, usually from the company that sold you the two networks.

A *router,* for Internet purposes, sends IP messages from one Internet network host to another. Most commercial routers also know how to translate messages coming from other kinds of networks (non-IP). Making routers efficient involves zillions of tricks, and if you're reading this book, it's probably somebody else's job to learn them.

The Internet Business Wish List

This short catalog lists products ranging from the absurdly simple to the simply absurd. Give it a quick scan, and you should be able to talk a good line in the conference room.

Taking it easy with Intercon

Intercon (800-468-7266) has two products that make it easy to connect a business to the Internet. The first is WorldLink, a $29.95 software product that works with Intercon's own Internet host (monthly charges range from $9 to $29, depending on the services you order). As Figure 14-1 shows, WorldLink can handle e-mail, newsgroups, mailing lists, and FTP. (That's Bob from the Church of the Subgenius [see newsgroup alt.religion.slack] operating the miscellaneous information box in the figure.)

WorldLink is as easy to use as a consumer on-line service like Prodigy. The difference between using WorldLink and a national on-line service for Internet access is that WorldLink doesn't bombard you with ads and fun facts — it's a basic, real-Internet communications tool, and it contains only the information you request. This feature makes it more appropriate for business than America Online, for example.

File Edit WorldLink Mailboxes Messages Window

WorldLink Status

Connection
Waiting for Prompt...

Administrative
Waiting...

Incoming Mail
Waiting...

Outgoing Mail
Waiting...

Incoming News
Waiting...

Outgoing News
Waiting...

File Requests
Waiting...

Misc. Information
Tuesday, June 14, 1994 12:58:45 PM

Hang Up

Figure 14-1:
WorldLink is a no-brainer connection utility.

Intercon's TCP/Connect II package of programs manages SLIP or direct IP connection to the Internet. TCP/Connect II Extended ($495) includes terminal emulation, e-mail, and a NetNews reader. For $195, you get *smart* "dumb terminal" software (a great oxymoron, no?), the TCP/Connect II Basic package. If you want to pick one person from a small office to be the official connection to the Internet, TCP/Connect II is a good choice.

Talking PowerTalk

Apple has built all sorts of amazing communication tricks into PowerTalk in System 7 Pro. They all amount to the same thing — you can send a message to someone simply by dragging a document to that person's icon on your screen (see Figure 14-2). And the person can be anywhere on any network, as long as you tell (or your system administrator tells) PowerTalk how to connect. It's just amazing. For example, you can drag a folder on the desktop from your hard drive to a someone's e-mail In-box on a Mac in Australia.

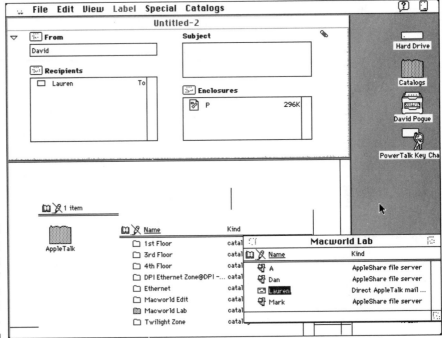

Figure 14-2:
PowerTalk
is your
gateway to
the
Gateway.

StarNine Technologies (510-649-4949) is one of the first companies to take advantage of PowerTalk for Internet access. Mail*Link Internet for PowerTalk* is a *personal gateway* that allows System 7 Pro users to exchange messages with Internet mail users if they're working on a network that uses the Internet's Simple Mail Transfer Protocol (SMTP). At $65 for a single-user pack and $595 for a ten pack, Mail*Link Internet for PowerTalk* effectively makes Internet e-mail a simple option on your Macintosh desktop.

Buying for bigger nets and serious hardware

For Internet connection, most networks simply need to be upgraded to support TCP/IP, the native language of the Internet. Shiva Corporation (800-458-3550), for example, now offers an upgrade to its LanRover software that lets corporate Mac users at remote sites dial into a company network (using AppleTalk or IP) and then get from the company network out to the Internet or national on-line services. Sitting in a motel in Sedona, Arizona, your Mac is just as connected as if you were back in the home office in midtown Manhattan (Sedona's prettier, but Manhattan has more places to do lunch). You pay a bit more than $3,000 to install the whole LanRover/E package (as you can see, as I proceed down the list I keep raising the prices), but then your whole company is as wired as it gets.

For $7,000 or so, network pioneer Cisco Systems (408-526-4000) sells you a hardware-plus-software package that lets you hook up, from scratch, a few hundred computers to each other and to the Internet. Instructional CD-ROMs make the network approach a do-it-yourself one. Ya' got a bunch of Macs using AppleTalk? No problem! There's a CD-ROM to explain exactly how to implement this setup. I did not intend to make this list of products comprehensive. If you're serious about internetworking hardware and software, your best bet is to follow network news in *Macworld* every month. The scene changes every few weeks as new vendors try to stake out claims in the great Internet gold rush.

Business: Twilight Zone of the Internet

The Internet is ready for lots of business information uses, but the academic/research orientation of the original Net users makes business something of a mystery area. Let me give you a little anecdote. As a devoted student of statistics, I hate one-shot examples being offered as evidence of *anything*. So here's a three-shot case. In the early months of 1994, I had three separate consulting assignments on Internet topics in the San Francisco Bay area. Every market-research company, every ad agency, and every forward-looking corporation suddenly became convinced that Internet awareness is a key to survival. Actually, they're probably right. In each case, someone in a company had assigned Steve ("that guy from systems services who knows everything") to check out the Internet for business data. The search never turned up as much material as expected, so I was usually called in to decide whether old Steve was losing it or whether there really was a problem.

There was indeed a problem. Very often, you can conduct a Gopher search and open folder after folder that says "Advertising" or "Marketing," going deeper and deeper in the hierarchy of folder names, only to find an empty folder at the end of the chase. Empty, as in nada, zilch, zip . . . melted ice cubes and nothing else.

As an information resource, the Internet is wondrously rich in C-language UNIX programming utilities. As yet, however, it is a tough place to find out how many VCRs were sold in Rhode Island last year. The Internet has a great variety of searching tools, but in the next few years lots of people will have to toil mightily to give you something to search other than the computer-interest group stuff that is its current strong point.

Good news, however, is starting to trickle in for business users. The most recent encouraging development is CommerceNet (Figure 14-3), a properly organized WWW server that's a new kind of corporate forum and marketplace. Unlike the servers based at universities, this one was designed (brilliantly) from scratch to be a business service. You can still drill plenty of dry holes at traditional Internet sites when wildcatting for business info, but by mid-1995 CommerceNet will have made that problem irrelevant. Direct your Mosaic or MacWeb (use the open URL command) to `http://www.commerce.net/` and browse to your heart's content.

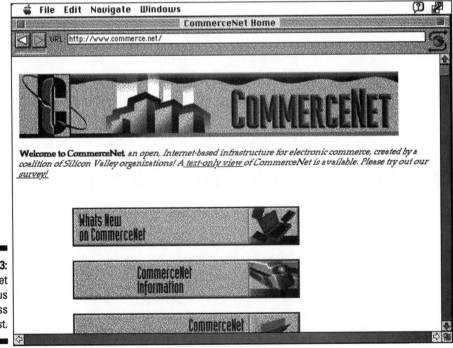

Figure 14-3:
CommerceNet
— Serious
Business
Internet at last.

Chapter 15

At the Frontier — The Future of the Internet

- -

- -

*T*he Internet is too new to have many traditions, but one tradition is free expression of opinion. In the spirit of this tradition, I will now treat you to a few pages of unfiltered speculation about what comes next in this huge, anarchic, nonsystem.

Whatever else can be said about the Internet, it certainly has a future. I don't know what its exact future will be — platoons of hucksters, idealists, bureaucrats, and others have visions of the Internet that may or may not materialize. Plenty of visions are more entertaining than those you read in the newspapers, too.

Wired

You owe it to yourself to read a science-fiction novel called *Snow Crash* by Neal Stephenson. I usually can't stand science fiction, but Stephenson happened to hypothesize a sort of Internet world in which most people's computers are a hundred times more powerful than a Macintosh Performa 475. Those computers will be here within a decade, so the speculation is a little closer to home than old-time classics like Ray Bradbury's *The*

Martian Chronicles. I believe that you'll see faster computers; I don't believe that you'll see Martians.

In *Snow Crash,* people move around in their own interactive movie with other people on the Net. This capability has, to put it mildly, far-reaching social consequences. The book is also a cult favorite among early Internet enthusiasts, so you advance your hipness quotient by taking a look.

Growing like a Weed

When I agreed to do this book in 1994, the generally accepted figure was that about 12 million people had some sort of Internet access. As I finish the last chapters in July 1994, I've seen quotes from 25 to 50 million.

This inexactitude isn't really a problem, at least in terms of fundamental Internet structure. There are still plenty of addresses for one and all, at least. The big problem concerns access.

The Mac: A special Internet case

Access takes on a special meaning for Macintosh users because the Internet has just a handful of large, Mac file repositories. The Internet hosts at Stanford, Dartmouth, the University of Michigan, and the University of Illinois (through the National Center for Supercomputing Applications), together with Apple Computer itself, pretty much define the world of general-interest Mac files.

Mac archives will probably migrate to other Internet sites in the years to come, but these sites set the standards. If you take the number of UNIX users and divide it by the number of UNIX-archive Internet sites, you get a number in the thousands. If you divide the number of Mac users by the number of important Mac-archive sites, you get a number in the millions. Are you going to see ACCESS DENIED everywhere you turn, even as a result of (gulp!) this book?

A solution for the rest of us

Nope. You'll be just fine. Although there are only a few big sites and also just a few "mirror" sites with copies of the original archives, the national on-line services are de facto mirror sites for the most often accessed files. Getting files on astrophysics and Turkish linguistics will, of course, still require real Internet access. But studies of Internet traffic and traffic at CompuServe have shown that the on-line service can handle 98 percent of Internet file requests for Mac topics. That capability puts the users/archives quotient back to the same ratio that the UNIX people enjoy, *as long as you check for the files you want in the libraries of your own on-line service first!*

If you follow this simple rule, everything will be fine.

Is the Internet a Market?

Anytime enough people do the same thing, they constitute a market. Vastly more people in the United States, for example, use the Internet than play golf. (My editors didn't believe me, but it's true: Internet 35 million, golf 15-20 million. People in the Midwest chronically overestimate the percentage of golfers in the population.) Some Internet users may be underpaid graduate students, and others may be there because they want stuff for free, but in the eyes of the business community, a marketing opportunity has identified itself within the last year.

First, lots of businesses want to find a way to buy advertising space, which is currently prohibited. If you join a newsgroup like `rec.tennis`, you're an obvious target for electronic junk-mail offers.

Second, businesses want to find a way to use the communications network for their own organizations. Why should you install your own nationwide business network if you can scatter employees all over the country and connect them with Internet accounts? Who needs an office when you can put all your employees on Delphi?

The reason more businesses haven't done that is security. The thought of competitors reading your communications is unnerving. In real life, this stuff happens, too — cellular phones in Silicon Valley have been the source of all kinds of corporate leaks, through random and purposeful eavesdropping.

Locking it up

A company called Terisa Systems, a joint venture of RSA Data Security and Enterprise Integration Technologies, announced recently that it will sell software tools to help programmers design security systems into Internet telecommunications applications. This way, business e-mail would be absolutely private.

Ironically, RSA was a pioneer in the kind of encryption technology that the government is trying to impose on all telecommunications with the controversial Clipper chip (the Clipper chip lets you put messages into code that no one but the intended recipient and law enforcement agencies can read). The biggest organization of Internet users, Computer Professionals for Social Responsibility, has issued a statement against the Clipper that includes 50,000 signatures (it looks like a Who's Who of the computer business).

In late-breaking news, a mathematician at AT&T reported a fundamental flaw in the Clipper plan, anyway. Historically, the Internet itself is nearly the only government-backed computer initiative that's been a major success. Maybe leaving well enough alone is an unanticipated but brilliant move.

Other Shady Business

Recent newspaper reports claim that police in large U.S. cities have taken to signing onto different local bulletin boards and Internet Relay Chat sessions in an attempt to identify pedophiles who want to lure 12-year-olds into motel rooms. You may confidently expect to read plenty of lurid stories in the months ahead, as police departments react to the need to present themselves as high-tech. Stories about other plans to entrap drug traffickers on the Internet are certain to be part of TV broadcasts soon. The accumulated weight of these stories will be used as a justification for more Internet regulation.

The first two or three of these stories reported in the San Francisco area are demonstrably false based on the evidence presented and appear to be wishful thinking dutifully relayed into print by gullible reporters (trust me, few newspaper reporters have a proper UNIX background). Because we live in a Spooky Monster society in which unspeakable peril lurks at every turn (at least on TV news), crime tales of the Internet are, unfortunately, going to be a big part of forthcoming publicity.

InterTerror

The following is your guide to the inevitable scary Internet stories of the next few years.

First, you need to know an interesting fact. In the early 1980s, the *Los Angeles Times* did a retrospective study of every Halloween-candy tampering incident it had reported in the previous ten years. Every story, *every one,* was found to be unverifiable. Researchers in criminology report that no incident has ever been verified nationally, either.

Honest, they don't occur. It's been thoroughly documented. The most typical case is that some kid's older brother tampers with the candy and claims they got it from mean Mr. Johnson, the PE teacher. The *LA Times*, the *New York Times*, and the two standard college textbooks on criminology all agree about the Halloween stuff. And no one ever dried a poodle in a microwave either.

Everybody knows that bad guys are out there doing these things every year. In fact, whether everybody knows it or not, it just doesn't happen, or at least it happens about 0.1% as much as people fear. Don't take my word for it — join an urban myth newsgroup and see for yourself.

Similarly, everybody knows that terrorists are everywhere these days, kept at bay only by expensive services that X-ray your underwear at every airport. The members of the Libyan hit squad who were said to be roaming the U.S. in the mid-1980s to assassinate President Reagan are now presumably using Internet Relay Chat or the newsgroup alt.kill.everyone to plan other fictitious capers. The historical record shows that various intelligence agencies do not hesitate to plant terror stories themselves. There are indeed some real terrorists in the world, but they won't be stopped by government security assaults on the Internet as long as there are still pay phones in New York.

The Internet and Education

Now some good news. No, really, I mean it. After all this talk about crowding and cops and Clipper chips, I'll tell you about the biggest single bright spot in the Internet's future: education.

Ten years ago, I was involved in a noble effort to provide college-credit classes over a network. It was great fun and a worthwhile service — I ran a statistics class, sending out lessons, correcting homework, and designing an on-line final exam.

The system design had one problem, however. With the 300-bps modems of 1985, the service lost about a nickel in connect charges on every homework assignment. In the classic business joke, I guess we made it up on volume!

These days, when half the students at large universities skip the lectures and buy class notes from professional note-taking services anyway, the fundamental idea of remote classes looks better than ever. With a 14.4-Kbps modem (that's 48 times faster than the old modems), you can even do so at a profit.

I bring excellent news to everyone who took a job right after high school, every lab technician who's supposed to take classes every few years to stay certified, every real-estate agent who wants to become a mortgage broker, and every middle-aged engineer who now needs a skill-set overhaul. Help is on the way! The same universities that make up the backbone of the Internet finally have found a convenient way to deliver their services to *you*. For anyone willing to crack the electronic books, great opportunities lie ahead.

The 5th Wave   **By Rich Tennant**

I DON'T KNOW- SOME PARTS OF THE NETWORK SEEM JUST FINE, AND OTHER PARTS SEEM TO BE COMPLETELY OUT OF CONTROL

NETWORK MANAGER

In fact, one of America's most progressive institutions, the New School for Social research in New York (despite the name, it's a full function, general-purpose collage), has started an Internet-based degree program. If you live in a big city, look through the Sunday newspaper book reviews — you're likely to see an ad for this school. What's exciting about this is that such a program will actually be fairly easy to copy, so administrators at Clueless U. can just see what NSSR has done and hire someone to produce a replica. To round out the spectrum of college activities, I personally will design an on-line campus coffeehouse, an interactive football game and virtual cheerleader software. Licences available soon — watch this space!

Part IV
The Part of Tens

In this part...

The Part of Tens, a patented Dummies feature, is a concentrated dose of Internet trivia, serious matters, and convenience.

I provide some alternate ways to find information so that as you and I use the Net, we can avoid colliding at peak times.

Chapter 16
Top Ten Internet Fun Files

- -

In This Chapter

▶ Net Trek

▶ SoundMaster

▶ Klingon Moov.sit

▶ Stand-Alone Grouch.sit

▶ Monroe

▶ BiorhythmII-5.0.sit

▶ Go Moku.sit

▶ City Defense.sit

▶ BlackJack.sit

▶ PippinPuss.sit

▶ Simpsons Clock DA

- -

*T*he Internet is easily the best source for finding the latest astronomical data. If you want to find out how the Hubble Space Telescope was repaired, the Internet is the place. Similarly, the most recent postings from the Quantum Chemistry Group at Indiana University are available in all their glory.

Yeah, well, uh-huh. It's not all serious out there. I suspect that plenty of people use their free Internet connections to goof off — a necessary activity to maintain one's creative faculties.

In this chapter, I describe some of my favorite files. I don't give a version number; just search on the name. Before you try to fetch these little gems, check the bulletin board or on-line service closest to you. You can find these files at practically every site, so don't go pulling them out of the University of Michigan archives in the middle of the afternoon, OK?

Net Trek

In this shareware game, your starship battles other users' starships on a network. Programs like this one, which is stupendously popular in networked offices, may be a reason that U.S. service-sector productivity hasn't improved much in the last ten years despite heavy investment in computers.

SoundMaster

This Macintosh control panel lets you play all sorts of sounds to accompany Mac tasks, such as ejecting a disk, putting a file in the trash, and so forth. SoundMaster adds loads of personality to your computer.

Klingon Moov.sit

This impressive color QuickTime movie of a Klingon battle cruiser is worth a look. (FYI: Lots of Trekkies boldly surf the Internet.)

Stand-Alone Grouch.sit

If I tell you how to find this amusing, if ridiculous, little program (hey, it's Oscar the Grouch), will you please tell me how to get to Sesame Street?

Monroe

This QuickTime movie of Marilyn Monroe was produced by the same jolly jokers who created the Klingon battleship. You can attach this file as a little window in your Microsoft Word documents any time you need to present a less-than-professional appearance.

BiorhythmII-5.0.sit

This is a complete program for computing biorhythms, providing you with an excellent excuse for bad hair days. You can use BiorhythmII-5.0 for two months for free; after that, the authors would like a shareware payment.

Go Moku.sit

This game, similar to the commercial game Othello, is a sort of beginner's entry to the more elaborate game Go.

City Defense.sit

City Defense, in which you defend a city against a missile attack, is one of the all-time most popular games despite (or, perhaps, because of) its simplicity.

BlackJack.sit

Don't leave home without this desk accessory, especially if you're running away from home to become a gambler in Las Vegas.

PippinPuss.sit

In this funny HyperCard stack, you create silly faces — a la the classic Mr. Potato Head. (Mostly for kids.)

Simpsons Clock DA

 If you need to gain a little respect around the office, use this desk accessory to display the Simpson family on a clock.

Six years ago, when Matt Groening was still an underground cartoonist working only on *Life In Hell* comics, I met him outside his modest office in Santa Monica. He was standing on the sidewalk in his stocking feet because his secretary wouldn't let him smoke inside. Now he could probably buy Santa Monica. Is this a great country or what?

Chapter 17

Top Ten Mac Software Sites

Most of the sites listed in Table 17-1 are universities, so please try to tap in sometime after dinner or early in the morning. The directory given is where you can find the goodies.

In general, you should log in as anonymous and give your own Internet address as the password.

The Stanford site has practically everything worth having. But everyone knows this fact, so I marked three sites with an asterisk that are *mirrors,* or copies, of the Stanford collection. By the way, I included sites in different time zones, so you can access what you want without staying up round the clock.

Table 17-1	Ten Mac Software Sites	
Location	*Number*	*Directory*
`mac.archive.umich.edu`	**141.211.32.2**	`/mac`
`sumex-aim.stanford.edu`	**36.44.0.6**	`/info-mac`
`ftp.apple.com`	**130.43.2.3**	`/dts`
`ftp.ncsa.uiuc.edu`	**141.142.20.50**	`/Mac (Mosaic)`
`ftp.funet.fi`	**128.214.6.100**	`/pub/mac`
`ftp.dartmouth.edu`	**129.170.16.54**	`/pub/mac (Dartmouth`
`boombox.micro.umn.edu`	**128.101.95.95**	`/pub (gopher, more)`
`ftp.rrzn.uni-hannover.de (*)`	**130.75.2.2**	`/ftp1/mac [sumex]`
`ftp.ucs.ubc.ca (*)`	**137.82.27.62**	`/pub/mac/info-mac`
`shark.mel.dit.csiro.au (*)`	**144.110.16.11**	`/info-mac [sumex]`

Chapter 18

Ten Communications Software Tips

Communications software is still full of bugs. The fact that shareware programs compete seriously with commercial applications indicates the unsettled state of things. If Apple had any sense of shame, it would have distributed a trouble-free communications program as part of System software long ago.

Anyway, give thanks to the clever people who write shareware. And be a good sport: Send them the modest registration fee if you use their software regularly.

Deflaking Your Modem

For a variety of reasons, communications software doesn't always reset your modem correctly when it starts up, and it doesn't always hang up properly at the end.

The solution: Keep your modem close enough to turn it off between sessions. Crude advice, I know, but sometimes it's the only way to get the darn thing to reset.

Sometimes the modem doesn't hang up. *If you're still connected, you're paying for it!* Make sure that you turn it off when you're done.

Deflaking Your Session Files, Part 1

Any good communications software keeps a *session log*, which is a record of all the stuff you saw on-screen while you were connected. Mastering your software's session log can save you untold grief. For example, there's nothing like watching a 10K text file roll past you on-screen and then finding that your software only logged the last page.

If you look under the File menu in your program, there will usually be a choice like Save Archive As... or Save Log File As... This choice lets you set the program to capture the entire session.

Deflaking Your Session Files, Part 2

As a Macintosh user, you are familiar with proportionally spaced fonts. Most of the computers running around the Internet, however, have never even heard of these lovely things. On Unix computers, all the spacing considerations for laying out tables and lists assume that every character has the same width. When you capture a session file and open it with Geneva or Times as the font, all the tables and lists look ragged because the spacing has been changed by using a font in which *l* is narrower than *w*.

If you have a table of some sort in your session file, open the file in a word processor, select the table, and pick the Monaco font. Presto! All the text in the columns aligns properly.

Dealing with Weird Files

Stuff on the Internet comes in a baffling array of file formats. You may see .zip, .z, .tar, and all sorts of non-Mac creatures. You can collect a whole set of utilities for dealing with this situation (including HQXer, uuencode, and a half dozen others). Or, as soon as you have an account anywhere, you can download StuffIt Lite, which can turn the majority of these files into something you can recognize.

Upgrading Your Communications Software

StuffIt Lite can solve lots of file decoding problems. I also recommend downloading ZTerm if you are using the communications module in an integrated (Works-type) program.

Experiment with Downloads

Most communications programs support several download protocols, among them XMODEM, YMODEM, and Kermit. There are considerable differences in the actual download speed from one on-line service to the next, depending on the protocol you use. It's worth doing several experiments with small files to compare speeds.

Serious Money

CompuServe, Delphi, and GEnie have special interface applications that let you design searches off-line and set up e-mail message handling at high speed. My measurements with CompuServe Navigator, for example, show that the actual on-line time can be crunched down by a factor of ten!

These kinds of programs can type faster than you, and they don't sit there staring at the screen wondering what to do next: you can already have devised a plan, at no charge, off-line. If you take advantage of these timesaving applications, you can typically get all your on-line work done inside the "free" time allotment.

Modem Speed Optimism

Don't you just hate it when you sign on with your brand-new 14.4 Kbps modem, only to be told that the service is still running at 2400 bps? But don't despair, national on-line services and bulletin boards upgrade their hardware all the time, often without telling you. As a result, try a faster modem setting every week or so — it costs you only a few seconds of connect time and can save you gobs of time and money if it works.

If you set your communications software for 9600 and the service is running at only 2400, either your modem drops down to the slower speed or you get some nonsense characters and are forced to turn the modem off to disconnect.

File Name Creativity

Most communications software give you a generic name for session logs. If you do on-line Archie searches in a shell account or telnet to look through some directory, the software assigns every session the same name. The solution: For your sanity, come up with filenames that clearly indicate the content of your session logs. And you should usually include the date in the filename, too.

Don't get lazy when you are naming your on-line files. After you cruise the Net for a month, you'll have so much stuff that you'll never find anything if you don't label your files clearly.

For Hotshots Only

If you're a hard-core Mac hotshot who bought this book just for a quick over-view of Internet access, be sure to get the shareware program Modem Maker. You can use it to write modem scripts that can be used as small Internet telecommunications applications.

Chapter 19
Ten Internet Service Providers

*M*ost Internet service providers are scrambling to accommodate the dramatic increase in Internet demand. Meanwhile, conflicting factors affect access and cost. On the one hand, it's more efficient to run a service with 1,000 subscribers than 50, especially if the providers aren't fussy about handing out busy signals. On the other hand, increased demand gives the providers incentive to keep the rates up as long as they can. (It's like running the only restaurant at the edge of a gold rush town: the owners want to charge $5 for an egg, but at some point the miners start raising their own chickens.)

My guess is that within a year you'll be paying $12 a month for a SLIP account and even less for a shell account. And soon, no one will be able to impose a 9600 bps surcharge.

Now, the game is to find a local number from your service provider and avoid 800-number charges (or worse, long-distance rates). Check out any humble local computer publication or even the business section of your newspaper.

Note that some on-line services provide 800 numbers so that you can avoid long-distance phone charges from the phone company. The catch is that the service charges you extra (beyond your standard per-hour charge) for using the 800 number. It used to be common to see 800-charges of $5 to $10 per hour, but increased competition is now bringing these charges down.

a2i Communications

This service is very popular in the San Francisco Bay area (area codes 408 and 415). I recommend calling 408-293-8078 for current rate information and high-speed dial-up numbers. Internet address is `rahul.net`.

CR Laboratories Dialup Internet Access

This is one of the few organizations practiced enough to get you on-line as a Macintosh SLIP user. And you can access it cheaply across the country via more and more local numbers (CR Laboratories does shell accounts, too). Call 415-381-2800 and ask someone to fax their spiel. Internet address is `crl.com`.

Delphi

Practically every computer magazine has instructions detailing Delphi's free trial offer. If you can't find any, call 800-544-4005. Delphi, basically a shell account with extensive hand-holding, is an excellent value. Send e-mail to `walthowe@delphi.com`; Walt Howe runs the Internet section.

DIAL n' CERF USA

Shell or SLIP access anywhere in the U.S. through an 800 number. Call 800-876-2373 or send e-mail to `help@cerf.net`. Very helpful staff, too.

HookUp Communication Corporation

This Canadian service has shell or SLIP access with an 800 number and a reasonable price. Call 519-747-4110 or send a note to info@hookup.net for information.

InterAccess

InterAcess has local numbers covering the Chicago area, with shell and SLIP accounts. Usually, I try to recommend services with an 800 number, but I'm from Chicago and I feel that Cubs fans deserve special consideration in view of the burden they carry. Call 800-967-1580 or e-mail info@interaccess.com.

Millennium Online

This is a shell service with a network of local numbers. Call 800-736-0122 or e-mail mill.com.

Netcom Online Communication Services

Netcom has local numbers in most big cities, shell and SLIP accounts, and customer support that knows something about Macintoshes. Call 800-501-8649 or e-mail info@netcom.com.

NovaLink

This Boston-based shell service, which uses Sprint for national access, has laudably modest access fees. Call 800-274-2814 or send e-mail to info@novalink.com. (Have you noticed a pattern in some of these e-mail addresses?)

The World

Last time I looked, this service charged $5 a month. Lots of advanced thinkers hang out at this service. Call 617-739-0202 or send e-mail to office@world.std.com.

Institute for Global Communications

OK, OK, I know that this is item 11 in the list. I just feel compelled to plug this service, which handles the nonprofit organizations PeaceNet, EcoNet, ConflictNet, LaborNet, and HomeoNet. It mostly carries newsgroups for this assortment of causes; you can find a remarkable diversity of opinion represented here. Call 415-442-0220 or e-mail support@igc.apc.org.

Chapter 20

Ten Good Causes on the Internet

● ●

● ●

*T*he current Internet is probably the most remarkable swords-into-plowshares situation in history. In one decade, the Net turned from a service facility for defense contracts into a service attracting vast numbers of society's most altruistic souls.

I don't have any political ax to grind here — hey, I already listed the name of the Rush Limbaugh newsgroup. This top-ten list just recognizes the social activism slant embraced by many Net residents. Myself, I am not a member of any organized political party (that's an old Will Rogers joke).

isoc@isoc.org

The Internet Society itself is worth joining. Drop them a line and see what you can contribute.

ask@eff.org

The Electronic Frontier Foundation (EFF) was founded in July 1990 to ensure that the principles embodied in the Constitution and the Bill of Rights are protected as new communications technologies emerge. This effort will take plenty of work by us all. Help out, please.

lemming.uvm.edu

EcoMUSE is a "virtual community dedicated to environmental education, natural science, geography, multiculturalism, research, and communication." MUSE (for *multiuser simulation environment*) is an Internet technology applied here to a bit of ecological consciousness raising.

802-862-2030

Call this phone number for information on the Together Foundation and its ECOLINE service. The Together Foundation is putting together an international database of ecological and other data.

support@igc.apc.org

Five (that's right, *five*) noble endeavors reside at this Internet e-mail address. All carry extensive newsgroup coverage from all over the globe in their areas of interest.

ConflictNet

ConflictNet is a computer-based information and communication network dedicated to promoting the resolution of conflict through nonadversarial processes.

PeaceNet

PeaceNet serves peace and social justice advocates around the world in such areas as human rights, disarmament, and international relations.

EcoNet

EcoNet serves individuals and organizations working for environmental preservation and sustainability. Important issues covered include global warming, energy policy, rain forest preservation, legislative activities, water quality, toxics, and environmental education.

LaborNet

LaborNet serves groups, unions, and labor advocates interested in information sharing and collaboration with the intent of enhancing workers' rights and economic justice. (I suppose I should balance this entry with an e-mail address for RichGuyNet, but it doesn't exist yet.)

Women's Issues Conferences

`support@igc.apc.org` also carries about 20 conferences on women's issues, representing a remarkable variety of political opinion.

Your Name Here

If you've made it this far through the book, you know more about the Internet than 99 percent of the people in your immediate community. Go to your local library and ask about its Internet plans and need for Net volunteers; or offer to give a talk at a high school. You'll be amazed at the way the MTV generation takes to this Internet stuff.

Chapter 21

Ten Absolutely Free Access Sites

In This Chapter

▶ Nyx

▶ Prairienet

▶ gorn

▶ m-net

▶ sdf

▶ Big Sky Telegraph

▶ O, Canada!

▶ O, Hio!

*I*n this chapter, I provide tips on contacting no-charge Internet hosts. If you're lucky, you may live in a community where this free access service is already established. If you're not lucky, you may be soon because organizations that provide free access are making new sites spring up every month.

If you don't see a site you can access conveniently, call your local library. As libraries put their own catalogs on-line, they find that it's relatively simple to get on-line access to remote catalogs, and from there it's a short step to full Internet access. In addition, pick up a copy of *Computer Currents*, *MicroTimes*, or a similar tabloid at a newsstand and check the bulletin board directories, which are always located near the want ads (in the last few pages).

By the time you read this book, someone probably will have started an Internet access site in your area code, but it takes six months before the site turns up in national lists.

Some of the sites listed here don't offer every possible Internet feature. But they don't want $20 a month either, so they're a good place to begin learning about the Net. Most of them allow you to have a shell account, and you only need basic communications software like ZTerm or the communications module of a "Works" package.

The people who provide these services are wonderful folks; their hospitality is not to be abused. If you sign onto one of these services and use it, for example, to send a chain letter to 20 million people, I will be obliged to track you down like a dog and smash your modem. Remember, my henchmen are everywhere.

Our motto: Be nice.

I selected these ten sites (out of about 40 or so) because I like them.

Nyx

Nyx is a site in Denver, Colorado, maintained by the University of Denver. The dial-up number is 303-871-3324, and the Internet address is `nyx.cs.du.edu`. Its volunteer staff accepts donations if you are moved to offer them.

Prairienet

Prairienet, which is free to Illinois residents, has pretty much the whole range of Internet services. Dial up 217-255-9000 and log in as "visitor." Internet address is `@uiuc.edu`. To ask for details, call 217-244-1962.

gorn

An interesting bulletin board in Santa Cruz, California. Dial-up number is 408-458-2289; Internet address is `gorn.echo.com`. Log in as "gorn," and you will be asked a few questions.

m-net

A reliable contact operated by a nonprofit organization, m-net accepts donations. Dial-up number is 313-996-4644; Internet address is `m-met.ann-arbor.mi.us`.

sdf

sdf is a bulletin board in Dallas, Texas, supported by user contributions. Dial-up number is 214-436-3281; Internet address is `sdf.lonestar.org`.

Big Sky Telegraph

I don't know what's going on in Montana, but it certainly is an Internet hot spot. Log in as "bbs" at the dial-up number 406-683-7680. For some reason, the Internet address is usually listed as `192.231.192.1`.

O, Canada!

The National Capital free Internet site (`freenet.carleton.ca`) lets you log in as "guest" at the dial-up number 613-780-3733. Out on the West Coast, the Victoria free net (`freenet.victoria.bc.ca`) is at the dial-up number 604-595-2300.

I also should point out that Saskatoon is a major center of free Internet activity. I included these sites in an attempt to shame U.S. locations into catching up with the Canadians.

O, Hio!

Cleveland has one of the largest free nets in the country. Somehow, when talking about free access, everywhere else seems to be ahead of New York or Los Angeles, which simply may not be as aggressive commercially. Dial-up number is 216-368-3888; Internet address is `freenet-in-a.cwru.edu`.

Part V

Appendixes

The 5th Wave   By Rich Tennant

"For further thoughts on that subject, I'm going to down-load Leviticus and go through the menu to Job, chapter 2, verse 6, file 'J', it reads..."

In this part...

L ots of information about the Internet is contained in Net documents and lists of various sorts. This part gives you the essentials you need to find interesting topics on the Net, and a few other tips to help you become a fine upstanding Internet citizen.

Appendix A

The Pedestrian's Guide to Internet Addresses

*I*nternet addressing can be confusing because it wasn't designed for you: it was designed for computers.

That explains everything.

I Want Oot, Find Me a Route!

After you get an account with an Internet service provider, you dial up the service, using your Mac and modem. At this point, you're connected to a network.

Now suppose that you want to use the telnet command to connect to another computer. For example, say that you want to visit the WELL in San Francisco as a guest. So you type

```
telnet well.sf.ca.us
```

to start the process.

Your network now calls another network — the main Internet high-speed network sponsored by the National Science Foundation.

Networks have relatively slow ports to the outside of modems (for your purposes, a *port* is just a phone number you can use) but faster connections inside the network. You may think that your 9600 bps modem is fast, but it's a poky little critter compared to real network-connection hardware. Networks call each other through a *router*, or a special hardware box that can connect networks that use the same plan for addresses and for message size. Technically, your messages are broken into little chunks called *packets*; the networks need to agree on the size of the packets.

You may think that you're calling up `well.sf.ca.us`. The machines involved, however, don't know a WELL from a bucket. The computer on the network won't tell you this, but inside the computer everything is a number. In the process of connecting to the WELL, both networks agree that the WELL is called

```
198.93.4.10
```

Strictly speaking, it's not even that user-friendly. The computers at either end of the transaction see a 32-digit *binary* number (0s and 1s).

The *real* Internet addresses, therefore, are numbers. But individuals can pick Internet addresses like

```
goofball@fishnet.org
```

and

```
starman@hollywood.ca.us
```

The routing system has translated the *Domain Names* (`fishnet` and `hollywood`) and the *Top-Level Domain Names* (`org` and `us`) into numbers. And it gets the numbers from a listing of Internet-assigned domain names, which are guaranteed to be unique.

When you issue a telnet command, the routing system gets the number of the site you're trying to reach; finding a file or a person at that site is up to you. When you send e-mail, the network at the other end calls up a table of *usernames* on that Net to determine that `goofball` is, in fact, Xenophon T. Biggles, cruelly nicknamed "goofball" in early childhood by playmates unable to pronounce the name of the great Athenian general.

What Domain Names Mean

You can usually count on the Top-Level Domain Name to be a type of group or else a country name. Country names are usually easy to guess, but some are a bit harder, like those little oval stickers you sometimes see on cars (*Hint:* the Germans don't call their country Germany, for example — it's Deutschland).

Here are some common Top-Level Domain names for groups:

.com	businesses
.edu	schools
.gov	government
.mil	military
.net	networks
.org	nonprofits

These are Top-Level Domain Names for countries you're likely to encounter:

.an	Australia
.au	Austria
.ca	Canada
.ch	Switzerland
.de	Germany
.fi	Finland
.it	Italy
.jp	Japan
.nz	New Zealand
.uk	United Kingdom
.us	United States

If you want to get the name for Brunei or other exotic climes (OK — you're dying of curiosity — Brunei is .bn), send a message to

```
isoc@isoc.org
```

the Internet Society itself.

Appendix B
Your Internet Phone Book

1 wish I could tell you that this was going to be easy. Well, I could tell you, but you would find out anyway and send me nasty letters at *Macworld*.

You can make up a text file of Internet names and addresses, and then just cut and paste them into the To: part of messages. You'll have your very own Internet phone book, and once you get the entries right in the first place, you won't make any typos (a truly dreaded Internet problem).This works not only if you have a service with a cool interface like America Online, but even if you're just using primitive terminal software on a shell account on a UNIX network somewhere.

That's the good news. The bad news is that after years of explosive growth, it is very difficult to track down names and Internet addresses. In this appendix, I tell you some resources to use, but you're on your own after that. Good luck!

Just Say What?

If you're talking to someone whom you think you may want to reach someday by e-mail, ask that person for an Internet address on the spot. Maybe you won't need it for months, but months from now you probably won't be able to get it. Also, at least for the next few years, before Internet numbers are assigned at birth, asking for an e-mail address will make you look cool.

I know that this plan sounds simple, but it's the most reliable.

Da Phone, Boss, Da Phone!

Many organizations provide lists of e-mail addresses; simply ask the receptionist at the other end of the phone. Take it from me, the boss's nephew who's answering the phone for the summer has more intelligence than the cleverest UNIX network utility. And if he doesn't know what you need to know, he can almost always find someone who does, if necessary.

(In case you couldn't tell, I just delivered a searing indictment of the pitiful lack of organization in modern on-line communications. Welcome to the information supersidewalk.)

IDG to the Rescue — Again

This fine organization recently published *The 1994 Internet White Pages* by Seth Godin and James McBride (don't worry, this book will be updated every year). This carefully edited 800-page, fine-print download is as accurate as humanly possible. In other words, the addresses are good for

- ✔ People who are willing to sit still for a few years at the same job
- ✔ People who want their address known

While perusing this magnificent collection, you will find that computer-school gypsies (you know the ones: they spent three months at Carnegie Mellon before taking a temporary job at Thinking Machines before enrolling at Berkeley) are typically represented under multiple goofy names at several sites.

Meanwhile, the footloose and, similarly, the secretive (hey, I *know* Henry Kissinger has an e-mail address, but will he tell us?) are badly represented. Nonetheless, this hefty tome costs a tiny fraction of a cent for each good address, so it's a bargain.

Secret Agent X.500

Many Internet sites have on-line directory services called X.500. If you know practically enough to guess the address anyway, try the command

```
person tim langly, apple, us
```

on your Internet host directories (lots of commercial shell service providers have X.500). If this method doesn't work, please notice that if you have the person's name and organization, you can track down the address with a phone call anyway.

Netfind: Just What the Name Implies

I have had pretty good luck with netfind. Telnet to

```
bruno.cs.colorado.edu
```

(Do this during off-peak hours, please.) Then log in as "netfind" — with no password. Follow the subsequent menu, in which you provide almost but not quite as much information as you need to search an X.500 directory.

The search procedure is quite easy to follow, and good old bruno delivers the goods more often than anything else I've tried.

Appendix C

Netiquette, or Playing Nicely Together

As the Internet expanded, it gradually shed its role as an on-line gentlemen's club whose members were university researchers. Old hands felt obliged, however, to post some of the informal rules of conduct that they had developed over the years.

Back when there were only a few million people on the Net, these considerations were simply good manners, like not leaving chewing gum on a subway seat. Now that there are 30 million Net denizens, these "rules" take on new importance, like signs that make sure that you drive on the right side of the freeway.

In essence, this thing ain't gonna work any more unless we all behave like proper little ladies and gentlemen.

Here are four simple rules. Please take them seriously as friendly advice.

Watch Your :) and : (

Probably 90 percent of the content of face-to-face messages lies in expression and tone (this is even more true in Japan, which is why Internet e-mail is not so popular there). When you send e-mail, all these little clues to meaning we have developed over the centuries are absent. My advice is: if you're saying anything that might be taken two ways, throw in a smile (see list below). And look over your mail carefully before you send it.

The Keyboard Symbol	What It Says
:)	smile
;)	wink
: *	kiss
: (	things are not OK
: >	fiendish grin

Download FAQs First and Read Them Off-Line

Every newsgroup has a file of FAQs (*f*requently *a*sked *q*uestions). You will be amazed (and I cast no aspersions on your originality) how often the things you want to know about rhododendrons or seismology are the *same things everyone else* wants to know. Don't bother the poor newsgroup moderators with questions that they've answered a hundred times.

In addition, you should read at your leisure the guide to local customs, a file usually called `etiquette.txt`.

Don't Send e-mail to Thousands of People at Once

After you use the Internet for a while, you will figure out how to post e-mail to platoons of potential victims automatically. I didn't tell you how to do so, though. And for a good reason. I don't want you to. Neither does anyone else.

Think about the Simplest Way to Get What You Want

When all the national on-line services support telnet, which I predict will happen by late 1994, you will be able to telnet to Finland (and elsewhere around the globe) to fetch chess games (and whatnot). Or you can find the same stuff on your own service.

If you want to get DNA sequence data from the molecular biology archives at Indiana University, please do so. Just don't bother the Hoosiers for calculator DAs, OK?

Appendix D

alt.newsgroups

*T*he alt newsgroups arose as a way to distinguish popular topics from the original core topics (physics, math, computer science, and other serious matters) in the Usenet universe. They loom large in the mythology of the Internet because they're where the fun is, among other things.

This list is a severely edited version of a list posted regularly to a newsgroup called news.lists, which you can join from any Internet provider that offers Usenet newsgroups. The list is maintained by a volunteer named David C. Lawrence (Internet address tale@uunet.uu.net), who is thus the person to notify when groups are created or disappear. It's another example of the remarkable way the Internet operates — the list is a key piece of information about the Internet, and it's not under the control of an organization or business.

If you want the full version of the list, you should download it yourself — just look for it in the Internet-files library of any national on-line service. The complete list has topics and descriptions that are too X-rated for this little fun-for-the-whole-family book, and there's also an amazing amount of repetition — very similar topics often appear in three or four separate newsgroups. The groups identified as "moderated" here have someone who edits out the worst flames or the most inappropriate postings. The rest are just the absolute, raw, unedited transcript of all the messages contributed to the newsgroup.

Social Issues

This list is about one-fourth of the social-issue groups on Usenet. Different types of activist communities staked out their turf fairly early in Internet history.

alt.abuse.recovery	Helping victims of abuse to recover.
alt.activism	Activities for activists.
alt.activism.d	A place to discuss issues in alt.activism.
alt.activism.death-penalty	For people opposed to capital punishment.

(continued)

(continued)

`alt.adoption`	For those involved with or contemplating adoption.
`alt.child-support`	Raising children in a split family.
`alt.censorship`	Discussion about restricting speech/press.
`alt.current-events.bosnia`	The strife of Bosnia-Herzegovina.
`alt.current-events.clinton.whitewater`	The Clinton Whitewater scandle.
`alt.current-events.russia`	Current happenings in Russia.
`alt.current-events.usa`	What's new in the United States.
`alt.dads-rights`	Rights of fathers. (Moderated)
`alt.discrimination`	Quotas, affirmative action, bigotry, persecution.
`alt.education.disabled`	Education for people with physical/mental disabilities.
`alt.education.distance`	Learning from teachers who are far away.
`alt.feminism`	Like `soc.feminism`, only different.
`alt.fraternity.sorority`	Discussions of fraternity/sorority life and issues.
`alt.individualism`	Philosophies where individual rights are paramount.
`alt.missing-kids`	Locating missing children.
`alt.parents-teens`	Parent-teenager relationships.
`alt.politics.greens`	Green-party politics and activities worldwide.
`alt.politics.usa.constitution`	U.S. Constitutional politics.
`alt.recovery`	For people in recovery programs (for example, AA, ACA, GA).
`alt.recovery.codependency`	Mutually destructive relationships.
`alt.sexual.abuse.recovery`	Helping others deal with traumatic experiences.
`alt.support`	Dealing with emotional situations and experiences.
`alt.support.cancer`	Emotional aid for people with cancer.
`alt.support.depression`	Depression and mood disorders.

`alt.support.divorce`	Discussion of marital breakups.
`alt.support.step-parents`	Helping people with their stepparents.
`alt.support.stuttering`	Support for people who stutter.
`alt.war`	Not just collateral damage.

At the Extremes

These groups contain plenty of interesting speculative material.

`alt.alien.visitors`	Space Aliens on Earth! Abduction! Gov't Cover-up!
`alt.conspiracy`	Be paranoid — they're out to get you.
`alt.out-of-body`	Out-of-body experiences.
`alt.paranet.skeptic`	"I don't believe they turned you into a newt."
`alt.paranet.ufo`	"Heck, I guess naming it 'UFO' identifies it."
`alt.paranormal`	Phenomena that are not scientifically explicable.
`alt.sci.physics.new-theories`	Scientific theories you won't find in journals.

Computer Stuff

Please note that these are discussion groups, rather than sources of software. You can, however, get plenty of advice if you want it.

`alt.bbs.internet`	BBSs that are hooked up to the Internet.
`alt.best.of.internet`	It was a time of sorrow, it was a time of joy.
`alt.gopher`	Discussion of the gopher information service.
`alt.irc.questions`	How-to questions for IRC (International Relay Chat).
`alt.lang.basic`	The language that would not die.
`alt.online-service`	Large commercial on-line services, and the Internet.
`alt.online-service.america-online`	Discussions and questions about America Online.

(continued)

(continued)

`alt.online-service.compuserve`	Discussions and questions about CompuServe.
`alt.online-service.delphi`	Discussions and questions about Delphi.
`alt.online-service.freenet`	Public FreeNet systems.
`alt.online-service.prodigy`	The Prodigy system.
`alt.sources.mac`	Source file newsgroup for the Apple Macintosh computers.

Critters

I expect that as more dog and cat owners get on the Internet, there will be postings of upcoming shows and the like. It's pretty hard to believe there's a skunks group and not at least one for Persian cat fanciers.

`alt.animals.badgers`	Badgers (meles meles and others).
`alt.animals.dolphins`	Flipper, Darwin, and all their friends.
`alt.animals.foxes`	Everything you ever wanted to know about vulpines.
`alt.aquaria`	The aquarium and related as a hobby.
`alt.fan.lemurs`	Little critters with BIG eyes.
`alt.pets.rabbits`	Coneys abound.
`alt.skunks`	Enthusiasts of skunks and other mustelidae.
`alt.wolves`	Discussing wolves and wolf-mix dogs.

Games

There are more groups actually playing games on the Internet than discussing them.

`alt.anagrams`	Playing with words.
`alt.games.mtrek`	Multi-Trek, a multiuser Star Trek-like game.
`alt.games.netrek.paradise`	Discussion of the paradise version of netrek.
`alt.games.video.classic`	Video games from before the mid-1980s.

`alt.sega.genesis`	Another addiction.
`alt.super.nes`	Like `rec.games.video.nintendo`, only different.

Sports

I'm only listing a few of the groups for professional sports teams. Your favorite team is almost certainly listed, in the same format as these, as `alt.sports.<sports>.<team-name>`.

`alt.archery`	Robin Hood had the right idea.
`alt.caving`	Spelunking.
`alt.fishing`	Like `rec.outdoors.fishing`, only different.
`alt.skate-board`	Discussion of all aspects of skateboarding.
`alt.sport.bowling`	In the gutter again.
`alt.sport.darts`	Look what you've done to the wall!
`alt.sport.falconry`	The taking of live game by using a trained raptor.
`alt.sport.jet-ski`	Discussion of personal watercraft.
`alt.sport.officiating`	Problems related to officiating athletic contests.
`alt.sport.pool`	Knock your balls into your pockets for fun.
`alt.sport.racquetball`	All aspects of indoor racquetball and related sports.
`alt.sport.squash`	With the proper technique, vegetables can go very fast.
`alt.sports.baseball.chicago-cubs`	Chicago Cubs major league baseball.
`alt.sports.basketball.nba.la-lakers`	Los Angeles Lakers NBA basketball.
`alt.sports.college.ivy-league`	Ivy League athletics.
`alt.sports.football.mn-vikings`	Minnesota Vikings football.
`alt.sports.football.pro.gb-packers`	Green Bay Packers NFL football.

(continued)

(continued)

`alt.sports.hockey.nhl.tor-mapleleafs`	Toronto Maple Leafs NHL hockey.
`alt.surfing`	Riding the ocean waves.

Fan Clubs

This listing represents roughly eight percent of the fan-club material on the lists. These were selected for no other reason than personal eccentricity.

`alt.books.anne-rice`	The vampire stuff.
`alt.elvis.king`	You've heard of this guy.
`alt.fan.blues-brothers`	Jake and Elwood ride again!
`alt.fan.disney.afternoon`	Disney Afternoon characters and shows.
`alt.fan.hofstadter`	Douglas Hofstadter, Godel, Escher, Bach and others.
`alt.fan.howard-stern`	Fans of the abrasive radio and TV personality.
`alt.fan.jimmy-buffett`	A white sports coat and a pink crustacean.
`alt.fan.laurie.anderson`	Will it be a music concert or a lecture this time?
`alt.fan.letterman`	One of the top ten reasons to get the alt groups.
`alt.fan.noam-chomsky`	Noam Chomsky's writings and opinions.
`alt.fan.oingo-boingo`	Have you ever played Ping-Pong in Pago Pago?
`alt.fan.penn-n-teller`	The magicians Penn and Teller.
`alt.fan.rush-limbaugh`	Just what it says.
`alt.fan.u2`	The Irish rock band U2.
`alt.fan.wodehouse`	Discussion of the works of humor author P.G. Wodehouse.
`alt.fan.woody-allen`	The diminutive director.
`alt.music.peter-gabriel`	Discussion of the music of Peter Gabriel.
`alt.ql.creative`	The "Quantum Leap" TV show.
`alt.tv.barney`	He's everywhere. Now appearing in several alt groups.

The Arts, More or Less

This list uses a fairly elastic definition of art.

`alt.artcom`	Artistic community, arts and communication.
`alt.arts.ballet`	All aspects of ballet and modern dance as performing art.
`alt.binaries.pictures.cartoons`	Images from animated cartoons.
`alt.binaries.pictures.fine-art.d`	Discussion of the fine-art binaries. (Moderated)
`alt.binaries.pictures.fine-art.digitized`	Art from conventional media. (Moderated)
`alt.binaries.pictures.fine-art.graphics`	Art created on computers. (Moderated)
`alt.books.reviews`	"If you want to know how it turns out, read it!"
`alt.folklore.urban`	Urban legends, a la Jan Harold Brunvand.
`alt.guitar`	Strumming and picking.
`alt.magic`	For discussion about stage magic.
`alt.music.a-cappella`	Like `rec.music.a-cappella`, only different.
`alt.music.alternative`	For groups having two or less platinum-selling albums.
`alt.music.blues-traveler`	For "All fellow travelers."
`alt.music.progressive`	Yes, Marillion, Asia, King Crimson, and so on.
`alt.music.synthpop`	Depeche Mode, Erasure, Pet Shop Boys, and much more!
`alt.music.techno`	Bring on the bass!
`alt.music.world`	Discussion of music from around the world.
`alt.prose`	Postings of original writings, fictional and otherwise.
`alt.tv.mst3k`	The finest cultural newsgroup on earth (author's opinion)!
`alt.zines`	Small magazines, mostly noncommercial.

Religion

This area is full of many lively discussions. It's sometimes strange to think of comments on ancient manuscripts flying back and forth on high-speed, fiber-optic links.

`alt.christnet`	Gathering place for Christian ministers and users.
`alt.christnet.bible`	Bible discussion and research.
`alt.christnet.philosophy`	Philosophical implications of Christianity.
`alt.christnet.theology`	The distinctives of God of Christian theology.
`alt.hindu`	The Hindu religion. (Moderated)
`alt.messianic`	Messianic traditions.
`alt.philosophy.zen`	Zen for everyone.
`alt.religion.christian`	Unmoderated forum for discussing Christianity.
`alt.religion.gnostic`	History and philosophies of the gnostic sects.
`alt.religion.islam`	Discussion of Islamic faith and society.

Funny Business

Humor is a giant newsgroup topic. If you're the only person in Nonesuch, Wyoming, who thinks Dave Barry is funny, you can find pals on the Net. In Usenet humor newsgroups like `alt.humor.best-of-usenet`, off-color jokes are typically encoded in a simple substitution cipher, so if you go to the trouble of decoding it, you don't have much business complaining about your sensibilities being assaulted.

`alt.comedy.british`	Discussion of British comedy in a variety of media.
`alt.comedy.british.blackadder`	The Black Adder programme.
`alt.comedy.firesgn-thtre`	Firesign Theatre — in all its flaming glory.
`alt.comedy.standup`	Discussion of stand-up comedy and comedians.
`alt.fan.dave_barry`	Electronic fan club for humorist Dave Barry.
`alt.fan.monty-python`	Electronic fan club for those wacky Brits.
`alt.fan.mst3k`	A forum of incisive cultural comment.
`alt.humor.best-of-usenet`	What the moderator thinks is funniest. (Moderated)

Appendix E

ClariNet — The News Source

*T*he alt newsgroups are fun, and the sci newsgroups are high-powered. But newcomers to the Internet are justified in wondering where they can find all the information that's relevant to the average hardworking citizen.

The answer is all that stuff — more than a megabyte a day — is on ClariNet. ClariNet is a commercial newsgroup service provider that collects news from all over, principally from wire services, such as UPI and Reuters. The news then is sorted into appropriate groups so that you don't drown in the sheer amount of text available.

ClariNet is a service with fees, so your Internet provider may or may not have secured access (but national on-line services now typically have a ClariNet connection). In this appendix, I list the newsgroups so that you can see what's available. If you're a serious news demon, you'll want to get the following:

- ✔ `clari.news.flash`
- ✔ `clari.news.bulletin`
- ✔ `clari.news.urgent`

This will put you about an hour ahead of television news and about eight hours ahead of the newspapers. Also look in the list for the designation "top" in different categories, such as sports or business.

I think the real value of ClariNet, however, is providing news that is not frequently reported by the mainstream press. During the O.J. Simpson pretrial hearings, for example, you may have thought that whole continents had ceased to exist and that the national research community had disbanded. They were still on ClariNet, though. So you can use ClariNet as a way to insulate yourself a bit from the pack journalism of the major networks and newspapers. There's also a reasonable amount of humor, including `clari.feature.dave_barry` and "Dilbert," the only good comic strip left (IMHO).

Anyway, look over the list in Table E-1 and use features like America Online's Newsgroup Expert Add to create your own tailored information service.

Table E-1   Guide to ClariNet Newsgroups

ClariNet Newsgroup	Description
clari.biz.briefs	Business newsbriefs.
clari.biz.commodity	Commodity news and price reports.
clari.biz.courts	Lawsuits and business-related legal matters.
clari.biz.earnings	Businesses' earnings, profits, losses.
clari.biz.economy	Economic news and indicators.
clari.biz.economy.world	Non-U.S. economy stories.
clari.biz.features	Business feature stories.
clari.biz.finance	Finance, currency, corporate finance.
clari.biz.finance.earnings	Earnings & dividend reports.
clari.biz.finance.personal	Personal investing & finance.
clari.biz.finance.services	Banks and financial industries.
clari.biz.industry.agriculture	Agriculture, fishing, forestry.
clari.biz.industry.automotive	The car and truck industry.
clari.biz.industry.aviation	Airlines and airports.
clari.biz.industry.banking	Banks and S&Ls.
clari.biz.industry.broadcasting	The television and radio industry.
clari.biz.industry.construction	The construction industry.
clari.biz.industry.dry_goods	Consumer goods, clothing, furniture.
clari.biz.industry.energy	Oil, gas, coal, alternatives.
clari.biz.industry.food	Food processing, markets, restaurants.
clari.biz.industry.health	The health care business.
clari.biz.industry.insurance	The insurance industry.
clari.biz.industry.manufacturing	Heavy industry.
clari.biz.industry.mining	Mining for metals, minerals.

ClariNet Newsgroup	*Description*
`clari.biz.industry.print_media`	Newspapers, publishers, magazines.
`clari.biz.industry.real_estate`	Housing and real estate.
`clari.biz.industry.retail`	Retail stores and shops.
`clari.biz.industry.services`	Consulting, brokerages, services.
`clari.biz.industry.tourism`	The tourism and hotel industry.
`clari.biz.industry.transportation`	Trains, buses, transit, shipping.
`clari.biz.invest`	News for investors.
`clari.biz.labor`	Strikes, unions, and labor relations.
`clari.biz.market`	General stock market news.
`clari.biz.market.amex`	American Stock Exchange reports & news.
`clari.biz.market.commodities`	Commodity reports.
`clari.biz.market.dow`	Dow Jones NYSE reports.
`clari.biz.market.misc`	Bonds, money market funds, and so on.
`clari.biz.market.news`	News affecting financial markets.
`clari.biz.market.ny`	NYSE reports.
`clari.biz.market.otc`	NASDAQ reports.
`clari.biz.market.report`	General market reports, S&P, and so on.
`clari.biz.market.report.asia`	Asian market reports.
`clari.biz.market.report.europe`	European market reports.
`clari.biz.market.report.top`	Overview of the markets.
`clari.biz.market.report.usa`	U.S. market reports.
`clari.biz.market.report.usa.nyse`	NYSE reports.
`clari.biz.mergers`	Mergers and acquisitions.
`clari.biz.misc`	Other business news.
`clari.biz.products`	Important new products and services.

(continued)

Table E-1 *(continued)*

ClariNet Newsgroup	Description
clari.biz.review	Daily review of business news.
clari.biz.top	Top business news.
clari.biz.urgent	Breaking business news.
clari.biz.world_trade	GATT, free trade, trade disputes.
clari.canada.biz	Canadian business summaries.
clari.canada.features	Alamanac, Ottawa Special, Arts.
clari.canada.general	Short Canadian news stories.
clari.canada.gov	Government-related news (all levels).
clari.canada.law	Crimes, courts, and the law.
clari.canada.newscast	Regular newscast for Canadians.
clari.canada.politics	Political and election items.
clari.canada.trouble	Mishaps, accidents, and serious problems.
clari.feature.dave_barry	Columns of humorist Dave Barry.
clari.feature.dilbert	The comic strip "Dilbert" (MIME/uuencoded GIF).
clari.feature.mike_royko	Chicago opinion columnist Mike Royko.
clari.feature.miss_manners	Judith Martin's humorous etiquette advice.
clari.living	Fashion, leisure, lifestyle.
clari.living.animals	Human interest stories about animals.
clari.living.arts	News of the arts.
clari.living.bizarre	Unusual or funny news stories.
clari.living.books	News about books and authors.
clari.living.celebrities	Famous people in the news.

ClariNet Newsgroup	Description
clari.living.consumer	Consumer issues and products.
clari.living.entertainment	Entertainment news.
clari.living.goodnews	Stories of success and survival.
clari.living.history	News and human interest about history.
clari.living.history.today	Today in history feature.
clari.living.human_interest	General human interest stories.
clari.living.movies	News of film and movies.
clari.living.music	News of the music scene.
clari.living.tv	News of TV programs and events.
clari.local.alabama	News of Alabama.
clari.local.alaska	News of Alaska.
clari.local.alberta.briefs	Local newsbriefs.
clari.local.arizona	Local news.
clari.local.arizona.briefs	Local newsbriefs.
clari.local.arkansas	News of Arkansas.
clari.local.bc.briefs	Local newsbriefs.
clari.local.california	Local news.
clari.local.california.briefs	Local newsbriefs.
clari.local.chicago	Local news.
clari.local.chicago.briefs	Local newsbriefs.
clari.local.colorado	News of Colorado.
clari.local.connecticut	News of Connecticut.
clari.local.delaware	News of Delaware.
clari.local.florida	Local news.
clari.local.florida.briefs	Local newsbriefs.
clari.local.georgia	Local news.
clari.local.georgia.briefs	Local newsbriefs.
clari.local.hawaii	News of Hawaii.
clari.local.headlines	Various local headline summaries.

(continued)

Table E-1 *(continued)*

ClariNet Newsgroup	Description
clari.local.idaho	News of Idaho.
clari.local.illinois	Local news.
clari.local.illinois.briefs	Local newsbriefs.
clari.local.indiana	Local news.
clari.local.indiana.briefs	Local newsbriefs.
clari.local.iowa	Local news.
clari.local.iowa.briefs	Local newsbriefs.
clari.local.kansas	News of Kansas.
clari.local.kentucky	News of Kentucky.
clari.local.los_angeles	Local news.
clari.local.los_angeles.briefs	Local newsbriefs.
clari.local.louisiana	Local news.
clari.local.maine	News of Maine.
clari.local.manitoba.briefs	Local newsbriefs.
clari.local.maritimes.briefs	Local newsbriefs.
clari.local.maryland	Local news.
clari.local.maryland.briefs	Local newsbriefs.
clari.local.massachusetts	Local news.
clari.local.massachusetts.briefs	Local newsbriefs.
clari.local.michigan	Local news.
clari.local.michigan.briefs	Local newsbriefs.
clari.local.minnesota	Local news.
clari.local.minnesota.briefs	Local newsbriefs.
clari.local.mississippi	News of Mississippi.
clari.local.missouri	Local news.
clari.local.missouri.briefs	Local newsbriefs.
clari.local.montana	News of Montana.
clari.local.nebraska	Local news.
clari.local.nebraska.briefs	Local newsbriefs.

ClariNet Newsgroup	Description
clari.local.nevada	News of Nevada.
clari.local.new_england	Local news.
clari.local.new_hampshire	Local news.
clari.local.new_jersey	Local news.
clari.local.new_jersey.briefs	Local newsbriefs.
clari.local.new_mexico	News of New Mexico.
clari.local.new_york	Local news.
clari.local.new_york.briefs	Local newsbriefs.
clari.local.north_carolina	News of North Carolina.
clari.local.north_dakota	News of North Dakota.
clari.local.nyc	Local news (New York City).
clari.local.nyc.briefs	Local newsbriefs.
clari.local.ohio	Local news.
clari.local.ohio.briefs	Local newsbriefs.
clari.local.oklahoma	News of Oklahoma.
clari.local.ontario.briefs	Local newsbriefs.
clari.local.oregon	Local news.
clari.local.oregon.briefs	Local newsbriefs.
clari.local.pennsylvania	Local news.
clari.local.pennsylvania.briefs	Local newsbriefs.
clari.local.rhode_island	News of Rhode Island.
clari.local.saskatchewan.briefs	Local newsbriefs.
clari.local.sfbay	Stories datelined San Francisco Bay Area.
clari.local.south_carolina	News of South Carolina.
clari.local.south_dakota	News of South Dakota.
clari.local.tennessee	News of Tennessee.
clari.local.texas	Local news.
clari.local.texas.briefs	Local newsbriefs.
clari.local.utah	Local news.
clari.local.utah.briefs	Local newsbriefs.

(continued)

Table E-1 *(continued)*

ClariNet Newsgroup	Description
`clari.local.vermont`	News of Vermont.
`clari.local.virginia+dc`	Local news.
`clari.local.virginia+dc.briefs`	Local newsbriefs.
`clari.local.washington`	Local news.
`clari.local.washington.briefs`	Local newsbriefs.
`clari.local.west_virginia`	News of West Virginia.
`clari.local.wisconsin`	Local news.
`clari.local.wisconsin.briefs`	Local newsbriefs.
`clari.local.wyoming`	News of Wyoming.
`clari.matrix_news`	Monthly journal on the Internet.
`clari.nb.apple`	Newsbytes Apple/Macintosh news.
`clari.nb.business`	Newsbytes business & industry news.
`clari.nb.general`	Newsbytes general computer news.
`clari.nb.govt`	Newsbytes legal and government computer news.
`clari.nb.ibm`	Newsbytes IBM PC World coverage.
`clari.nb.review`	Newsbytes new product reviews.
`clari.nb.summary`	Daily summary of Newsbytes news.
`clari.nb.telecom`	Newsbytes telecom & on-line industry news.
`clari.nb.top`	Newsbytes top stories (cross-posted).
`clari.nb.trends`	Newsbytes new developments & trends.
`clari.nb.unix`	Newsbytes UNIX news.
`clari.net.admin`	Announcements for news admins at ClariNet sites.

ClariNet Newsgroup	Description
clari.net.announce	Announcements for all ClariNet readers.
clari.net.answers	Monthly postings for ClariNet readers.
clari.net.info	Occasional announcements for readers.
clari.net.newusers	On-line info about ClariNet.
clari.net.products	New ClariNet products.
clari.net.talk	Discussion of ClariNet — not moderated.
clari.net.talk.admin	Discussion of adminstrative topics — not moderated
clari.net.talk.news	Discussion of events in the news — not moderated
clari.news.aging	News of senior citizens and aging.
clari.news.alcohol	Drunk driving, alcoholism.
clari.news.almanac	Daily almanac — quotes, this date in history, and so on.
clari.news.arts	Stage, drama, & other fine arts.
clari.news.aviation	Aviation industry and mishaps.
clari.news.blacks	Black news.
clari.news.books	Books & publishing.
clari.news.briefs	Regular news summaries.
clari.news.bulletin	Major breaking stories of the week.
clari.news.canada	News related to Canada.
clari.news.cast	Regular U.S. news summary.
clari.news.censorship	Censorship, government control of media.
clari.news.children	Stories related to children and parenting.
clari.news.civil_rights	Freedom, civil rights, human rights.

(continued)

Table E-1 (continued)

ClariNet Newsgroup	Description
`clari.news.conflict`	War, conflict, peace talks.
`clari.news.consumer`	Consumer news, car reviews, and so on.
`clari.news.corruption`	Corruption in government.
`clari.news.crime.abductions`	Kidnappings, hostage-taking.
`clari.news.crime.abuse`	Spouse and child abuse.
`clari.news.crime.issue`	The social issue of crime.
`clari.news.crime.juvenile`	Crimes by children and teenagers.
`clari.news.crime.misc`	Other crimes.
`clari.news.crime.murders`	Murders and shootings.
`clari.news.crime.organized`	Organized crime.
`clari.news.crime.sex`	Sex crimes, child pornography.
`clari.news.crime.top`	Well-known crimes.
`clari.news.crime.white_collar`	Insider trading, fraud, embezzlement.
`clari.news.demonstration`	Demonstrations around the world.
`clari.news.disaster`	Major problems, accidents, & natural disasters.
`clari.news.drugs`	Drug abuse and social policy.
`clari.news.economy`	General economic news.
`clari.news.education`	Primary and secondary education.
`clari.news.education.higher`	Colleges and universities.
`clari.news.election`	News regarding U.S. and international elections.
`clari.news.entertain`	Entertainment industry news & features.
`clari.news.ethnicity`	Ethnicity issues.
`clari.news.europe`	News related to Europe.
`clari.news.family`	Families, adoption, marriage.

ClariNet Newsgroup	*Description*
clari.news.features	Unclassified feature stories.
clari.news.fighting	Clashes around the world.
clari.news.flash	Ultra-important once-a-year news flashes.
clari.news.gays	Homosexuality and gay rights.
clari.news.goodnews	Stories of success and survival.
clari.news.gov	General government-related stories.
clari.news.gov.agency	Government agencies, FBI, and so on.
clari.news.gov.budget	Budgets at all levels.
clari.news.gov.corrupt	Government corruption, kickbacks, and so on.
clari.news.gov.international	International government-related stories.
clari.news.gov.officials	Government officials & their problems.
clari.news.gov.state	State government stories of national importance.
clari.news.gov.taxes	Tax laws, trials, and so on.
clari.news.gov.usa	U.S. government news. (high volume).
clari.news.group	Special-interest groups.
clari.news.group.blacks	News of interest to black people.
clari.news.group.gays	Homosexuality and gay rights.
clari.news.group.jews	Jews & Jewish interests.
clari.news.group.women	Women's issues and abortion.
clari.news.guns	Gun control and other gun news.
clari.news.headlines	Hourly list of the top U.S./world headlines.
clari.news.hot.east_europe	News from Eastern Europe.
clari.news.hot.laquake	News on the L.A. earthquake.

(continued)

Table E-1 *(continued)*

ClariNet Newsgroup	Description
`clari.news.hot.somalia`	News from Somalia.
`clari.news.hot.ussr`	News from the Soviet Union.
`clari.news.immigration`	Refugees, immigration, migration.
`clari.news.interest`	Human interest stories.
`clari.news.interest.animals`	Animals in the news.
`clari.news.interest.history`	Human interest & history in the making.
`clari.news.interest.people`	Famous people in the news.
`clari.news.interest.people.column`	Daily "people" column — tidbits on celebs.
`clari.news.interest.quirks`	Unusual or funny news stories.
`clari.news.issues`	Stories not covered elsewhere.
`clari.news.issues.civil_rights`	Freedom, racism, civil rights issues.
`clari.news.issues.conflict`	Conflict between groups around the world.
`clari.news.issues.family`	Family, child abuse, and so on.
`clari.news.jews`	Jewish news.
`clari.news.labor`	Unions, strikes.
`clari.news.labor.layoff`	Layoffs in the news.
`clari.news.labor.strike`	Strikes.
`clari.news.law`	General group for law-related issues.
`clari.news.law.civil`	Civil trials & litigation.
`clari.news.law.crime`	Major crimes.
`clari.news.law.crime.sex`	Sex crimes and trials.
`clari.news.law.crime.trial`	Trials for criminal actions.
`clari.news.law.crime.violent`	Violent crime & criminals.
`clari.news.law.drugs`	Drug-related crimes & drug stories.
`clari.news.law.investigation`	Investigation of crimes.

ClariNet Newsgroup	Description
clari.news.law.police	Police & law enforcement.
clari.news.law.prison	Prisons, prisoners, & escapes.
clari.news.law.profession	Lawyers, judges, and so on.
clari.news.law.supreme	U.S. Supreme Court rulings & news.
clari.news.lifestyle	Fashion, leisure, and so on.
clari.news.military	Military equipment, people, & issues.
clari.news.movies	Reviews, news, and stories on movie stars.
clari.news.music	Reviews and issues concerning music & musicians.
clari.news.politics	Politicians & politics.
clari.news.politics.people	Politicians & political personalities.
clari.news.poverty	Poverty, homelessness, hunger.
clari.news.punishment	Prison conditions, torture, death penalty.
clari.news.religion	Religion, religious leaders, televangelists.
clari.news.reproduction	Abortion, contraception, fertility.
clari.news.review	Daily news review.
clari.news.sex	Sexual issues, sex-related political stories.
clari.news.smoking	Smoking and tobacco issues.
clari.news.terrorism	Terrorist actions & related news around the world.
clari.news.top	Top U.S. news stories.
clari.news.top.world	Top international news stories.
clari.news.trends	Surveys and trends.
clari.news.trouble	Less major accidents, problems, & mishaps.
clari.news.tv	TV news, reviews, & stars.

(continued)

Table E-1 *(continued)*

ClariNet Newsgroup	Description
clari.news.urgent	Major breaking stories of the day.
clari.news.usa.gov.financial	U.S. financial policy.
clari.news.usa.gov.foreign_policy	U.S. foreign policy .
clari.news.usa.gov.misc	Miscellaneous U.S. domestic policy.
clari.news.usa.gov.personalities	Personalities and private lives.
clari.news.usa.gov.politics	Party politics and electioneering.
clari.news.usa.gov.state+local	State and local governments.
clari.news.usa.gov.white_house	Presidential news.
clari.news.usa.law	Legal news and U.S. lawsuits.
clari.news.usa.law.supreme	The U.S. Supreme Court.
clari.news.usa.military	News of the U.S. military.
clari.news.weather	Weather and temperature reports.
clari.news.women	Womens' issues: sexism, harassment.
clari.sfbay.briefs	Twice-daily news roundups for SF Bay Area.
clari.sfbay.entertain	Reviews and entertainment news for SF Bay Area.
clari.sfbay.fire	Stories from the fire depts. of the SF Bay.
clari.sfbay.general	Main stories for SF Bay Area.
clari.sfbay.misc	Shorter general items for SF Bay Area.
clari.sfbay.police	Stories from the police depts. of the SF Bay.
clari.sfbay.roads	Reports from Caltrans and the CHP.
clari.sfbay.short	Very short items for SF Bay Area.

ClariNet Newsgroup	*Description*
`clari.sfbay.weather`	SF Bay and California weather reports.
`clari.sports.baseball`	Baseball scores, stories, stats.
`clari.sports.baseball.games`	Baseball games and box scores.
`clari.sports.basketball`	Basketball coverage.
`clari.sports.basketball.college`	College basketball coverage.
`clari.sports.briefs`	General sports scoreboard.
`clari.sports.features`	Sports feature stories.
`clari.sports.football`	Pro football coverage.
`clari.sports.football.college`	College football coverage.
`clari.sports.football.games`	Coverage of individual pro games.
`clari.sports.golf`	Golf coverage.
`clari.sports.hockey`	NHL coverage.
`clari.sports.misc`	Other sports, plus general sports news.
`clari.sports.motor`	Racing, motor sports.
`clari.sports.olympic`	The Olympic Games.
`clari.sports.review`	Daily review of sports.
`clari.sports.tennis`	Tennis news & scores.
`clari.sports.top`	Top sports news.
`clari.tw.aerospace`	Aerospace industry and companies.
`clari.tw.biotechnology`	Biotechnology news.
`clari.tw.computers`	Computer industry, applications, and developments.
`clari.tw.defense`	Defense industry issues.
`clari.tw.education`	Stories involving universities & colleges.
`clari.tw.electronics`	Electronics makers and sellers.
`clari.tw.environment`	Environmental news, hazardous waste, forests.

(continued)

Table E-1 *(continued)*

ClariNet Newsgroup	*Description*
`clari.tw.health`	Disease, medicine, health care, sick celebs.
`clari.tw.health.aids`	AIDS stories, research, political issues.
`clari.tw.misc`	General technical industry stories.
`clari.tw.new_media`	On-line services, multimedia, the Internet.
`clari.tw.nuclear`	Nuclear power & waste.
`clari.tw.science`	General science stories.
`clari.tw.space`	NASA, astronomy, & spaceflight.
`clari.tw.stocks`	Regular reports on computer & technology stock prices.
`clari.tw.telecom`	Phones, satellites, media, & general telecom.
`clari.tw.top`	Top technical stories.
`clari.world.africa`	Translated reports from Africa.
`clari.world.africa.south_africa`	News from South Africa.
`clari.world.americas`	News on the Americas.
`clari.world.americas.canada`	General Canadian news.
`clari.world.americas.canada.business`	Canadian business news.
`clari.world.americas.canada.review`	Daily review of Canadian news.
`clari.world.americas.caribbean`	News of the Caribbean island nations.
`clari.world.americas.central`	News of Central America.
`clari.world.americas.mexico`	News of Mexico.
`clari.world.americas.south`	News of South America.
`clari.world.asia`	News from Asia and the Pacific Rim.
`clari.world.asia.central`	Ex-Soviet republics in Central Asia.

ClariNet Newsgroup	Description
clari.world.asia.china	News of China.
clari.world.asia.hong_kong	News of Hong Kong.
clari.world.asia.india	News of India.
clari.world.asia.japan	News of Japan.
clari.world.asia.koreas	News of North and South Korea.
clari.world.asia.south	News of South Asia (Pakistan, Bangladesh, and so on).
clari.world.asia.southeast	News of Vietnam, Cambodia, Laos, Thailand.
clari.world.asia.taiwan	News of the Republic of China (Taiwan).
clari.world.briefs	World events.
clari.world.europe.alpine	Austria, Switzerland, Liechtenstein.
clari.world.europe.balkans	Former Yugoslavia, Romania, Bulgaria.
clari.world.europe.benelux	Belgium, the Netherlands, Luxembourg.
clari.world.europe.central	Poland, Czech Rep., Slovakia, Hungary.
clari.world.europe.eastern	Translated reports from Eastern Europe.
clari.world.europe.france	News of France and Monaco.
clari.world.europe.germany	News of Germany.
clari.world.europe.greece	News of Greece.
clari.world.europe.iberia	Spain, Portugal, Andorra.
clari.world.europe.ireland	News of the Republic of Ireland.
clari.world.europe.italy	News of Italy and San Marino.
clari.world.europe.northern	Scandinavia, Finland, Iceland.
clari.world.europe.russia	News of Russia.
clari.world.europe.uk	News of the United Kingdom.

(continued)

Table E-1 *(continued)*

ClariNet Newsgroup	Description
clari.world.europe.union	News about the European Union.
clari.world.europe.western	Stories on western Europe.
clari.world.mideast	News from the Middle East.
clari.world.mideast.arabia	News of the Arabian Peninsula.
clari.world.mideast.iran	News of Iran.
clari.world.mideast.iraq	News of Iraq.
clari.world.mideast.israel	News of Israel and occupied lands.
clari.world.mideast.turkey	News of Turkey.
clari.world.oceania	News of Oceania.
clari.world.oceania.australia	News of Australia.
clari.world.organizations	The UN and other organizations.
clari.world.top	Top news from around the world.

Appendix F

A New Kind of Service

*J*ames Gleick, the very capable fellow who wrote the best-seller *Chaos*,
decided about a year ago to put a decent Internet service together in New
York. He did a great job, proving once again that some of the best software is
designed to meet one person's specifications rather than a committee's. I'm
including a brief description of the service — called the Pipeline (212-267-3636) —
for three reasons:

✔ Gleick set it up as a Windows service first; there still isn't an official Mac
release (at the time of this writing).

✔ It's not like the national on-line services — it's a pure Internet effort.

✔ It's likely to be a prototype for many Internet providers in the next few years.

Guided Tour

I'll step you through a series of screens that show what's available on the
Pipeline. I used a Pipeline Mac interface that was still a fairly scratchy beta in
June, but I expect that by the fall of 1994 things will be pretty well refined. (*Beta*
software, by the way, is software that is still in development.)

The essence of the Pipeline is its simplicity (Figure F-1).There are only eight
areas in the interface picture, but because one of them is a gateway to all other
gophers, this little screen gives you access to the complete power of the Internet.

Note the relatively elevated tone of the interest areas — Society, Law, Politics,
and Arts and Leisure give the package a highfalutin tone, at least compared to
something like the sign-on screen in Prodigy. Beneath this screen is a standard
Internet shell system, and the tools in the second area are the old standbys —
Archie (Figure F-2), FTP, and Gopher.

Figure F-1:
The Pipeline welcomes you to the Internet.

Figure F-2:
The Archie interface: simplicity itself.

The hierarchy of menus in the Pipeline is self-explanatory. Click on News, and a News window opens. Click on a topic with little follow-on signs (++), and you get another window (Figure F-3).

Gleick reports that he hired a programmer who stuck together the original Windows interface in about six months — it makes you wonder what everyone else has been doing in the shell-account trade in the last five years, other than telling people that they'll have to learn UNIX.

The same connected-windows approach is the way to navigate other areas of the Pipeline. Once again, the selection of topics at the upper levels (Figure F-4) is rather elevated and "Manhattan" by the standards of national on-line services.

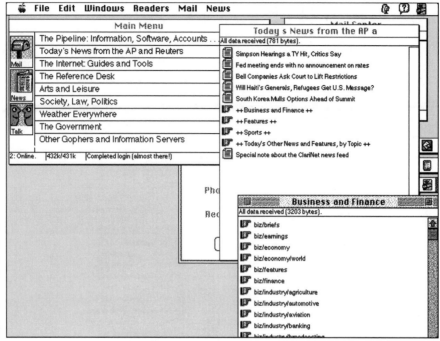

Figure F-3:
The news
window
opens to a
business
window.

Figure F-4:
The ACLU
and other
serious
matters.

Men (and Women) at Work

Tantalizing glimpses of the future remain to be implemented. Under Arts and Leisure there's a timid concession to the idea of fun, wherein one can find a list of .gif files (Figure F-5) of the comic strip "Dilbert," the definitive commentary on high-tech labor relations (at least there's a rat called Ratbert). The catch is that when you try to get one of these files, an error message tells you that there's no way (not yet anyway) to get the files down to your Mac.

Figure F-5:
Dilbert
himself
would
appreciate
the
situation.

Other oddities are just part of the new world of the Internet. You can try to telnet to an on-line game (Figure F-6), but there's a good chance you won't connect.

Partly because Mr. Gleick is clearly fascinated with them and partly because they're a valid part of antique Internet folklore, the Pipeline includes the notorious Coke machines (Figure F-7). That's right, believe it or not, there are some sites on the Internet that have Coke machines that report on their inventory of Cokes in response to Internet commands. This doesn't do you much good if you can't take delivery, but if you're at one of the sites, it can save you a trip down the hall.

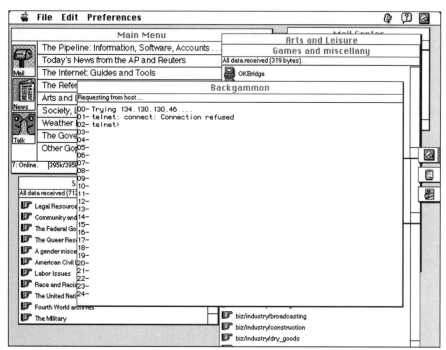

Figure F-6:
No luck at
backgammon.

Figure F-7:
Coke
machines.
Now you
know.

Enough of this undergraduate tomfoolery. Let us return to the loftier realms of the Pipeline. The Architectural resources file, for example, is where you may peruse the archive of the works of Wassily Kandinsky (see Figure F-8). Moving down the list (would the stragglers in back try to stay with the group, please — this is the *last* time I agree to do this Docent nonsense . . .), we see equally elevating artistic vistas.

Figure F-8:
It's the top,
it's the Met
museum.

Toward the Year 2000

The point of this quick tour of the Pipeline is that the software under construction will serve equally well as a model for other regional services or special-interest Internet services. Mac users can probably look forward to TexasNet or ChemNet or ChessNet, with favorite topics represented by icons at the top level and general-purpose Internet access also available somewhere on the menu.

I hope the Pipeline recoups some of Gleick's investment by licensing the software framework to other services — but even if it doesn't, it can expect hordes of imitators soon.

Glossary

These are terms you are likely to encounter while roaming the Net or planning your next adventure.

a2i

A major Internet service provider. See Chapter 19.

account

There are two main kinds of Internet access for civilians: shell accounts and SLIP accounts. In a shell account, you usually dial up a computer with your modem and then navigate with UNIX commands. With a SLIP account (see SLIP), you are a real Internet site yourself, so you can use special Mac software for graphical-interface access.

address

A person's Internet address is the line with the @, as in chseiter@aol.com. From the Internet's point of view, an address is a set of four numbers, such as 132.34.115.31. The numbers correspond to a name that you can remember, such as zapp.com or simple.net. Check Appendix A for more on addresses.

alt

The newsgroups with the highest entertainment value are all in the unofficial alternative newsgroup hierarchy, and their names start with alt. Look in Appendix D for examples.

Anarchie

Anarchie is a Macintosh shareware program (see Chapter 5) that performs Archie searches. It's very good, and every national on-line service has it in Mac software libraries.

anonymous FTP

Anonymous FTP (see Chapter 5) is a procedure for logging into computers that maintain file archives that are accessible to anyone. You use *anonymous* as your user name and your e-mail address as your password.

AppleLink

Apple's own on-line service, soon to be merged into eWorld.

AppleTalk

Apple's own set of hardware and software for managing local-area networks. It's a slow protocol, best for smaller networks.

Archie

Archie is the basic Internet system for finding files. An Archie server is a computer that has lists of available archived files all over the Internet.

archive

An archive is a collection of files. At a site that maintains archives, someone is responsible for updating files and checking the archive for viruses.

ARPA

The Advanced Research Projects Agency, the government agency that funded ARPANET, a precursor to the Internet.

ARPANET

The ARPANET was the basis for networking research in the 1970s. The ARPANET has esentially disappeared into the Internet.

ASCII

ASCII stands for *A*merican *S*tandard *C*ode for *I*nformation *I*nterchange, a definition that associates each character with a number from 0 to 255. An ASCII file is a text file of characters.

backbone

A high-speed set of network connections. On the Internet, this usually means the NSFNET, a government-funded set of links between large computer sites.

BBS

Shorthand for *b*ulletin *b*oard *s*ystem. A BBS can be an old Mac II in a garage or a gigantic system with 10,000 users.

Big Sky Telegraph

A public-access Internet service, located in Montana. One of the best of its kind.

binary file

A file of 0s and 1s, which can represent pictures and sound, as well as text.

binhex

A file transmission fix-up. Most mail programs can only handle ASCII, so a binhex utility program converts binary programs to ASCII so that people can mail you a binary file. At the receiving end, you have to decode the file back to binary with the programs BinHex (4.0 or 5.0), HQXer, or uudecode.

BITNET

A large network that passes material back and forth to the Internet. See Chapter 2.

biz

A newsgroup where you find discussions that have to do with (gasp!) money. Generally, you're not supposed to use other newsgroups for commercial purposes.

bounce

When you send a piece of e-mail and it comes back as undeliverable, it is said to have "bounced," much like an uncashable check.

bridge

A bridge is a set of hardware and software that lets two different networks appear to be a single larger network to people connecting from outside the system.

bug

A software programming or design problem. Unfortunately, bugs are plentiful in communications software.

chat

If you send messages to an electronic mailbox, that's e-mail. If you're sending messages back and forth to someone in real time, that's chat. See IRC.

ClariNet

ClariNet is a special newsgroup system that provides first-rate, commercially important news and charges a fee. Some Internet service providers carry it; some don't.

ClarisWorks

ClarisWorks is an integrated software package with a communications module that's better than some but not particularly useful in a world where you can get older versions of ZTerm for free.

com

This is the top-level domain name that identifies businesses.

communications software

The software that controls your modem and dials out to other networks. Mac examples are ZTerm, Microphone, White Knight, and the communications modules of Microsoft Works and ClarisWorks.

comp

The term comp in the middle of a newsgroup name means that the discussions will be computer-oriented. I'm sorry to report that the majority of these groups are oriented towards UNIX or PCs, not Macintoshes.

Computer Currents

A tabloid-format computer magazine that turns up on newspaper racks in big cities. A good source of local bulletin board numbers.

country code

A top-level domain name that identifies a site by country: well.sf.ca.us, for example, has the country code us because San Francisco is physically, if not emotionally, part of the United States.

.cpt

The file extension .cpt at the end of a filename means that the file was compressed with Compact Pro. You can expand it either with that program or with one of the StuffIt series from Aladdin Software.

CR Laboratories

A shell and SLIP account provider in Larkspur, California, with local dial-up numbers all over the United States. They're *my* SLIP provider, and they know how to set up MacTCP and InterSLIP for you.

cyberspace

This somewhat overworked term first appeared in the science fiction novel *Neuromancer,* by William Gibson. It refers to the digital world represented by all computers and their interaction.

dial-up

A dial-up connection is one that works only while you're connected by phone. The other type of connection is direct, where you're wired to a network and are connected all the time.

Dial 'n' cerf

A national Internet access provider (see Chapter 19).

DIALOG

A huge information service, managed by Lockheed, with lots of technical databases.

DNS

The domain name system, used to convert Internet names to their corresponding Internet numbers.

domain

An Internet site address has two parts, the domain and the top-level domain name. For America Online — `aol.com` — `aol` is the domain name and `com` is the top-level part. The domain roughly corresponds to the name of a particular network.

DOS

The original operating system that Microsoft cooked up (actually, Microsoft bought it in a one-sided deal) for IBM PCs. Don't bother looking in DOS file collections.

dotted quad

Every now and then you'll hear an old-time Internet hipster refer to the four numbers of an Internet address as a "dotted quad."

Electronic Frontier Foundation (EFF)

This organization is something like the conscience of the Internet, as opposed to its administration. Go look for the EFF area on your Internet service provider.

elm

This is considered a "good" UNIX e-mail utility, meaning that as a Mac user you've probably never seen anything as cryptic or difficult.

e-mail

Electronic mail. It's a message you compose on your computer to be received on someone else's computer, although some services let your message be delivered as a fax or (this sounds weird, but it's true) *an actual piece of paper!*

edu

Usually this is the Internet address identifier for a university. The universities of the United States are the reason the Internet is the vast wonderland it is today.

Ethernet

An Ethernet network is a very common, much faster alternative to Apple's original built-in networking stuff. Newer Macs for business now have Ethernet capability as part of the system.

Eudora

A Macintosh program for handling e-mail. The first versions were shareware, but now it's a commercial program from QualComm software.

FAQ

*F*requently *a*sked *q*uestion. Trust me, your questions will be just like anyone else's. When you sign up with an Internet service provider — and before you make any contributions to newsgroups— read the FAQ files that are prominently displayed in menus. This saves you embarrassment and saves everyone else from your three-millionth-time newbie questions.

Fetch

A truly wonderful Macintosh FTP program from Dartmouth, available from all Internet service providers.

file transfer protocol

See FTP.

finger

On UNIX-based Internet systems, finger is a utility that lets you get a profile of a user (including the user's real name).

firewall

You may wonder how other computers you can reach by telnet keep you out of private areas. Networks have *firewalls* in different places to block access to unauthorized users.

flame

A flame is the sort of extreme opinion that the sender probably wouldn't have the nerve to deliver in person. Although some Internet old-timers seem to generate four flames a day, I think that as a matter of decorum you should never flame (it's a verb or a noun) anyone ever, no matter what.

freenet

There are about 30 or 40 freenets around the United States. These are networks that don't charge you a monthly or per-hour fee. Cool, huh? Your local librarian is likely to have the phone numbers.

freeware

Freeware is software that is offered by its author for no charge. This is different from shareware (see shareware). There's some amazingly good freeware on the Net.

FTP

FTP stands for *file transfer protocol*. On the Internet, it usually refers to a UNIX-system utility program that lets you collect files from archives at other sites (see Chapter 5).

FTP-by-mail

FTP-by-mail, explained in Chapters 7 and 8, is a way to use e-mail to get files sent to you automatically from FTP sites, even if your own Internet service provider doesn't have FTP implemented.

gateway

A gateway is hardware that lets messages be sent between two different kinds of networks. You need a gateway, for example, to communicate at network speeds between a Macintosh AppleTalk-based network and a UNIX-based network.

Graphic Interchange Format (GIF)

GIF stands for graphics interchange format — you see it as a file extension on picture files as `flower.gif`. GIF files are very common on the Internet, and most sites offer a shareware program called GIFwatcher to read them. Adobe Photoshop and other large image-handling programs also can work with GIF files.

gnu

Every time you look in a big archive, you see gnu folders. The Free Software Foundation has developed gnu as a sort of UNIX-clone operating system, complete with C-language compiler and lots of utilities, that it distributes for free, as a matter of principle.

Gopher

A Gopher is a file search-and-retrieval system that's usually the right basic Internet tool for finding the file you want. For the Macintosh, there's TurboGopher.

gopherspace

Gopherspace is a cutesy name for the total of all the gophers in the world and the information in them.

gov

Gov is the top-level name, or zone, for any type of government organization.

host

Most kinds of Internet access using a modem will have you dialing a host computer, which is a big computer with its own Internet address.

.hqx

When you see this as a file extension, it means that the file is in binhex (see binhex) format. You have to decode it to get the original file, and the easiest way to decode it is with HQXer.

HQXer

As you can guess from the name, this shareware utility processes files into and out of .hqx format. It's available in the libraries of every Internet service provider.

hypertext

Hypertext is a set of text files in which individual words link one file to the next.

HyTelnet

This program can be used to manage telnet functions, but it can also be used off-line as a comprehensive directory of telnet sites.

information superhighway

No one knows what this means, including me, so I thought I'd put it in the glossary. Internet fans think it means the Internet, cable TV companies think it's what will happen when cable fibers carry data, and phone companies think it's what will happen when they can force you to buy computers from them. The Internet fans are closest.

Internet protocol (IP)

A set of definitions that govern transmission of individual packets of information on the Internet.

Internet Society

A bunch of good people who discuss policies and make recommendations about Internet management.

InterNIC

The name stands for *Inter*net *Network Information Center*. The word *InterNIC* turns up on the menus of many Internet service providers, and it's a good place to look for the history and future of the Net.

InterSLIP

A freeware program from Intercon that works with MacTCP to give your Mac a SLIP connection.

IRC

IRC stands for *Internet Relay Chat*, an on-line forum of almost unimaginable liveliness that's offered by real Internet providers, such as Delphi.

jpeg

A compressed file format for images.

Jughead

Because there was a program called Archie and another called Veronica, someone decided that Jughead would be a good name for a Gopher searching tool.

Kermit

A slow but reliable file transfer protocol named, in fact, after the frog on "The Muppet Show."

LISTSERV

LISTSERV programs manage mailing lists by sending messages automatically to everyone on a given list.

log in

Log in and log on are different terms for making contact with a remote computer. They're used interchangeably.

lurking

In Internet jargon you are said to be lurking if you join a discussion group and just read other people's messages. Oh, well, better a lurker than a flamer.

Mac Binary

A special format for storing Macintosh binary files on other computers.

MacTCP

Apple's program (a Control Panel, actually) that you need to use a SLIP account (see Chapter 13). MacTCP translates your files and messages into Internet-compatible chunks of information.

MacSLIP

An alternative to InterSLIP.

MacWAIS

An excellent shareware program for WAIS, the *w*ide *a*rea *i*nformation *s*erver.

mail server

A mail server is a program on a host computer that saves your mail for you until you make a dial-up connection and have a chance to download your mail and read it.

Matrix

Lots of early Net visionaries use the term Matrix to denote the total of all connected computers in the world. It used to be used as a cool name for the Internet plus everything else.

Metaverse

A graphical version, more or less, of the Internet, but with a better plot. This electronic structure is the basis of Neal Stephenson's science fiction masterpiece *Snow Crash*.

MicroTimes

A tabloid-format computer magazine that turns up on newspaper racks in big cities. A good source of local bulletin board numbers.

mil

The top-level domain name of military sites on the Internet. Just about all U.S. military sites are Internet sites.

MIME

This acronym stands for *M*ultipurpose *I*nternet *M*ail *E*xtension, an Internet standard that lets you add sound and images to e-mail. It's not widely implemented yet, but it will be.

mirror

A mirror site is an archive that keeps a copy of the files in another site.

misc

Newsgroups that don't fit under any other recognizable category get put into misc.

modem

The device that lets your computer make telephone calls to other computers.

moderated

A moderated newsgroup has someone who filters out the really pointless or offensive material, leaving only moderately pointless or offensive messages.

Mosaic

Mosaic is the original freeware program for access to the World Wide Web hypertext system. Commercial versions of Mosaic will appear in 1994.

MUD

Multi-User Dungeons are on-line fantasy games that can have dozens of players.

Multi-User Simulated Environment (MUSE)

A *Multi-User Simulated Environments* is a sort of highbrow MUD. A multiplayer version of the Mac game SimCity would be a MUSE.

NCSA

National Center for Supercomputing Applications, managed by the University of Illinois, is the home of Mosaic, along with lots of big computers.

Netcom

A large national Internet service provider, and a big FTP server.

network

Any set of computers that can communicate directly with each other constitutes a network.

newbie

A faintly derogatory term for users in their first months on the Internet, employed freely by people who have been on the system one week longer.

newsgroup

A collection of people and messages on a particular topic of interest.

node

The term *node* in Internet context means a central computer that's part of an Internet-connected network. Sometimes used interchangeably with site or host.

NovaLink

A big-time Internet service provider. Look in Chapter 19 for the phone number.

NSFNET

The *National Science Foundation Net* is a principal Internet traffic carrier.

packet

A block of information, complete with addresses for destination and source, traveling over the Internet.

page

The basic unit of the World Wide Web information service is the page. Pages are linked by hypertext references to other pages.

password

OK, you know what a password is. Just try to think of a nonobvious password (usually, it shouldn't be a real word from a dictionary, much less your nickname) to save yourself potential grief.

PDIAL

The PDIAL list, available on every Internet service, is a regularly updated registry of public Internet access providers.

ping

An Internet program that is used to determine if a site is still active.

poker

OK, you may be wondering why I keep putting definitions next to their acronyms. Years ago at Caltech, I asked a French postdoc in my research group if he wanted to join the lunchtime graduate student poker game. He looked puzzled (he was just learning vernacular English, although he could write better than we could). I wrote the word "poker" on a blackboard, he looked at it, frowned, and looked it up in a bilingual dictionary, where the entry read (I'm not kidding)

poker (n.) *poker*

The light bulb went off, he said "Ah, poker!", sat down, and cleaned us out.

point of presence

A local phone number for high-speed access maintained by an Internet provider.

POP

Post Office Protocol is an e-mail protocol used for downloading mail from a mail server.

PPP

Point to Point Protocol is an alternative to SLIP for dial-up full Internet access. You would use MacPPP instead of InterSLIP or MacSLIP for this kind of connection. Your Internet service provider's system administrator will tell you which to use.

protocol

A protocol is a definition that controls communication on a network.

rec

Newsgroups for recreational purposes are signaled with `rec`. There's plenty of overlap between `rec` and `alt`, in practice.

RFC/RFD

Requests For Comment and *Requests For Discussion* are study-group documents with an important role in settling general Internet questions about design and use.

rlogin

An alternative to telnet, rlogin is a UNIX command for connecting to remote computers.

router

A router is a gateway (see gateway) between two networks that use Internet protocol.

sci

Serious research newsgroups in science and mathematics belong to this newsgroup hierarchy.

.sea

This file extension stands for *self-extracting archive*. If you double-click on a .sea file, it usually turns itself into a folder containing an application and some documentation files.

server

A computer that stores files as a central resource for other computers, called clients, that can connect to the server to get files for themselves.

shareware

Shareware is software you can download free to test. If you like it and use it, you are obliged as a matter of honor to send the requested payment to the author.

.sit

Files compressed with StuffIt from Aladdin Software show this file extension. You can expand them with UnStuffIt, available from all the national on-line services and most bulletin boards.

SLIP

Serial Line Internet Protocol lets you become a dial-up Internet site. You also need MacTCP to make a SLIP connection with a Macintosh (see Chapter 13). SLIP is an alternative to PPP.

SMTP

The *Simple Mail Transport Protocol* is the e-mail protocol standard for the Internet.

soc

The `soc` newsgroups on social issues overlap many of the `alt` social issue newsgroups.

.tar

This file extension indicates files compressed with a special UNIX program. You can expand them with StuffIt Deluxe.

TCP/IP

The whole system, *Transport Control Protocol* and *Internet Protocol*, makes up a standard guideline for network hardware and software design.

telnet

The core of all Internet services is the UNIX utility telnet, a program that lets users connected to one host dial up a different Internet host.

terminal

In the old days, a terminal could only receive and send characters to the real computer at the other end of the wires. A terminal program lets your sophisticated Macintosh mimic this primitive arrangement.

thread

A series of connected messages in a newsgroup.

TurboGopher

A brilliant Macintosh Gopher program for searching all the files of the Internet. As freeware, TurboGopher is available everywhere in the libraries of on-line services.

UNIX

The operating system that runs the Internet. Developed over many years, it's capable of meeting any networking challenge and is very thrifty with computing resources. The downside consequence of these virtues is that UNIX is hard for beginners to use.

Usenet

The network, linked at different points to the Internet, that supports all the newsgroups.

uuencode

Uuencode is a program that turns binary files into ASCII files so that you can send them through e-mail. Uudecode takes the files back to binary. Mac shareware utilities for this function are available in most libraries.

Veronica

Veronica is a program that searches for files over all available Gopher servers, making it the program to use whenever it's available. Higher-level searches are preferable to direct use of Archie.

VT-100/102

These are two very common terminals and, hence, two very common terminal-software options. As a first guess, pick vt100 as the terminal setting when you dial up almost any service using standard communications software.

WAIS

*W*ide *a*rea *i*nformation *s*ervers are text databases with a superior search method that looks inside the text rather than just looking at document titles.

WELL

A very popular Bay Area bulletin board with full Internet access. About half the computer journalists on earth seem to hang out on this service.

Windows

An attempt to stick a Macintosh-like face on the ugly reality of DOS.

WWW

*W*orld *W*ide *W*eb is an Internet service consisting of hypertext-linked documents. When we all have faster Macs and faster connections, WWW will probably be the best kind of Internet facility because it's so easy for beginners to operate.

whois

A command available on some Internet services to find the real name of a user based on the user's screen name.

X, Y, and ZMODEM

XMODEM is a 15-year-old file transfer protocol; YMODEM is newer; and ZMODEM is the fastest and best.

.z

Another type of UNIX-system compressed file extension, also expandable with UnStuffIt.

zip

The most common compressed-file format for PCs. Unless it's a text file, you probably won't be able to do anything with a .zip file on a Mac even if you expand it, so don't bother unless there's a compelling reason to put yourself through the trouble.

ZTerm

The favorite communications software for many Mac users. It's reliable and fast for downloading large files from bulletin boards.

Index

• X •

• Y •

• Z •

Notes

Internet Society

Application for Individual Membership

❏ Please enroll me as an individual member of the Internet Society. I understand that membership, in addition to fostering the evolution of the Internet and its use, entitles me to receive the quarterly Internet Society News, reduced fees for attendance at Internet Society conferences and other benefits. Membership will extend for 12 months from the month of application receipt. I am applying for:

❏ Individual membership at $35.00

❏ Student individual membership at $25.00

Name: _____

Postal Address: _____

_____

_____

Internet Email address: _____

Fax (optional): _____ Telephone (optional): _____

Payment Information

Payment of annual dues may be made by check, money order, credit card or wire transfer.

❏ Payment is included with this application   ❏ Please bill me

For credit card payments

❏ VISA   ❏ MasterCard   ❏ AMEX   ❏ Diner's Club   ❏ Carte Blanche

Card Number: _____

Name on Card (please print): _____

Expiration Date: _____

Signature: _____

Send wire transfers to:

Riggs Bank of Virginia   Bank ABA number: 056001260
8315 Lee Highway   Account number: Internet Society 148 387 10
Fairfax VA 22031
USA

Please telephone toll-free or send by post, fax or email to:

Email: <**membership@isoc.org**>
Fax: +1 703 648 9887
Tel: +1 703 648 9888
Tel: 800 468 9507 (USA only)

Internet Society
12020 Sunrise Valley Dr, suite 270
Reston VA 22091
USA

MicroPhone ™ Pro for Macintosh

The World's No. 1 Communications Software — from Software Ventures — *Now available for $89.95!*

MicroPhone™ Pro for Macintosh is, simply, the most powerful and comprehensive communications program available. With a complete suite of TCP/IP tools for easy Internet connectivity, a powerful scripting language and graphical interfaces for information services, MicroPhone will take you where you want to go with point-and-click Macintosh ease. We're so convinced that you'll love our product that we're prepared to let users of other communications software packages try us out for a special price. Send this coupon with proof of ownership of a competing Macintosh product — a photocopy of your master disks will do — and we'll upgrade you to MicroPhone Pro for $89.95. *That's a savings of at least $100!*

Just complete the enclosed coupon and mail to the address below. California residents add 8.25% state sales tax. US customers: $5 shipping. Canadian customers: $20 shipping (includes 7% GST); payment in US dollars, please. One product per coupon. Offer expires December 31, 1995.

How to Place Your Order
Mail this ENTIRE form with your payment to: Software Ventures, Attn: MicroPhone Pro MFD Upgrade, 2907 Claremont Ave., Berkeley, CA 94705. For faster service, use our (510) 601-1088 fax number.

Customer Information *(print clearly, please no P.O. boxes)*

Name _____ Company _____

Address _____

City _____ State/Province _____ Zip/Postal Code_____

Phone (   ) _____ Fax (   ) _____

Payment Information *(no purchase orders or CODs)*

☐ Check enclosed *(payable to Software Ventures)*
☐ Bill my credit card ☐ Visa ☐ MasterCard

Credit Card Number _____/ _____/ _____/ _____ Exp. Date _____

Signature_____ Cardholder Name _____

GEnie
The most fun you can have with your computer on.

No other online service has more cool stuff to do or more cool people to do it with than GEnie. Join dozens of awesome special interest RoundTables on everything from scuba diving to Microsoft to food and wine, download over 200,000 files, access daily stock quotes, talk to all those smart guys on the Internet, play the most incredible multi-player games, and so much more you won't believe your eyeballs.

And GEnie has it all at a standard connect rate of just $3.00 an hour.[1] That's one of the lowest rates of all the major online services! Plus, because you're a reader of *The Internet For Macs For Dummies*, you get an even cooler deal[2]. If you sign up before December 31, 1995, we'll waive your first monthly subscription fee (an $8.95 value) and include ten additional hours of standard connect time (another $30.00 in savings). That's fourteen free hours during your first month — *a $38.95 value!*

You can take advantage of this incredible offer immediately — just follow these simple steps:

1. Set your communications software for half-duplex (local echo) at 300, 1200, or 2400 baud. Recommended communications parameters 8 data bits, no parity and 1 stop bit.
2. Dial toll-free in the U.S. at 1-800-638-8369 (or in Canada at 1-800-387-8330). Upon connection, type **HHH** (please note: every time you use GEnie, you need to enter the HHH upon connection).
3. At the U#= prompt, type **JOINGENIE** and press <Return>.
4. At the offer code prompt, enter GDF225 to get this special offer.
5. Have a major credit card ready. In the U.S., you may also use your checking account number. (There is a $2.00 monthly fee for all checking accounts.) In Canada, VISA and MasterCard only.

Or, if you need more information, contact GEnie Client Services at 1-800-638-9636 from 9am to midnight, Monday through Friday, and from noon to 8pm Saturday and Sunday (all times are Eastern).

[1] U.S. prices. Standard connect time is non-prime time: 6pm to 8am local time, Mon. - Fri., all day Sat. and Sun., and selected holidays.
[2] Offer available in the United States and Canada only.
[3] The offer for ten additional hours applies to standard hourly connect charges only and must be used by the end of the billing period for your first month. Please call 1-800-638-9636 for more information on pricing and billing policies.

Effective date as of 7/1/93. Prices subject to change without notice. Offer limited to new subscribers only and one per customer.

©1994 by General Electric Company   Printed in the USA

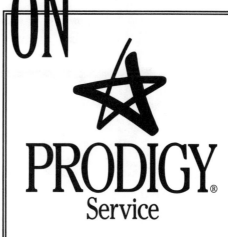

EXPLORE the INTERNET
——— FREE! ———

DELPHI is the only major online service to offer you full access to the Internet. And now you can explore this incredible resource with no risk. You get 5 hours of evening and weekend access to try it out for free!

Use electronic mail to exchange messages with over 20 million people throughout the world. Download programs and files using "**FTP**" and connect in real-time to other networks using "**Telnet**." Meet people from around the world with "**Internet Relay Chat**" and check out "**Usenet News**," the world's largest bulletin board with over 10,000 topics.

If you're not familiar with these terms, don't worry; DELPHI has expert **online assistants** and a large collection of help files, books, and other resources to help you get started. After the free trial you can choose from two low-cost membership plans. With rates as low as $1 per hour, no other online service offers so much for so little.

5-Hour Free Trial!
Dial by modem, **1-800-365-4636**
Press return a few times
At *Password*, enter DG965

Put the world at your fingertips.

Join the world's largest international network of people with personal computers. Whether it's computer support, communications, entertainment, or continually updated information, you'll find services that meet your needs.

Your introductory membership will include one month of free basic services plus a $15 usage credit for extended and premium CompuServe services.

To get connected, complete and mail the card below. Or call **1-800-524-3388** and ask for Representative 370.

CompuServe®

☐YES!

Send me my FREE CompuServe Introductory Membership including a $15 usage credit and CompuServe basic services membership free for one month.

Name:_____

Address:_____

City:_____State:_____ZIP:_____

Phone:_____

Clip and mail this form to: CompuServe
P.O. Box 20212
Dept. 370
Columbus, OH 43220

Offer is limited to first-time members only. One per customer. Original reply cards only please.

The fun & easy way to learn about computers and more!

Windows 3.1 For Dummies,™ 2nd Edition
by Andy Rathbone

ISBN: 1-56884-182-5
$16.95 USA/$22.95 Canada

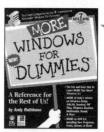

MORE Windows For Dummies™
by Andy Rathbone

ISBN: 1-56884-048-9
$19.95 USA/$26.95 Canada

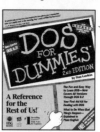

DOS For Dummies,® 2nd Edition
by Dan Gookin

ISBN: 1-878058-75-4
$16.95 USA/$21.95 Canada

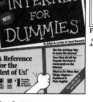

The Internet For Dummies™ 2nd Edition
by John R. Levine & Carol Baroudi

ISBN: 1-56884-222-8
$19.99 USA/$26.99 Canada

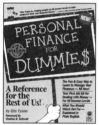

Personal Finance For Dummies™
by Eric Tyson

ISBN: 1-56884-150-7
$16.95 USA/$21.95 Canada

PCs For Dummies,™ 2nd Edition
by Dan Gookin & Andy Rathbone

ISBN: 1-56884-078-0
$16.95 USA/$21.95 Canada

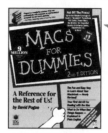

Macs For Dummies,® 2nd Edition
by David Pogue

ISBN: 1-56884-051-9
$19.95 USA/$26.95 Canada

Over 12 Million in print!

Here's a complete listing of IDG's ...For Dummies Titles

Title	Author	ISBN	Price
DATABASE			
Access 2 For Dummies™	by Scott Palmer	1-56884-090-X	$19.95 USA/$26.95 Canada
Access Programming For Dummies™	by Rob Krumm	1-56884-091-8	$19.95 USA/$26.95 Canada
Approach 3 For Windows For Dummies™	by Doug Lowe	1-56884-233-3	$19.99 USA/$26.99 Canada
dBASE For DOS For Dummies™	by Scott Palmer & Michael Stabler	1-56884-188-4	$19.95 USA/$26.95 Canada
dBASE For Windows For Dummies™	by Scott Palmer	1-56884-179-5	$19.95 USA/$26.95 Canada
dBASE For Windows Programming For Dummies™	by Ted Coombs & Jason Coombs	1-56884-215-5	$19.99 USA/$26.99 Canada
FoxPro 2.6 For Windows For Dummies™	by John Kaufeld	1-56884-187-6	$19.95 USA/$26.95 Canada
Paradox 5 For Windows For Dummies™	by John Kaufeld	1-56884-185-X	$19.95 USA/$26.95 Canada
DESKTOP PUBLISHING / ILLUSTRATION / GRAPHICS			
CorelDRAW! 5 For Dummies™	by Deke McClelland	1-56884-157-4	$19.95 USA/$26.95 Canada
CorelDRAW! For Dummies™	by Deke McClelland	1-56884-042-X	$19.95 USA/$26.95 Canada
Harvard Graphics 2 For Windows For Dummies™	by Roger C. Parker	1-56884-092-6	$19.95 USA/$26.95 Canada
PageMaker 5 For Macs For Dummies™	by Galen Gruman	1-56884-178-7	$19.95 USA/$26.95 Canada
PageMaker 5 For Windows For Dummies™	by Deke McClelland & Galen Gruman	1-56884-160-4	$19.95 USA/$26.95 Canada
QuarkXPress 3.3 For Dummies™	by Galen Gruman & Barbara Assadi	1-56884-217-1	$19.99 USA/$26.99 Canada
FINANCE / PERSONAL FINANCE / TEST TAKING REFERENCE			
QuickBooks 3 For Dummies™	by Stephen L. Nelson	1-56884-227-9	$19.99 USA/$26.99 Canada
Quicken 8 For DOS For Dummies™, 2nd Edition	by Stephen L. Nelson	1-56884-210-4	$19.95 USA/$26.95 Canada
Quicken 5 For Macs For Dummies™	by Stephen L. Nelson	1-56884-211-2	$19.95 USA/$26.95 Canada
Quicken 4 For Windows For Dummies™, 2nd Edition	by Stephen L. Nelson	1-56884-209-0	$19.95 USA/$26.95 Canada
The SAT I For Dummies™	by Suzee Vlk	1-56884-213-9	$14.99 USA/$20.99 Canada
GROUPWARE / INTEGRATED			
Lotus Notes 3/3.1 For Dummies™	by Paul Freeland & Stephen Londergan	1-56884-212-0	$19.95 USA/$26.95 Canada
Microsoft Office 4 For Windows For Dummies™	by Roger C. Parker	1-56884-183-3	$19.95 USA/$26.95 Canada
Microsoft Works 3 For Windows For Dummies™	by David C. Kay	1-56884-214-7	$19.99 USA/$26.99 Canada

FOR MORE INFORMATION OR TO ORDER, PLEASE CALL ▶ 800.762.2974

For volume discounts & special orders please call
Tony Real, Special Sales, at 415. 312. 0650

Title	Author	ISBN	Price

11/11/94

INTERNET / COMMUNICATIONS / NETWORKING

Title	Author	ISBN	Price
CompuServe For Dummies™	by Wallace Wang	1-56884-181-7	$19.95 USA/$26.95 Canada
Modems For Dummies™, 2nd Edition	by Tina Rathbone	1-56884-223-6	$19.99 USA/$26.99 Canada
Modems For Dummies™	by Tina Rathbone	1-56884-001-2	$19.95 USA/$26.95 Canada
MORE Internet For Dummies™	by John R. Levine & Margaret Levine Young	1-56884-164-7	$19.95 USA/$26.95 Canada
NetWare For Dummies™	by Ed Tittel & Deni Connor	1-56884-003-9	$19.95 USA/$26.95 Canada
Networking For Dummies™	by Doug Lowe	1-56884-079-9	$19.95 USA/$26.95 Canada
ProComm Plus 2 For Windows For Dummies™	by Wallace Wang	1-56884-219-8	$19.99 USA/$26.99 Canada
The Internet For Dummies™, 2nd Edition	by John R. Levine & Carol Baroudi	1-56884-222-8	$19.99 USA/$26.99 Canada
The Internet For Macs For Dummies™	by Charles Seiter	1-56884-184-1	$19.95 USA/$26.95 Canada

MACINTOSH

Title	Author	ISBN	Price
Macs For Dummies®	by David Pogue	1-56884-173-6	$19.95 USA/$26.95 Canada
Macintosh System 7.5 For Dummies™	by Bob LeVitus	1-56884-197-3	$19.95 USA/$26.95 Canada
MORE Macs For Dummies™	by David Pogue	1-56884-087-X	$19.95 USA/$26.95 Canada
PageMaker 5 For Macs For Dummies™	by Galen Gruman	1-56884-178-7	$19.95 USA/$26.95 Canada
QuarkXPress 3.3 For Dummies™	by Galen Gruman & Barbara Assadi	1-56884-217-1	$19.99 USA/$26.99 Canada
Upgrading and Fixing Macs For Dummies™	by Kearney Rietmann & Frank Higgins	1-56884-189-2	$19.95 USA/$26.95 Canada

MULTIMEDIA

Title	Author	ISBN	Price
Multimedia & CD-ROMs For Dummies™, Interactive Multimedia Value Pack	by Andy Rathbone	1-56884-225-2	$29.95 USA/$39.95 Canada
Multimedia & CD-ROMs For Dummies™	by Andy Rathbone	1-56884-089-6	$19.95 USA/$26.95 Canada

OPERATING SYSTEMS / DOS

Title	Author	ISBN	Price
MORE DOS For Dummies™	by Dan Gookin	1-56884-046-2	$19.95 USA/$26.95 Canada
S.O.S. For DOS™	by Katherine Murray	1-56884-043-8	$12.95 USA/$16.95 Canada
OS/2 For Dummies™	by Andy Rathbone	1-878058-76-2	$19.95 USA/$26.95 Canada

UNIX

Title	Author	ISBN	Price
UNIX For Dummies™	by John R. Levine & Margaret Levine Young	1-878058-58-4	$19.95 USA/$26.95 Canada

WINDOWS

Title	Author	ISBN	Price
S.O.S. For Windows™	by Katherine Murray	1-56884-045-4	$12.95 USA/$16.95 Canada
MORE Windows 3.1 For Dummies™, 3rd Edition	by Andy Rathbone	1-56884-240-6	$19.99 USA/$26.99 Canada

PCs / HARDWARE

Title	Author	ISBN	Price
Illustrated Computer Dictionary For Dummies™	by Dan Gookin, Wally Wang, & Chris Van Buren	1-56884-004-7	$12.95 USA/$16.95 Canada
Upgrading and Fixing PCs For Dummies™	by Andy Rathbone	1-56884-002-0	$19.95 USA/$26.95 Canada

PRESENTATION / AUTOCAD

Title	Author	ISBN	Price
AutoCAD For Dummies™	by Bud Smith	1-56884-191-4	$19.95 USA/$26.95 Canada
PowerPoint 4 For Windows For Dummies™	by Doug Lowe	1-56884-161-2	$16.95 USA/$22.95 Canada

PROGRAMMING

Title	Author	ISBN	Price
Borland C++ For Dummies™	by Michael Hyman	1-56884-162-0	$19.95 USA/$26.95 Canada
"Borland's New Language Product" For Dummies™	by Neil Rubenking	1-56884-200-7	$19.95 USA/$26.95 Canada
C For Dummies™	by Dan Gookin	1-878058-78-9	$19.95 USA/$26.95 Canada
C++ For Dummies™	by Stephen R. Davis	1-56884-163-9	$19.95 USA/$26.95 Canada
Mac Programming For Dummies™	by Dan Parks Sydow	1-56884-173-6	$19.95 USA/$26.95 Canada
QBasic Programming For Dummies™	by Douglas Hergert	1-56884-093-4	$19.95 USA/$26.95 Canada
Visual Basic "X" For Dummies™, 2nd Edition	by Wallace Wang	1-56884-230-9	$19.99 USA/$26.99 Canada
Visual Basic 3 For Dummies™	by Wallace Wang	1-56884-076-4	$19.95 USA/$26.95 Canada

SPREADSHEET

Title	Author	ISBN	Price
1-2-3 For Dummies™	by Greg Harvey	1-878058-60-6	$16.95 USA/$21.95 Canada
1-2-3 For Windows 5 For Dummies™, 2nd Edition	by John Walkenbach	1-56884-216-3	$16.95 USA/$21.95 Canada
1-2-3 For Windows For Dummies™	by John Walkenbach	1-56884-052-7	$16.95 USA/$21.95 Canada
Excel 5 For Macs For Dummies™	by Greg Harvey	1-56884-186-8	$19.95 USA/$26.95 Canada
Excel For Dummies™, 2nd Edition	by Greg Harvey	1-56884-050-0	$16.95 USA/$21.95 Canada
MORE Excel 5 For Windows For Dummies™	by Greg Harvey	1-56884-207-4	$19.95 USA/$26.95 Canada
Quattro Pro 6 For Windows For Dummies™	by John Walkenbach	1-56884-174-4	$19.95 USA/$26.95 Canada
Quattro Pro For DOS For Dummies™	by John Walkenbach	1-56884-023-3	$16.95 USA/$21.95 Canada

UTILITIES / VCRs & CAMCORDERS

Title	Author	ISBN	Price
Norton Utilities 8 For Dummies™	by Beth Slick	1-56884-166-3	$19.95 USA/$26.95 Canada
VCRs & Camcorders For Dummies™	by Andy Rathbone & Gordon McComb	1-56884-229-5	$14.99 USA/$20.99 Canada

WORD PROCESSING

Title	Author	ISBN	Price
Ami Pro For Dummies™	by Jim Meade	1-56884-049-7	$19.95 USA/$26.95 Canada
MORE Word For Windows 6 For Dummies™	by Doug Lowe	1-56884-165-5	$19.95 USA/$26.95 Canada
MORE WordPerfect 6 For Windows For Dummies™	by Margaret Levine Young & David C. Kay	1-56884-206-6	$19.95 USA/$26.95 Canada
MORE WordPerfect 6 For DOS For Dummies™	by Wallace Wang, edited by Dan Gookin	1-56884-047-0	$19.95 USA/$26.95 Canada
S.O.S. For WordPerfect™	by Katherine Murray	1-56884-053-5	$12.95 USA/$16.95 Canada
Word 6 For Macs For Dummies™	by Dan Gookin	1-56884-190-6	$19.95 USA/$26.95 Canada
Word For Windows 6 For Dummies™	by Dan Gookin	1-56884-075-6	$16.95 USA/$21.95 Canada
Word For Windows For Dummies™	by Dan Gookin	1-878058-86-X	$16.95 USA/$21.95 Canada
WordPerfect 6 For Dummies™	by Dan Gookin	1-878058-77-0	$16.95 USA/$21.95 Canada
WordPerfect For Dummies™	by Dan Gookin	1-878058-52-5	$16.95 USA/$21.95 Canada
WordPerfect For Windows For Dummies™	by Margaret Levine Young & David C. Kay	1-56884-032-2	$16.95 USA/$21.95 Canada

FOR MORE INFORMATION OR TO ORDER, PLEASE CALL ▶ 800. 762. 2974

For volume discounts & special orders please call
Tony Real, Special Sales, at 415. 312. 0650

Fun, Fast, & Cheap!

CorelDRAW! 5 For Dummies™ Quick Reference
by Raymond E. Werner

ISBN: 1-56884-952-4
$9.99 USA/$12.99 Canada

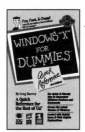

Windows "X" For Dummies™ Quick Reference, 3rd Edition
by Greg Harvey

ISBN: 1-56884-964-8
$9.99 USA/$12.99 Canada

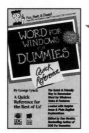

Word For Windows 6 For Dummies™ Quick Reference
by George Lynch

ISBN: 1-56884-095-0
$8.95 USA/$12.95 Canada

WordPerfect For DOS For Dummies™ Quick Reference
by Greg Harvey

ISBN: 1-56884-009-8
$8.95 USA/$11.95 Canada

Title	Author	ISBN	Price
DATABASE			
Access 2 For Dummies™ Quick Reference	by Stuart A. Stuple	1-56884-167-1	$8.95 USA/$11.95 Canada
dBASE 5 For DOS For Dummies™ Quick Reference	by Barry Sosinsky	1-56884-954-0	$9.99 USA/$12.99 Canada
dBASE 5 For Windows For Dummies™ Quick Reference	by Stuart J. Stuple	1-56884-953-2	$9.99 USA/$12.99 Canada
Paradox 5 For Windows For Dummies™ Quick Reference	by Scott Palmer	1-56884-960-5	$9.99 USA/$12.99 Canada
DESKTOP PUBLISHING / ILLUSTRATION/GRAPHICS			
Harvard Graphics 3 For Windows For Dummies™ Quick Reference	by Raymond E. Werner	1-56884-962-1	$9.99 USA/$12.99 Canada
FINANCE / PERSONAL FINANCE			
Quicken 4 For Windows For Dummies™ Quick Reference	by Stephen L. Nelson	1-56884-950-8	$9.95 USA/$12.95 Canada
GROUPWARE / INTEGRATED			
Microsoft Office 4 For Windows For Dummies™ Quick Reference	by Doug Lowe	1-56884-958-3	$9.99 USA/$12.99 Canada
Microsoft Works For Windows 3 For Dummies™ Quick Reference	by Michael Partington	1-56884-959-1	$9.99 USA/$12.99 Canada
INTERNET / COMMUNICATIONS / NETWORKING			
The Internet For Dummies™ Quick Reference	by John R. Levine	1-56884-168-X	$8.95 USA/$11.95 Canada
MACINTOSH			
Macintosh System 7.5 For Dummies™ Quick Reference	by Stuart J. Stuple	1-56884-956-7	$9.99 USA/$12.99 Canada
OPERATING SYSTEMS / DOS			
DOS For Dummies® Quick Reference	by Greg Harvey	1-56884-007-1	$8.95 USA/$11.95 Canada
UNIX			
UNIX For Dummies™ Quick Reference	by Margaret Levine Young & John R. Levine	1-56884-094-2	$8.95 USA/$11.95 Canada
WINDOWS			
Windows 3.1 For Dummies™ Quick Reference, 2nd Edition	by Greg Harvey	1-56884-951-6	$8.95 USA/$11.95 Canada
PRESENTATION / AUTOCAD			
AutoCAD For Dummies™ Quick Reference	by Bud Smith	1-56884-198-1	$9.95 USA/$12.95 Canada
SPREADSHEET			
1-2-3 For Dummies™ Quick Reference	by John Walkenbach	1-56884-027-6	$8.95 USA/$11.95 Canada
1-2-3 For Windows 5 For Dummies™ Quick Reference	by John Walkenbach	1-56884-957-5	$9.95 USA/$12.95 Canada
Excel For Windows For Dummies™ Quick Reference, 2nd Edition	by John Walkenbach	1-56884-096-9	$8.95 USA/$11.95 Canada
Quattro Pro 6 For Windows For Dummies™ Quick Reference	by Stuart A. Stuple	1-56884-172-8	$9.95 USA/$12.95 Canada
WORD PROCESSING			
Word For Windows 6 For Dummies™ Quick Reference	by George Lynch	1-56884-095-0	$8.95 USA/$11.95 Canada
WordPerfect For Windows For Dummies™ Quick Reference	by Greg Harvey	1-56884-039-X	$8.95 USA/$11.95 Canada

FOR MORE INFORMATION OR TO ORDER, PLEASE CALL ▶ 800. 762. 2974

For volume discounts & special orders please call
Tony Real, Special Sales, at 415. 312. 0650

Macworld System 7.5 Bible, 3rd Edition
by Lon Poole

ISBN: 1-56884-098-5
$29.95 USA/$39.95 Canada

NATIONAL BESTSELLER!

Macworld Mac & Power Mac SECRETS,™ 2nd Edition
by David Pogue & Joseph Schorr

ISBN: 1-56884-175-2
$39.95 USA/$54.95 Canada

Includes 3 disks chock full of software.

Macworld Complete Mac Handbook + Interactive CD, 3rd Edition
by Jim Heid

ISBN: 1-56884-192-2
$39.95 USA/$54.95 Canada

Includes an interactive CD-ROM.

Macworld Ultimate Mac CD-ROM
by Jim Heid

ISBN: 1-56884-477-8
$19.99 USA/$26.99 Canada

CD-ROM includes version 2.0 of QuickTime, and over 65 MB of the best shareware, freeware, fonts, sounds, and more!

Macworld Networking Bible, 2nd Edition
by Dave Kosiur & Joel M. Snyder

ISBN: 1-56884-194-9
$29.95 USA/$39.95 Canada

Macworld Photoshop 3 Bible, 2nd Edition
by Deke McClelland

ISBN: 1-56884-158-2
$39.95 USA/$54.95 Canada

Includes stunning CD-ROM with add-ons, digitized photos, new filters from Kai's Power Tools, and more.

NEW!

Macworld Photoshop 2.5 Bible
by Deke McClelland

ISBN: 1-56884-022-5
$29.95 USA/$39.95 Canada

NATIONAL BESTSELLER!

Macworld FreeHand 4 Bible
by Deke McClelland

ISBN: 1-56884-170-1
$29.95 USA/$39.95 Canada

Macworld Illustrator 5.0/5.5 Bible
by Ted Alspach

ISBN: 1-56884-097-7
$39.95 USA/$54.95 Canada

Includes CD-ROM with QuickTime tutorials.

Macworld QuarkXPress 3.2/3.3 Bible

by Barbara Assadi & Galen Gruman

ISBN: 1-878058-85-1
$39.95 USA/$52.95 Canada

Includes disk with QuarkXPress XTensions and scripts.

Macworld PageMaker 5 Bible

by Craig Danuloff

ISBN: 1-878058-84-3
$39.95 USA/$52.95 Canada

Includes 2 disks with Pagemaker utilities, clip art, and more.

Macworld FileMaker Pro 2.0/2.1 Bible

by Steven A. Schwartz

ISBN: 1-56884-201-5
$34.95 USA/$46.95 Canada

Includes disk with ready-to-run databases.

Macworld Word 6 Companion, 2nd Edition

by Jim Heid

ISBN: 1-56884-082-9
$24.95 USA/$34.95 Canada

Macworld Guide To Microsoft Word 5/5.1

by Jim Heid

ISBN: 1-878058-39-8
$22.95 USA/$29.95 Canada

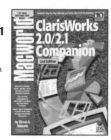

Macworld ClarisWorks 2.0/2.1 Companion, 2nd Edition

by Steven A. Schwartz

ISBN: 1-56884-180-9
$24.95 USA/$34.95 Canada

Macworld Guide To Microsoft Works 3

by Barrie Sosinsky

ISBN: 1-878058-42-8
$22.95 USA/$29.95 Canada

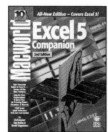

Macworld Excel 5 Companion, 2nd Edition

by Chris Van Buren & David Maguiness

ISBN: 1-56884-081-0
$24.95 USA/$34.95 Canada

Macworld Guide To Microsoft Excel 4

by David Maguiness

ISBN: 1-878058-40-1
$22.95 USA/$29.95 Canada

FOR MORE INFORMATION OR TO ORDER, PLEASE CALL ▶ 800. 762. 2974

For volume discounts & special orders please call
Tony Real, Special Sales, at 415. 312. 0650

Order Center: **(800) 762-2974** *(8 a.m.–6 p.m., EST, weekdays)*

Quantity	ISBN	Title	Price	Total

Shipping & Handling Charges

	Description	First book	Each additional book	Total
Domestic	Normal	$4.50	$1.50	$
	Two Day Air	$8.50	$2.50	$
	Overnight	$18.00	$3.00	$
International	Surface	$8.00	$8.00	$
	Airmail	$16.00	$16.00	$
	DHL Air	$17.00	$17.00	$

*For large quantities call for shipping & handling charges.
**Prices are subject to change without notice.

Ship to:

Name _____

Company _____

Address _____

City/State/Zip _____

Daytime Phone _____

Payment: ☐ Check to IDG Books (US Funds Only)

☐ VISA   ☐ MasterCard   ☐ American Express

Card # _____ Expires _____

Signature _____

Subtotal _____

CA residents add
applicable sales tax _____

IN, MA, and MD
residents add
5% sales tax _____

IL residents add
6.25% sales tax _____

RI residents add
7% sales tax _____

TX residents add
8.25% sales tax _____

Shipping _____

Total _____

Please send this order form to:

IDG Books Worldwide
7260 Shadeland Station, Suite 100
Indianapolis, IN 46256

Allow up to 3 weeks for delivery.
Thank you!